100 THINGS
CHIEFS FANS
SHOULD KNOW & DO
BEFORE THEY DIE

100 THINGS
CHIEFS FANS
SHOULD KNOW & DO
BEFORE THEY DIE

Matt Fulks

TRIUMPH
BOOKS

The Library of Congress has catalogued the previous edition as follows:

Names: Fulks, Matt.
Title: 100 things Chiefs fans should know & do before they die / Matt Fulks.
Other titles: One hundred things Chiefs fans should know and do before they die
Description: Chicago, Illinois : Triumph Books, [2014]
Identifiers: LCCN 2014020750 | ISBN 9781629370156
Subjects: LCSH: Kansas City Chiefs (Football team—Miscellanea.
Classification: LCC GV956.K35 F85 2014 | DDC 796.332/6409778/411
—dc23 LC record available at https://lccn.loc.gov/2014020750

This book is available in quantity at special discounts for your group or organization. For further information, contact:
Triumph Books LLC
814 North Franklin Street
Chicago, Illinois 60610
(312) 337-0747
www.triumphbooks.com

Printed in U.S.A.
ISBN: 978-1-62937-852-7
Design by Patricia Frey
Photos courtesy of Getty Images unless otherwise indicated

To Libby. A lot of authors dedicate their first or second book to their significant other. This is my 20th book, and we celebrated our 20th anniversary as I was finishing it. Those numbers aren't coincidences. Although I dedicated an earlier book to you, there's no way I could've written a first book, let alone a 20th, without your constant love and support.

Contents

Foreword

There's no greater place to play in the NFL than Arrowhead Stadium. For the home team at least. There are great stadiums with terrific fans, but there's something unique, something magical about coming out of that tunnel and running onto the field to a stadium of 75,000 fans, clad in red, making a deafening sound. I'm getting chills thinking about it.

Arrowhead is one of the things that pops into my head immediately when I look back on my time with the Chiefs, along with my teammates and coaches, a few games, and the city overall.

First, I think about my teammates and coaches. A lot of my former teammates still live in the Kansas City area, and I stay in contact with many of those guys. The relationships that players build in the locker room are special. Those relationships and camaraderie in the locker room helped us succeed on the field while I was with the Chiefs—and what a great group of guys! During my time on the team from 2001–06, on defense we had Eric Hicks, Scott Fujita, Mike Maslowski, Shawn Barber, Jerome Woods, Jared Allen, Derrick Johnson, Kawika Mitchell, and Tamba Hali to name a few. On the offensive line, we had the best group in the NFL in Hall of Famers Willie Roaf and Will Shields, Chiefs Hall of Famer Brian Waters, plus Casey Wiegmann and John Tait. That was an incredible line. Speaking of offense, any quarterback would love to have the weapons we had with Priest Holmes, Tony Richardson, Chiefs and NFL Hall of Fame tight end Tony Gonzalez, Dante Hall, and Eddie Kennison. We were truly a multiple-personnel offense with a lot of versatility—multiple guys who could catch the ball and multiple guys who could run the ball—which put a strain on defenses. The success of our offense made that a special time to be a member of the Kansas City Chiefs.

The bulk of that success can be attributed directly to coach Dick Vermeil and offensive coordinator Al Saunders. I can't say enough positive things about each of these gentlemen. I talk with Coach Vermeil every couple weeks at least and more frequently during the season. That's a valuable relationship to me because, though we talk a lot about football, we also talk about each other's families and just about life. I've learned incredible lessons about dealing with people and handling adversity from Coach Vermeil. We share an appreciation for what each of us went through when we were together in St. Louis. So when he traded for me in Kansas City prior to the 2001 season, we'd already developed a strong bond.

Under Saunders our offense was complex, so it took some time to get everyone on the same page. Things began clicking, though, in 2002 as we led the NFL in scoring with 467 points. Defensively, we struggled with consistency that year. All three aspects of the game—offense, defense, and special teams—came around in 2003. We again led the league in scoring (484 points), but instead of finishing 8–8, we went 13–3, which was the second-best record in the AFC—and the NFL—behind New England. That year we were confident that we'd find a way to win every game. We believed that anybody on offense, defense, or special teams would make a big play. That's how it came together. A prime example of that is the Green Bay game at Lambeau Field. We were down by 17 points, 31–14, in the fourth quarter. Thanks to two big defensive plays—a Pick-6 by Woods and a fumble recovery by Maslowski—a field goal by Morten Andersen, a running touchdown by Holmes, and a receiving touchdown by Kennison, we tied the game and won it in overtime. You can read more about that game later in the book.

Unfortunately, we didn't get the job done against Indianapolis in the playoffs. The way things went for us that season, I felt good about our chances at New England the following week. That's not to say we overlooked Indy because we definitely were focused. But as I've replayed the scenario countless times, if we capitalize on at least one of two missed possessions offensively, and our defense makes a stop, we're at New England with a good chance of going to the Super Bowl. Needless to say, that loss to Indianapolis was hard to swallow in January 2004, and it's hard to swallow today. If there's one regret from my time with the Chiefs, it's that we didn't make a postseason run in '03 or any other year. The Hunt family, the fans, and Kansas City all deserve it.

So it was incredible to see how electric Kansas City became when the team finally made it back to the Super Bowl—and won it—at the end of the 2019 season. The excitement really began in 2018 when Patrick Mahomes took over as the team's starting quarterback. I can't tell you how many times I've marveled at Pat's poise, leadership, creativity, and just sheer natural ability. Having a father who was a major league pitcher and then having a year to learn under Alex Smith are two keys to what we've seen early in Pat's career. People use the term "generational talent" often in sports, but he truly is one.

Kansas City is a wonderful place. I grew up in St. Louis, but Kansas City has become our home. As a quarterback I always felt it was important to be around for all workouts and to be part of the community where you're playing. My wife and I have been active in the Kansas City community since 2001 through the Trent Green Family Foundation, and we'll continue to be.

One of the great things about this city, besides the people, is the experience of gameday at Arrowhead Stadium. There is an incredible energy that I didn't expect when I arrived. At that time I was coming off my fourth knee surgery, so I didn't participate in any of the Chiefs offseason workouts. Before my first Chiefs game—Raiders Week on Opening Day 2001—the team was supposed to meet for a pregame meal at a restaurant on the Plaza.

Since we drove separately to breakfast and I was still new to the city, I wanted to drive on my own from the Plaza to the stadium. I was stubborn enough that I didn't want to follow anyone. Guys tried telling me where exactly to go, how to maneuver the traffic, and then to pull up to the gate, and tell the person who I was. I listened to part of what they were saying, but I missed most of it. As a result, I made the mistake of going to the gate near the practice facility...and I was stuck. There was no type of shoulder, and I was pinned with countless other cars—all fans waiting to get into the parking lot. Players were supposed to be there no later than 10:00 for a noon game. At this point it's almost 9:00. I called the head of security to let the coaches know that I was at the stadium but I was stuck in traffic and then I pulled out my playbook and started listening to the pregame show on radio *for nearly an hour and a half.* Luckily, I was only about 15 minutes late. Of course the guys started laughing and busting my chops. Needless to say, that didn't happen again.

Funny stories aside, gameday at Arrowhead is unlike any other stadium in the NFL. You want to play in stadiums where they're passionate about football because it makes it more fun. That was every game day at Arrowhead. From the quarterback warm-ups to running out of the tunnel for the introductions, it's an indescribable and incredible experience. When I go to games now, whether I'm broadcasting or simply there as a spectator, I want to be back on the field.

Because of the offense we had with the Chiefs, my name is in the team's record books alongside guys like Len Dawson, Joe Montana, and now Mahomes. That's very humbling. I was a guy who was the third-to-the-last draft pick and got my first start in the NFL when I was 28 years old. And then I had the hurdle with my knee. For me, 81 consecutive starts for the Chiefs is one of the things I'm most proud of after four knee surgeries. I started every game until I got the concussion in 2006 against Cincinnati. To sit here now and say that I played 15 years in the NFL, including six really productive years with the Chiefs, a franchise with such a long and rich history, is very cool. This is a special organization with some of the most passionate fans in the league. Throughout *100 Things Chiefs Fans Should Know & Do Before They Die*, you'll read more about the people and moments that have helped shape this organization—and why it's such a special place to play.

Go Chiefs!

—Trent Green
Chiefs quarterback, 2001–06

Introduction

I'm a big sports fan and I have been for as long as I can remember. Growing up in New Jersey, close to Philadelphia, the Chiefs weren't my team as a kid. For more than half of my life, however, since signing my first professional contract in 1981, I've been a proud fan of the Kansas City Chiefs.

The fraternity of men who have played in the National Football League is relatively small, and the number of us who were privileged enough to play for this organization that Lamar Hunt started is even smaller. It's amazing to me to think that I spent my entire 11-year career playing for one of the best franchises in professional sports and for the man who created the American Football League, which eventually became a major part of the NFL. When you talk about the Chiefs and *100 Things Chiefs Fans Should Know & Do Before They Die*, you're talking about that kind of history.

The journey started for me after I graduated from Rutgers. I went undrafted in 1981, but Chiefs linebackers coach Ted Cottrell, who had been our defensive coordinator at Rutgers, called me and said the Chiefs were looking for a punter. I flew to Kansas City the next day, and the team signed me as a punter. They ended up releasing me, but I called coach Marv Levy and said, "Coach, I know my punting wasn't what it should be, but I also played safety and I think I can contribute there." He said he'd think about it and call me back. Well, he called back and told me to come back in, and they'd work me both as a punter and as a safety. I can't tell you how many times I've thought over the years that if I hadn't made that call and, subsequently, if Marv Levy hadn't given me that opportunity, I wouldn't be where I am today. I got another opportunity in my third season. After I hadn't played much in 1981 and '82, defensive backs coach Walt Corey told management that I had the ability to play at this level and that I needed a chance. I ended up starting that season in 1983, and my career took off from there. Those opportunities don't come often, especially for a free-agent punter.

That 1983 season probably defines my career better than any other single season or any specific game. Halfway through the season, I led the league in interceptions before ending the year with seven. That started a four-year streak of at least seven interceptions and a streak of six straight Pro Bowls. For me that whole year was big because it gave me a chance to get the respect of the guys around me, who had been playing with the guy I replaced, Gary Barbaro, a three-time All-Pro and one of the best safeties in all of football. That year put me on the NFL map, but it also served as validation to my teammates and coaches that I could play in this league. It showed that I could make a strong contribution and be a leader on the team, even though I was one of the youngest guys in a secondary that featured All-Pro players. Later in this book, you'll read more about my career and that incredible secondary we had during the 1980s.

Although I think 1983 defines my career, there are Chiefs fans who could debate the most important game of my career, whatever they think that moment is. That's the beauty of sports. As fans we can argue why this player was better than that one, or whether this moment or that moment was bigger for a team or a player. That's the cool thing about a book like *100 Things Chiefs Fans Should Know & Do Before They Die*. If I were to compile a list and rank the top 100 moments, players, and things to do for Chiefs fans, my list likely would look a little different than the one Matt Fulks has compiled in this book. But you know what? As with most sports-related debates, we both could make solid arguments to support our lists.

The order and content of the chapters that follow might be debatable. One thing that no Chiefs fan can debate, however, is No. 1 on the list: founder and owner Lamar Hunt. When I think about Lamar, two moments in particular stand out. The first was my second road trip during my rookie year in 1982. As we got off the bus at the hotel in Seattle, I saw this guy on his hands and knees pulling luggage out from under the bus. I couldn't tell who it was, but I figured it was the driver because all I could see were gray pants. Turns out it was Lamar. I thought, *This guy's the owner of the team. Doesn't he have someone who can pull luggage for him?* But that's how he was—very humble and very unassuming. Here's a billionaire who's not waiting on someone to take care of him. He's on his hands and knees, getting dirty, grabbing luggage from under the bus. I learned a lesson about humility and other things when I saw that.

The other moment was after my playing career, when Jacksonville was trying to get an NFL team and I was going to become one of the minority owners. Lamar was someone on whom I leaned heavily for guidance and advice. In fact, the Jaguars' majority owner at the time, Wayne Weaver, came to Kansas City and sat down with Lamar, who was very gracious with his time and support. I'll never forget this as long as I live, but when we were in Chicago and they were announcing the newest team to enter the NFL, commissioner Paul Tagliabue stood at the podium and said, "The 32nd team in the NFL will be the Jacksonville Jaguars," I was so excited that I jumped in the air. When I turned around, the person who was standing behind me, watching me with joy, was Lamar Hunt. He hugged me and congratulated me. That's a moment I'll never forget.

Lamar has meant everything to me. I appreciate what he did for me and the opportunities he gave me and, more importantly, his friendship. As every Chiefs player who played for Lamar would say, he would always welcome you. His door was always open. He was a special person.

Although he wasn't here to see it, it was so special when Norma and Clark Hunt were able finally to raise the Lamar Hunt Trophy after the Chiefs won the AFC Championship Game at Arrowhead in January 2020 and then the Lombardi Trophy as Super Bowl LIV champs two weeks later. I've no doubt that Lamar would've been incredibly proud of the team but more excited for this city and Chiefs fans everywhere.

As far as I'm concerned, there's no other family that I would've wanted to be a part of than the Chiefs family. That starts with Lamar and the Hunt family, to the front office, to the players, to the fans. The entire Chiefs Nation has supported me through all of my years here from playing and even after retiring. There's no better fan base in the National Football League than the Chiefs. You see it year in and year out, regardless of the team's record. When the Chiefs are in town to play, Chiefs Nation shows up throughout stadiums in the NFL, and they support the team, current and former players alike. Even though we didn't win any titles when I played, I feel very fortunate that I spent 11 years of my life in a truly great place and with the fans of this city. That's a remarkable feeling. Thank you.

—Deron Cherry
Chiefs Hall of Fame, 1996

1 Lamar Hunt

Lamar Hunt, a native Texan and resident of Dallas throughout the time he owned the Chiefs, did an incredible amount of good for Kansas City during his lifetime. Of course, there are the Chiefs, which started out as the Dallas Texans in the American Football League. Oh, yeah, there's the American Football League, which Hunt founded and helped foster to what is now (basically) the NFL's American Football Conference. "It starts with Lamar Hunt," said Hall of Fame quarterback Len Dawson. "I've said many times: what would professional football be today without Lamar Hunt?"

But there's also Worlds of Fun. And Oceans of Fun.

Then there are the Wiz, Kansas City's pro soccer team, which has morphed into Sporting Kansas City and plays in the league that Hunt helped start, Major League Soccer (MLS). "To Kansas City, he's more than just the owner of a professional franchise," said the Chiefs' former president and general manager, Carl Peterson. "He's committed himself there with other businesses such as Hunt Midwest Enterprises, creating thousands of jobs throughout the Kansas City community. He's been one of the most philanthropic people I've ever been involved with."

He also encouraged his players to get involved in the Kansas City community with charitable endeavors. Really, there's no telling how many lives in Kansas City have been touched—directly or indirectly—by Lamar Hunt, the most unassuming and unsuspecting son of a billionaire oil man. "When you looked at the guy, you wouldn't think he had 20 cents on him, and he never did to my knowledge," Dawson said. "But he was a very humble person who wanted to win."

Hunt's humility helped shape the Chiefs franchise. Along the way, whether in the early days of the organization when they were his contemporaries or in his later years when he was a fatherly figure, Hunt left an impression that remains today.

"The difference between Lamar and all of the other owners I've had the opportunity to meet," said former defensive back Jayice Pearson, "is that he genuinely cared about the players. That's something that is rare. He would walk up to you and know your name, know where you're from. He'd come up to us after a game, almost apprehensive like a fan...and here's the dude who's signing the checks! He could talk to us any way he wanted to, but he was a really humble guy and cared about people."

The son of wealthy oil baron H.L. Hunt, Lamar used that money to purchase an AFL team, an understandable investment, considering he played college football at SMU. His impact on football was immeasurable. He would even coin the term "Super Bowl," a term originated from the Super Ball toy with which his children played. While owning the Chiefs, Hunt became one of the more popular and respected figures—both within the NFL and his own franchise.

"Lamar Hunt was a wonderful man; I love Lamar Hunt and his wife Norma," said former quarterback Bill Kenney. "Great people and great for this city. When I decided to run for the Missouri Senate, I called Lamar and asked him if he'd support me. He said he would, so I asked if he'd host a fund-raiser for me at his suite. He agreed to do it. The event was kicking off, and Lamar and I were standing there, looking at the field [at Arrowhead]. They were just putting down grass. I had played on artificial turf my entire career here. I joked and said, 'Lamar, if we had grass when I was playing, I might still be collecting a paycheck from you.' He chuckled and said, 'Yeah, but you never would've gotten into politics.' I asked what he meant. He said, 'Bill, I think you hit your head one too many times on that artificial turf.'"

From left to right: Chiefs founder Lamar Hunt, Chiefs coach Hank Stram, and NFL commissioner Pete Rozelle pose prior to the Chiefs' 23–7 victory on January 11, 1970, against the Vikings in Super Bowl IV. (AP Images)

No one worked closer with Lamar Hunt than Jack Steadman, who had been working for Hunt Oil for about five years before joining Hunt and the Texans with the AFL endeavor. Steadman, of course, became the team's general manager and president. "When God created man," Steadman has said many times, "he had Lamar Hunt in mind. He was one of the most humble, gracious, caring persons that I've ever been around. In all of the 47 years that I worked with Lamar—it was always *with*—there was never a time that he made me feel I was working *for* him. It was a very unique quality for him to have. He was a visionary beyond all of the people I've ever known. He could see things beyond where I could even comprehend. He was very, very quiet, which is interesting because we'd be having discussions in a meeting, and Lamar would just sit there and listen. They would think that he wasn't paying attention. I will guarantee that his mind was going 100 miles an hour on everything that was said. He also had an incredible photographic memory. He could remember plays years after they occurred…He might be presenting an award to one of the players and he'd bring back things that I'd forgotten a long time ago. He was a brilliant man, fun to work with because he was so creative."

Among Hunt's other contributions to the sports world, he co-founded World Championship Tennis and the North American Soccer League (1967–84) and he was one of the original investors in the NBA's Chicago Bulls. Hunt was inducted into the Pro Football Hall of Fame in 1972 and into the National Soccer Hall of Fame in 1992.

Hunt passed away on December 13, 2006, following a long battle with prostate cancer. "[He was] arguably the greatest sportsman of this last half-century, although he never sought fame or recognition for the improvements and changes he brought to the world's sports institutions," Peterson said. "His was a creative, constructive, and loving life not nearly long enough, and we will likely never see one like it again."

2 Super Bowl LIV

A lot happened in the 50 years since 1970. The VCR came and went. So did the Sony Walkman. Mobile phones came and shrank. The Rubik's Cube was invented. As were the McDonald's Quarter Pounder and Reese's Pieces. Shoot, Elvis Presley has had 25 songs in the top 40 between Super Bowls IV and LIV. Then there are the Kansas City Royals and the Truman Sports Complex. The two stadiums hadn't been built yet. And the Royals? They had just finished their inaugural season when the Chiefs last went to the Super Bowl. There have been countless heartbreaks and close moments for the Chiefs, including two AFC Championship Game appearances.

But, oh, this was so worth the wait.

For posterity sake, as if any Chiefs fan could ever forget this score: Kansas City Chiefs 31, San Francisco 49ers 20. As happens so many times, though, the score is deceiving. In fact, there was plenty of anxiety for Kansas City and plenty of celebration for San Francisco, particularly during the fourth quarter. The Chiefs scored the first touchdown of the Super Bowl on, fittingly, a one-yard run by quarterback Patrick Mahomes. That gave Kansas City a 7–3 lead in the closing seconds of the opening quarter. Each team scored again and went into the locker room at halftime tied at 10. Just like that, though, in the third quarter, the 49ers went up by 10 with 2:40 left. They carried that 20–10 lead well into the fourth quarter.

No biggie, right? After all, the Chiefs, winners of the AFC West, overcame double-digit deficits in their two previous postseason games—24 points against the Houston Texans and 10 against the Tennessee Titans. This one, though, felt different. Since taking a 10–3 lead on a 31-yard field goal by Harrison Butker with 9:36 left in the second quarter, the Chiefs were outscored 17–0, and Mahomes and the offense couldn't get things going. On their first three offensive possessions after Butker's field goal in the second quarter, the Chiefs punted, and Mahomes threw two interceptions.

But then something incredibly fortuitous happened. After Mahomes connected with Tyreek Hill on a second and 15 that seemingly put the Chiefs at midfield with a little more than seven minutes remaining, San Francisco challenged the catch. While awaiting the call, Mahomes went over to offensive coordinator Eric Bieniemy to discuss the next play. "What are we thinking?" He asked as Bieniemy looked over the extensive play chart. "Do we have time to run *Wasp?*"

That one suggestion from the 24-year-old Mahomes completely flipped the momentum and put a play in Chiefs fans' lexicon that'll remain as famous as *65 Toss Power Trap*. *Wasp*, which the Chiefs ran rarely—but had during the previous season's AFC Championship Game against the New England Patriots—was designed to sting the defense with a deep pass to Hill. After the 49ers won the challenge, forcing third and 15 from the Chiefs' 35, Mahomes hit Hill on *Wasp* for a 44-yard gain. "We were in a bad situation, especially with that pass rush," Mahomes said. "You knew those guys had their ears pinned back, and they were going to be rushing. I think the offensive line gave me enough time to throw a really deep route and I just put it out there, and Tyreek made a really great play, and so that got us going there."

After the 49ers committed defensive pass interference on third down, putting the Chiefs on the 1-yard line, Mahomes hit Travis Kelce for a touchdown that made it 20–17. Kansas City's defense, which improved dramatically throughout the season, forced the 49ers to punt with 6:13 remaining. A little more than two minutes later, General Mahomes marched his offense 65 yards and completed a five-yard touchdown play to running back Damien Williams. Butker's extra point gave the Chiefs a 24–17 lead with 2:44 left in regulation.

Kansas City's defense came up big once again on the ensuing possession. They allowed San Francisco to creep inside the 50, but after 49ers quarterback Jimmy Garoppolo overthrew Emmanuel Sanders on third and 10 with 1:39 remaining, Frank Clark sacked Garoppolo.

The old adage of "defense wins championships" couldn't be more appropriate for the 2019 Chiefs. Under coordinator Bob Sutton in 2018, the Chiefs' maligned defense ranked 24th in points allowed and 31st in yards allowed. With a new scheme under new

Comeback Kingdom

"Was it over when the Germans bombed Pearl Harbor?" Like that famous scene in *Animal House*, Chiefs fans should've learned before Super Bowl LIV that with Patrick Mahomes no deficit was too much during the postseason. Even though the 10-point deficit against the San Francisco 49ers was late in the game, the Chiefs had come out of similar holes in their two previous playoff games.

AFC Divisional Playoff vs. the Houston Texans
Down 24–0
Chiefs Kingdom was stunned pretty early in the game against the Texans. Barring an injury, the game could not have started any worse for the home team. An early 54-yard touchdown play from Deshaun Watson to Kenny Stills was followed by a blocked punt that Houston recovered in the end zone, the Texans recovered a dropped punt, which turned it into another Watson touchdown pass, and was followed by another field goal. Kansas City's offense looked tight like it had never been on that stage before. But something clicked in the second quarter, and the Chiefs scored four touchdowns in nine minutes, 11 seconds, erasing the largest first-half deficit in NFL history. But they weren't done. Kansas City scored 41 straight points en route to a 51–31 whooping of the Texans.

AFC Championship Game vs. the Tennessee Titans
Down 10–0 and 17–7
This wasn't as dramatic—save for the fact that the Chiefs did it in the conference championship game. Much like the previous week against Houston, Tennessee seemed to throw off Kansas City's offensive rhythm. The touchdown that cut the Titans' lead to 17–7 was the first of three consecutive touchdowns for Kansas City's offense. The third, which gave the Chiefs a lead going into halftime, was a hallmark 27-yard run down the sidelines by Mahomes, which ended with him spinning and then falling into the end zone. The Chiefs won 35–24, punching their ticket to Super Bowl LIV.

coordinator Steve Spagnuolo and with new players, including Clark and Tyrann Mathieu, Kansas City's defense developed throughout 2019 into the seventh best in points and 17th in yards allowed. "The defense is unbelievable," Kelce said after the game. "From Spags to five-five [Clark] to Honey Badger [Mathieu] bringing that championship swagger, he brought that here, and Brett Veach did a great job of bringing the right guys to change the culture in this locker room and win the Lombardi."

The Chiefs added to their lead with 1:20 left. After San Francisco took a timeout, the Chiefs were trying to eat the clock and get another first down, when Williams found a hole and scampered 38 yards for a touchdown. "Honestly, it's funny because Sherm [Chiefs fullback Anthony Sherman] came in the game and was like, 'Follow me.' That's exactly what I did. I followed him," Williams said of the clinching touchdown run. "The run was supposed to go inside. He went outside. So I went outside and I said, 'Forget it. I'm taking it to the house.'"

Ironically, the defense came up with one more huge play as Kendall Fuller went over Deebo Samuel for an interception on San Francisco's next possession and sealed the game. "It wasn't pretty, but it was gritty," Spagnuolo said of his unit making plays in the last quarter. "The guys were gritty at the end; our guys never gave up. And the one good thing about coaching defense and playing defense for the Kansas City Chiefs is we have Patrick Mahomes. You have the confidence that he's going to find a way to get some points on the board, and if we can just hang in there and keep not letting them score, you're going to find a way to win games."

And what a win it was. For the first time in 50 years, the Chiefs were Super Bowl champions! The win gave Mahomes one more accolade in his young career as he became the youngest player in NFL history to win the NFL MVP and Super Bowl MVP. And it was the first Super Bowl win for legendary coach Andy Reid. "I had two goals when I became the starting quarterback for the Kansas City Chiefs," Mahomes said after the game. "And the first goal was to win the Lamar Hunt trophy. I wanted to bring it home, the one that has our founder's name on it. I wanted to bring it to this family and this organization. And the second most important thing was to get Coach Reid a Super Bowl trophy. He's one of the greatest coaches of all time. I don't think he needed the Lombardi Trophy to prove that. But just to do that, it puts all doubt aside, and he's going to be listed as one of the all-time great coaches in history whenever he wants to be done, which I hope is not anytime soon."

As locals celebrated a Super Bowl win for the first time in 50 years, fireworks, car horns, banging pots and pans, and sobbing—a lot of sobbing—could be heard around 9:30 PM throughout Kansas City. A few days later, Reid, Mahomes, and the rest of the Chiefs received a hero's welcome in Kansas City, when hundreds of thousands of people took on the 20-degree temperatures and snow for the victory parade in downtown. And more tears were shed. It was worth the wait.

65 Toss Power Trap

The night before the Chiefs took on the Minnesota Vikings in Super Bowl IV in New Orleans, safety Johnny Robinson was chatting with his road roommate, quarterback Len Dawson. "Can you score any damn points against these guys?" Robinson asked Dawson.

"Yes, I can," said Dawson. "We're going to put some points on the board. What about you guys on defense against Joe Kapp? They killed the NFL in the playoffs. Can you guys stop him?"

Robinson looked Dawson in the eyes and, in a tone full of more sincerity than bravado, said: "I've seen him all week and I think we might just shut them out."

With an outstanding offense and their defensive "Purple People Eaters," the Vikings seemed like a team of destiny. In 1969 they ranked first in both offense (379 points) and defense (133 points) in the NFL. The only time they allowed more than 14 points in a game came during a 24–23 season-opening loss to the New York Giants. Offensively, they scored more than 50 points three times in 1969. So Robinson's comment might've seemed crazy if it weren't for what the Chiefs had done that season.

Kansas City had the top-ranked defense (177 points) and the second-ranked offense (359 points) in the AFL that year. The Chiefs defense was so good in 1969 that not only were they the only team that gave up fewer than 200 points in the wide-open AFL, they were the only team that gave up less than 240 points. "We still had that shadow of the 'Mickey Mouse League' following us around," said wide receiver Frank Pitts, referring to the AFL's nickname. "We were determined to let everybody know we were going to take care of business."

And the Chiefs did just that during the 23–7 victory.

The confidence they felt going into the contest with Minnesota came out during the game's first two possessions. After Minnesota marched to the Kansas City 39-yard line, the Chiefs defense woke up and stopped the Vikings. The Chiefs, after starting on their own 17, promptly moved the ball into Minnesota territory, thanks largely to a 20-yard pass play from Dawson to Pitts. Four plays later, Jan Stenerud booted a 48-yard field goal, giving the Chiefs an early 3–0 lead. Stenerud's field goal remained a Super Bowl record for distance until Super Bowl XXI. It also gave the Chiefs a lead that they wouldn't relinquish.

Kansas City scored on three of its next four possessions, including two more Stenerud field goals. The third score in that stretch

Dawson's Distraction

The day before the 1969 AFL Championship Game at Oakland, a league official told coach Hank Stram that Len Dawson's name had surfaced in a betting scandal involving Detroit gambler Donald Dawson (no relation). Shortly before the Raiders game, however, the league official, Mark Duncan, called Stram and told him that everything had been resolved.

It was. Until the Chiefs arrived in New Orleans. "When we got off the bus in New Orleans, we heard the same thing again about Lenny and this betting nonsense," Stram said 30 years after Super Bowl IV. "Only this time it was all over the papers. The story was absolutely absurd!"

In hopes of putting it behind them so they could focus on the game, Stram and Dawson decided to hold a press conference to squash the rumors. NFL commissioner Pete Rozelle, whom Stram called a "great friend" and who was the former public relations director for the Los Angeles Rams, suggested that if they held a press conference, they shouldn't talk about the scandal, only the upcoming game with the Vikings. "[Rozelle] didn't look at us like we had done something wrong," Stram said. "He was mainly concerned about having a good Super Bowl. I was, too, but I didn't agree with his thoughts on Lenny's press conference."

So the press conference went on as Stram had envisioned at 11 PM. The media seemed satisfied with Dawson's comments. "Of course he handled everything with typical class and style and grace and dignity," Stram said, "and did a fantastic job as everybody knows."

Stram's biggest concern then was his team's reaction—and possible distraction—due to the reports and all of the questions from the media. So he addressed his squad at the team breakfast the morning after the press conference.

"I told [our team] what we did the night before," Stram said. "Then I asked if anybody had any questions. E.J. Holub, our center, said, 'Yeah, I've got a question, Coach. When are we going to eat?'... That's how distracted they were. It was amazing how they responded to the situation and rallied around Lenny. The whole team just did a fantastic job of not letting the story affect them, which was obvious in the game."

has become one of the most memorable moments in Super Bowl history, when head coach Hank Stram sent wide receiver Gloster Richardson into the game on third and goal from the 5 and said: "Gloster, come on; 65 Toss Power Trap. Get in there; 65 Toss Power Trap."

Because of Minnesota's defense, Stram felt it would work. "Their great defensive tackle, Alan Page, occasionally lined up between the guard and the tackle on short yardage downs instead of between the guard and center. So he would be on the shoulder of our tackle, Jim Tyrer," Stram wrote in his autobiography *They're Playing My Game*. "Page had quick reactions. If Tyrer pulled, Page would chase him along the line of scrimmage, and we could run a trap play to the inside. I watched Page at work several more times to confirm this, then put in a play based on it—65 Toss Power Trap."

"When I told Lenny the play, he looked at me like I was crazy and asked if I'm sure that's what [Stram] called," Richardson said. "We didn't normally run it in the red zone. We usually called it in the open field." And, really, 65 Toss Power Trap wasn't a play the Chiefs used often. "We hadn't worked on that play in weeks," Dawson said. "He called that out of nowhere. So, yes, when Gloster brought the play in, I said, 'Gloster, are you sure that's what he called?' He told me it was."

The play has become an iconic part of Chiefs and Super Bowl history—mainly because it worked. Mike Garrett ran the ball five yards for a touchdown that gave Kansas City a 16–0 lead at half-time. "I remember the run, but it wasn't a big run," Garrett said. "What I remember most about scoring is thinking about how the city of Kansas City was going to be beside themselves. They loved us, and it was great to be a part of a team that represented Kansas City the way it should be."

The day definitely belonged to Kansas City and the Chiefs. Even after Minnesota scored on a touchdown late in the third quarter, the Chiefs answered on their next possession with a

46-yard pass play from Dawson, the game's MVP, to Otis Taylor. A 7-yard reverse by Pitts on third and 7 set up the play.

The convincing win gave the city of Kansas City its first pro sports championship since the Monarchs won the 1942 Negro World Series. With the Chiefs winning Super Bowl IV, a year after the New York Jets became the first AFL team to win the championship by beating the Baltimore Colts, the AFL gained the respect that it deserved.

Super Bowl IV marked the end of the AFL vs. the NFL. The two leagues merged following that season. Since Lamar Hunt had the foresight to start the AFL, it was only fitting that the Chiefs reach this particular game. "It was poetic justice that we were the first team to play and represent the American Football League in Super Bowl I," Stram said. "So it also seemed appropriate that we were the team to win Super IV, the last championship game before the two leagues officially merged. There was a lot of satisfaction in that."

Speaking of Stram, perhaps the main reason "65 Toss Power Trap" remains embedded in Super Bowl history—besides the play working—is that NFL Films had a microphone on Stram. (As the story goes, Minnesota coach Bud Grant was asked, but he declined because of his penchant for cussing.) The players didn't know about it during the game. Even though they thought Stram was acting a little more animated than usual, they didn't find out until a few months after the win over the Vikings.

"That spring they showed the highlights at the Lyric Theatre in downtown Kansas City," Dawson said. "We didn't know it before then. He didn't tell anybody. He also had the rights to edit what was used or to even let something be used. It explained a lot."

Because of that we can go back and hear such now famous lines—including his misuse of the word that actually means to enroll—as, "Just keep *matriculating* the ball down the field, boys," and "Here comes a reverse from tight-I," and perhaps the most famous play in Chiefs history: 65 Toss Power Trap.

4 Len Dawson

It could be said that Len Dawson was destined to be a quarterback. That really seems to be the most logical reason he went from a hesitant 125-pound fifth-string quarterback during his sophomore year in high school—with more passion and ability to play baseball and basketball—to a Pro Football Hall of Famer. Well, destiny unless you believe in luck for the seventh son of a seventh son.

Len Dawson, who was from Alliance, Ohio, went to Purdue after being recruited by a relatively unknown assistant coach named Hank Stram. While at Purdue, Dawson had an outstanding career, starting with his first game. In his first varsity game, Dawson threw for 185 yards and four touchdowns in Purdue's 31–0 win against Missouri. Dawson went on to throw for more than 3,000 yards, led the Big Ten in passing for three seasons, and led the Boilermakers to an upset over top-ranked Notre Dame in South Bend. Before the draft the Pittsburgh Steelers and the Cleveland Browns were among the teams that contacted Dawson to see if he'd be interested in playing if they drafted him.

The Steelers beat the Browns in a coin flip to see which team would draft fifth in 1957. Pittsburgh won and picked Dawson. Walt Kiesling, Pittsburgh's coach at the time of the draft, resigned before the season because of health reasons. When training camp opened, Buddy Parker had taken over. "Buddy was going to do it his way, and Buddy was known as a coach who didn't play rookies, particularly at quarterback," Dawson said. "They made a trade to get Earl Morrall. So there's Earl Morrall, me, and another rookie quarterback named Jack Kemp. They ended up releasing Kemp, so I was the understudy to Morrall."

Part of the Chiefs franchise for more than 50 years, Len Dawson transitioned from a Super Bowl-winning quarterback to a Hall of Fame broadcaster.

The next season Kemp was long gone after, allegedly, not obeying Parker's request to punt a ball out of bounds during a preseason game. He got cut on the spot, and the Steelers traded Morrall for another quarterback and a Parker friend, Bobby Layne. Dawson remained a backup. Let's put it this way: during his three years in Pittsburgh, Dawson played in just 19 games, starting one. He completed six of 17 passes for 96 yards and one touchdown.

In December 1959 the Steelers traded Dawson to Cleveland, where he spent two benchwarming seasons. "Five years into my pro career, and I really hadn't played much," he said.

Then came Dawson's break—a coaching convention in Pittsburgh, where he was living. "Hank was in town, and we had breakfast one morning," Dawson said. "He could see that I wasn't very happy, not getting a chance to play. He said, 'Well, if you ever get free, give me a call. We'd love to have you with the Texans.' Wanting to jump on that chance, I figured I had nothing to lose by asking Paul Brown for my release. He put me on waivers in June, when most the coaches for most teams were taking the month off for training camps. The other teams didn't even know I was on waivers, and I cleared. That's how I became a Dallas Texan."

Dawson joined the Texans before the 1962 season, and both he and the organization flourished. He promptly led the Texans to the '62 AFL Championship en route to becoming the league's Player of the Year by *The Sporting News*. "Lenny the Cool" led the Chiefs to Super Bowls I and IV, winning the MVP award after the Chiefs' victory over Minnesota.

Even 40 years after the end of his career, Dawson remains at or near the top of multiple categories for the Chiefs. Among Dawson's superlatives, he's first in: most games started as a quarterback (158); most seasons leading the league in passing (four—1962, '64, '66, and '68); most passing yards, career (28,507); most touchdown passes, career (237); most passes attempted, career (3,696); most completions, career (2,115); most consecutive passes completed (15, tied with Bill Kenney and Alex Smith); most seasons leading the league in completion percentage (eight, which is an NFL record); most consecutive seasons leading the league in completion percentage (six, also an NFL record); most seasons leading the league in touchdowns (four, also an NFL record); and most touchdown passes, game (six vs. Denver in November 1964, tied with Patrick Mahomes).

Dawson, whose No. 16 the Chiefs retired, finally was inducted into the Pro Football Hall of Fame in 1987.

As good as Dawson was on the field, he became just as good on the microphone. Starting in 1966 Dawson became a sports anchor and sports director on Kansas City's ABC affiliate, KMBC-TV. Shortly after his playing career ended, he became an analyst on NBC's football broadcasts and was a mainstay on HBO's *Inside the NFL* (1977–2001). He also became one of the top radio analysts in the NFL, serving as the color commentator on Chiefs broadcasts from 1983 to 2017.

Dawson's broadcast work was recognized by the Pro Football Hall of Fame in 2012 when he received the Pete Rozelle Radio-Television Award. He was the third person—along with Frank Gifford and Dan Dierdorf—to be in the Hall of Fame as both a player and a broadcaster. "This is an unbelievable award for me," Dawson said at the time. "To be in the Hall of Fame as a player was the highlight of my playing career, but now to be recognized by the Hall of Fame as a broadcaster—well, it's just a great, great honor."

5 Derrick Thomas

Neil Smith knows about heartbreak. He felt it professionally after the Chiefs lost six times in the playoffs during his career, including the 1993 AFC Championship Game. That pain goes away. But the pain—after the unexpected death of his former teammate and best friend Derrick Thomas—still lingers. "There's not a day that he doesn't cross my mind," Smith said. "I sometimes ask myself, *What would Derrick do in this situation.*"

The hurt for Smith, the Chiefs family, and Chiefs Nation started on Sunday afternoon, January 23, 2000. While en route to the airport on a snowy and icy Interstate-435 to go to St. Louis for the NFC Championship Game, Thomas, who turned 33 on New Year's Day, lost control of his Chevy Suburban, hit a median, and caromed out of control. Thomas and one of his passengers, Mike Tellis, were ejected from the vehicle. Thomas suffered a fractured neck and a fractured back. Tellis died at the scene. Neither was wearing his seatbelt. Another passenger, John Hagebusch, who was buckled up, suffered minor injuries.

The next day, paralyzed from the neck down, Thomas was taken to one of the nation's top spinal research centers at Jackson Memorial Hospital in Miami, his hometown.

Through reports almost daily on TV and radio and in *The Kansas City Star*, fans were told of Thomas' status and reminded of his long road toward recovery. General manager Carl Peterson had visited Thomas—Peterson's first draft pick who had become like a son to the Chiefs GM; "Derrick's dad died when Derrick was about four, and I didn't have a son," Peterson said—on February 7 at the hospital.

"I stepped out in the hall, and coming down the hall was Derrick Thomas in a wheelchair but upbeat," Peterson said at the time. "I said, 'Son, you're mobile.' And he said, 'Father, I am. I've got wheels.'"

Peterson reflected further on it years later. "Derrick was in such a better mood, very optimistic about his life ahead," he said. "I remember flying back to Kansas City…with [Chiefs doctor] Jon Browne, and we were truly amazed at Derrick's spirit and determination."

But something went horribly wrong. At 10:10 EST the next morning, February 8, Thomas died from a pulmonary embolism—a blood clot that lodged in an artery between his heart and a lung.

The Chiefs family has suffered unexpected losses during the organization's existence: Stone Johnson, Mack Lee Hill, and Joe

D.T. Downs Krieg—7x

If there ever was a day when Derrick Thomas looked possessed on the field, it would be Veterans Day 1990, during Thomas' second season in the NFL. Appropriately, on a day when Americans pay honor to those who served our country, Thomas had his father, Robert, on his mind. Robert Thomas was an Air Force captain whose plane was shot down during the Vietnam War on a mission called "Operation: Linebacker Two." (He was declared dead in 1980.)

Inspired by his father, D.T. went out and set a single-game record by sacking Seattle (and future Chiefs teammate) Dave Krieg seven times. On the final play of the game, Thomas had Krieg in his grasp for what would have been an eighth sack, but Krieg broke loose and launched a 25-yard touchdown prayer to Paul Skansi in the end zone, giving the Seahawks a 17–16 win. "I thought I had him," Thomas said. "He just stumbled back and caught his balance and threw the pass. That last sack I didn't get is the one I'm going to remember."

It was Seattle's first win at Arrowhead in a decade.

Thomas' third sack of the game helped give the Chiefs a 16–10 lead, when he stripped the ball from Krieg. It was picked up by Dan Saleaumua, who scored the Chiefs' first touchdown in three weeks.

After taking down Denver Broncos quarterback John Elway during the Chiefs' 24–22 home victory in 1997, Derrick Thomas celebrates his 100th career sack. (AP Images)

Delaney. But this one resonated a little more because of D.T.'s impact on the team.

On the field, Thomas, the Chiefs' first pick in 1989, quickly became a fan favorite and the face of the franchise. With incredible quickness, grace, and tenacity, he bullied offensive linemen and quarterbacks. Leading a renaissance of the Chiefs defense, he reminded longtime Chiefs fans of Hall of Fame linebackers Bobby Bell and Willie Lanier.

During his rookie season, Thomas recorded 13 tackles (six solo) in a game at Cleveland. Almost a year to the day later, he had a career-defining game when he sacked Seattle Seahawks quarterback Dave Krieg seven times, setting an NFL single-game record. During his 11-year career in which he went to nine Pro Bowls, Thomas set Chiefs records with 45 forced fumbles, 19 fumble recoveries, three safeties, and four touchdowns.

Thomas and Smith, the team's top pick in '88, formed one of pro football's all-time best pass rushing tandems. Opponents couldn't focus on one and not the other. "We felt we put the seven-step drop out of football," Smith said. "They dropped it down to three steps, and now it's one step. We felt we helped change a lot of [offensive strategies]."

Thomas and Smith accounted for 184.5 sacks between them. Smith finished his Kansas City career with 86.5 sacks. He's second on the team's all-time list behind Thomas, who had 126.5 in his career following the 1999 season.

On and off the field, Smith and Thomas were inseparable. "We kept each other out of trouble," Smith says.

They were like a couple of big kids, both always smiling and cutting up while endearing themselves to a city that was in the midst of going football crazy. Of course, acting like a big kid got Thomas in trouble a few times, privately and publicly. His play on the field, though, helped fans overlook his penchant for mischief.

But like most dynamic duos—Simon and Garfunkel, Elvis and Priscilla, Shaq and Kobe—Smith and Thomas separated, when Smith signed with Denver after the 1996 season. "Once we split up, I always said in my mind that Derrick made me what I was and I feel I was a key part in his career," Smith said. "But I never took over a ballgame. He could take over a game."

Even so, Smith helped the Broncos reach the Super Bowl, while Thomas' stock as a star athlete in the Kansas City community continued to rise. His name oftentimes was mentioned in the same breath as George Brett and Tom Watson. "He was a presence wherever he was," Smith said. "I told him that he was the only guy I knew that, when a president was in the city, he could get out of practice to go shake the president's hand, while the rest of us had to practice."

Indeed, the first president George Bush designated Thomas as his 832nd "Point of Light" for Thomas' work in the Kansas City community. The two met when President Bush was in Kansas City on September 11, 1992. In 1993 the NFL bestowed its highest honor on Thomas when the league selected him as the Edge NFL Man of the Year, which mainly takes into account a player's service in the community. "On-the-field accolades are great," Thomas said, "but in order to reach your full potential, you have to overstep the boundaries of football and go out into the community and be an All-Pro there, too."

Thomas served on numerous boards for non-profit groups and he took on countless charitable endeavors, including his Third and Long Foundation, which continued after his death. Appropriately, Smith's name was added to the foundation, and he became the chairman of the board. "I miss the friend and brother in him the most and his smile. He was a happy, fun guy to be around," Smith said. "Nobody can take his place."

In 2009 Thomas, whom the Chiefs selected for their Hall of Fame in 2001, was inducted into the Pro Football Hall of Fame. "Father" Peterson served as Thomas' presenter.

6 Super Bowl I

They'd heard the comments. They weren't good enough to be playing in this game. To get downright nasty about it, they were from a Mickey Mouse league. The Chiefs—along with every other American Football League team—knew they didn't get respect from their counterparts in the National Football League.

Hank Stram, the master motivator that he was, knew exactly which buttons to push and when. So in spite of the pressure on his Chiefs as the first representative from the AFL to play in the AFL-NFL Championship (now known as Super Bowl I)—and facing the powerhouse from Green Bay no less—Stram tried to lighten up his team's mood before the game. "I asked our equipment manager to go to the five-and-dime store and get some Mickey Mouse ears and the Mickey Mouse theme song," Stram said. "When the players walked into the locker room, the equipment guys were wearing the Mickey Mouse ears, while the theme song played in the background. I thought, *What the hell; we'll have a little fun with this and maybe get them relaxed to play like they're supposed to play.*"

The players certainly seemed to be a little relaxed. Heck, they were giddy.

Second-year receiver Frank Pitts, who played mainly on special teams during the Chiefs' 35–10 loss in Super Bowl I, remembered: "Before the game I ran by [Green Bay coach Vince] Lombardi on the sidelines and started rambling, 'I've seen you on TV so much and I'm out here in Los Angeles.' And I shook his hand. He said, 'It's great to have you out here. Now get back to the other side.'

"Then, on the kickoff I made the tackle on Elijah Pitts. When I got him, I was hugging him and falling to the ground and I said,

'This is your namesake making a tackle!' He said, 'Fine, get up.' That was a big highlight for me…[The game] was so new that anything and everything was exciting."

Defeating the Bills 31–7 on January 1, 1967 (the very day future Kansas City star Derrick Thomas was born) for the AFL championship, however, gave the Chiefs a belief that they belonged on the same field as the Packers. It also didn't hurt that the Chiefs scored more than 30 points in eight of their 14 regular-season games. In four of those, they scored at least 40.

"I was really happy that we were in the first so-called Super Bowl, playing for the world championship," Ed Budde said, "but I'm still disappointed that we lost. Green Bay had a great team, obviously, but we were a great team. All of a sudden, because it was the Green Bay Packers we were giving them a lot of respect."

The Chiefs knew they'd have to rely heavily on their offense if they were going to beat Green Bay. Kansas City's defense wasn't the team's strength, and the team knew it might not provide a worthy opponent to quarterback Bart Starr and his potent Packers offense.

The Chiefs kept the game close in the first half. They matched a Bart Starr to Max McGee touchdown with a Len Dawson to Curtis McClinton scoring play and then got a field goal from Mike Mercer just before halftime after another Green Bay touchdown. The Chiefs' concern about their defense came to fruition in the second half. In spite of the close 14–10 deficit at halftime, Kansas City couldn't slow down the Packers offense in the second half. Starr threw for 250 yards and two touchdowns on 16-for-23 passing. "That was such an emotional game because we knew the importance of it since we were competing with the NFL," said E.J. Holub, who played center and linebacker during his 10-year career with the Texans and Chiefs. "We made mistakes because we were overexcited. We got burned."

Possibly the biggest play of the game came in the third quarter when Green Bay's Willie Wood intercepted a pass attempt from Dawson to Fred Arbanas and ran it back to the Chiefs 5. "The game was relatively close then," Dawson said. "That might've been a different game if I hadn't called that play." The Packers scored during their next series and didn't look back.

Dawson said the interception still haunts him today. But he and others admit the Packers were the better team—something that showed on the scoreboard. "One thing about playing in a Super Bowl game is that if you have any shortcomings, they're going to be exposed," Stram said. "[Defense] was our shortcoming...[Super Bowl I] did provide us with a lot of impetus that we wanted to make it back to that championship again, and if we did make it back, we would win."

7 Bobby Bell

Bobby Bell could seemingly do it all. And before joining the Chiefs as a seventh-round selection in the 1963 AFL Draft, he did do it all at the University of Minnesota. Recruited as a running back out of high school in North Carolina, Bell switched to quarterback during his freshman year for the Gophers. By the time he won the Outland Trophy in 1962 as the nation's top lineman, Bell played center and tackle on both sides of the ball. It even took the Chiefs a couple seasons to decide where to put him. Originally a defensive end for the first two years of his pro career, Bell moved to outside linebacker where he became one of the best in the history of the NFL. During 168 career games, Bell intercepted 26 passes for 479 yards and recovered 15 fumbles. In 1983 Bell became the first Chiefs player to be enshrined in the Pro Football Hall of Fame.

How did Lamar Hunt recruit you to the AFL out of the University of Minnesota?

Bobby Bell: He came over to St. Paul, and when I opened the door, I immediately thought, "There's no way this guy owns a football team." He just looked like some guy off University Avenue. My mind didn't change when he started talking. "I'm Lamar Hunt and I just came by to see Bobby," he said, and then before we sat down he added, "Is there any place to get some ice cream around here?" I thought we were going to talk football. *And this guy wants to find ice cream?* We went to have some ice cream, and he told me right off the bat, "I have this new league and I want you to be part of our new team in Dallas." I said, "Well I don't know that much about it, so let's go talk to Mr. Lange. We'll talk together." Herman Lange was a business guy in Minneapolis who was like a father to me. As we sat there, Mr. Lange said we wanted a guaranteed contract because we didn't know if the league was going to last. Mr. Hunt said okay, and we talked for a little bit longer to come to terms. Mr. Lange said, "Do we have a deal?" Lamar said, "We have a deal." And we shook hands. Honest to God, we shook hands! That was it.

The next day I was going to New York for an All-American team function, and Lamar was going on some type of business. When we got there, we decided to share a cab to our hotels. On our way we went through a toll booth. The cab driver held out his hand and told us we needed to pay. I put my hands in my pockets while Lamar just sat there. So I paid the 15 cents. Then when we got to Lamar's hotel, which was the first stop, he came around the car and knocked on my window. He smiled and said, "Hey, do you have any cash on you?" I told him I did, so he said, "Good, you take care of the cab. I'll talk to you later." And he walked away. As soon as I got to the Waldorf, I checked in, went to my room, and called Mr. Lange. I said, "Mr. Lange, did I do the right thing, signing with Lamar Hunt?" He said, "Yeah, it's a good deal. Why?" I said, "Because Lamar is broke!"

There's a side story to that. Lamar used to write letters to me all the time, including every birthday. On my 60th birthday, guess what he sent me? A note with 15 cents taped to it. I still have it today.

What was fellow Hall of Famer Hank Stram like?

BB: As a coach, he was great. They talk about him being before his time. Look at the offense now, which is called the "West Coast Offense." That's what we ran, but it was called the "spread." On defense we ran a triple stack with three linemen and four linebackers. That's how I ended up at linebacker because Coach said he wanted to put me in a position to make the big plays. He treated all of us that way.

Didn't Stram, a very snazzy dresser, make you guys dress up on road trips?

BB: When we first got to Kansas City, we had to wear these red blazers with the big patch on the pocket. It was the ugliest thing. We were in Houston for a game, and a bunch of us were standing outside our hotel ready to go get something to eat. A lady pulled up in a cab, jumped out, and said to me, "Hey, boy, come and get my bag." I guess I looked like the doorman. I was thinking, *What the hell?* as I went over and picked up her bag. I took it to the counter and stood there with it as she checked in to the hotel. As she was finishing checking in, the guy behind the desk said, "Do you need anything else? Do you need help with your bag?" She said, "No, he has it." The guy looked at me funny; I shrugged my shoulders and followed this lady up to her room with her bag. I offered to get her some ice when we got to her room. I tell you what, though; she gave me a $5 bill. Back then $5 was a lot of money! I went back downstairs where the guys were waiting. I joked with them, "Shoot, you guys go on to dinner. I can make more money doing this."

What does it mean to be the first Kansas City Chiefs player to be inducted into the Pro Football Hall of Fame?

BB: You play for a team and give all that you have, and then to go into the Pro Football Hall of Fame is the very top of the pyramid. You have to understand, I grew up playing six-man football. I didn't even know if I could play at a big university, but I did at Minnesota, and then Lamar Hunt gave me a chance to play in Kansas City, and I ended up becoming the first Chiefs player to go into the Hall of Fame. That's something that my family and friends can take pride in after I'm gone. I played the game because I loved it. I was a good football player, sure, but I'd like people to remember me as a person who loved the game and gave everything I had.

MVPat

A high school kid in Texas sent a tweet on February 6, 2013, which likely went unnoticed at the time: "I bet it feels amazing to be the quarterback who says "I'm going to Disney World" after winning the Super Bowl #Qbs." Seven years and three days later, that kid, the 24-year-old, third-year quarterback for the Chiefs, got to say those words as the MVP of Super Bowl LIV.

Watching Patrick Mahomes—with his unique haircut and a voice that's a cross between Louis Armstrong and Kermit the Frog—became must-see TV simply because there was no telling what he would do. One week it might be a no-look pass. The next week it might be an incredible scramble down the sideline. The next week it might be a sidearm pass around a defender. The next it might be a 60-yard pass play for a touchdown. Shoot, it might be all three of those in one quarter.

Besides that God-given ability, though, Mahomes possesses other intangibles. Even during his first two years as a starter, he never seemed to get too rattled. The stage never seemed to be too big. And he became the vocal leader of the team. "He was encouraging us, telling us to believe," wide receiver Tyreek Hill said of Mahomes after Super Bowl LIV, a game that looked perilous for Kansas City midway through the fourth quarter. "He had seen it in some guys' eyes —They were getting down, including myself. I was like, 'Man, how are we going to pull this off?' He was like '10, you've got to believe, brother.' He brought the guys together, and you see what happened, man. We pulled it off."

Much of Mahomes' coolness under pressure likely comes from being around his dad, Pat Mahomes, who pitched in the major leagues for 11 years. Young Patrick grew up in big league clubhouses around the likes of Mike Piazza, Rickey Henderson, Ivan Rodriguez, and Alex Rodriguez. "I guess when you meet guys like Alex Rodriguez and Derek Jeter growing up, you don't get starstruck," the elder Mahomes told *USA TODAY*.

The Chiefs didn't know necessarily that they were getting a young player who was so cool under pressure. But they felt he could be the quarterback of the future. The fact that they ended up with him is somewhat magical. Mahomes wasn't exactly a household name coming out of Texas Tech as a junior. It must mean that Kansas City general manager Brett Veach either sold his soul or is a wizard. Those are the only two explanations for his decision to trade up to the 10th spot and select Mahomes. The Red Raiders have a history of producing quarterbacks who can throw for a gazillion yards but struggle in the NFL. But there was something special about Mahomes that Veach, who was Kansas City's co-director of player personnel at the time, noticed when he watched him of film after the 2015 season. That was Mahomes' sophomore year. It was love at first sight—for Veach anyway. It took him a long time to convince coach Andy Reid that Mahomes was the right pick in

2017. "At one point that December [2016]," Veach recalled on NBC's *Football Morning in America*, "I remember Coach calling me into his office and showing me a Kiper/McShay mock first round. He said, 'Your guy's not even in the first round!' They didn't have Patrick in the round. I just said, 'Coach, it's perfect! Don't worry. You don't want him on these lists now. It sets up perfect for us.'"

There was just one somewhat curious piece to this: the Chiefs had a dependable veteran quarterback, Alex Smith, with seemingly a few years left in his arm. Were they going trade up to draft a quarterback with the 10th pick and sit him? Were they going to trade Smith and throw the rookie into the fire? "We had a plan for Patrick," Veach said during the 2018 NFL Combine. "And that was to come in, to learn the offense, and to not go out there and play until you have a firm mental grasp of what you want to accomplish. All of the physical tools are there. He's one of the best players I've ever seen. You don't want to throw them out there too soon. You want them to really be who they are and not have to process too much, just play."

Thankfully, in Smith they had someone who could not only win games, but also one of the nicest people on the planet. He not only knew that he was helping to groom the team's next quarterback, but he also embraced the role. He made sure that he included Mahomes in all aspects of his preparation: early or late workouts, film sessions, etc. "That's a big ego position," Reid told *Sports Illustrated*. "The QB room can be a little snitty at times. But Patrick came into a great situation. Alex didn't make any demands of him, but he didn't close the door on him. Patrick can't pay him enough for that opportunity."

Mahomes rewarded Reid and Veach and the Chiefs by winning the league MVP in his first season as a starter, becoming the third quarterback in NFL history to throw for 50 touchdowns in a season. The early part of the following season, however, didn't go exactly to script. Mahomes injured his ankle in Week One of

2019 and then suffered a dislocated kneecap in Week 7 against the Denver Broncos. The Chiefs downplayed the ankle injury, but it was obvious that Mahomes didn't have the same mobility that fans grew accustomed to seeing in 2018. His completion percentage and passer rating declined with the bad ankle. Because of the knee injury, he missed two full games.

The Chiefs beat the Broncos despite Mahomes' injury, snapping a two-game losing streak, but then dropped two of the next three, including Mahomes' return in Week 10 against the Tennessee Titans. But Mahomes looked like his old self, completing 36-of-50 passes for 446 yards, three touchdowns, and no interceptions against Tennessee. And after that loss, the Chiefs looked like the '18 version—only with an improving defense. Mahomes led the team to nine consecutive wins, including avenging regular-season losses to the Houston Texans and Titans, and then won the MVP award in Super Bowl LIV. "You dream about this stuff when you're a little kid," Mahomes said after the game. "I just try to go out there and be the best person I can be every single day and I enjoy this every single day. I enjoy going to the facility. I enjoy watching film. I enjoy most of all the brotherhood a team builds. So for me, just to be here with these guys and win the Super Bowl, it's amazing."

Tony G.

Quarterback Trent Green remembers one of his first meetings with tight end Tony Gonzalez. At the time Gonzalez was coming off the best season of his four-year NFL career and a second straight Pro Bowl selection. With Elvis Grbac as the quarterback in 2000, Gonzalez racked up then-career highs with 1,203 receiving yards and 93 receptions. The year before, Tony G had 849 receiving yards and 11 touchdowns, which remained his single-season best throughout his 17-year career.

Green, whom the Chiefs acquired from St. Louis prior to the 2001 season, was coming from an offense with the Rams that

Tony Gonzalez's hands—once considered a flaw—improved to such an extent that many consider him the best receiving tight end of all time.

used tight ends as blockers. The early plan under head coach Dick Vermeil and offensive coordinator Al Saunders was to run a similar offense. "I told Tony I wasn't sure he'd get the same touches that he'd been getting," Green said. "He wasn't happy with that, but Tony is a pro. He's going to show up in great shape, ready to roll. He worked hard, and you knew he was going to give everything he had each day, regardless of his role and regardless of how he felt about it. Tony became a very good blocker. He didn't get enough credit for that.

"As far as his ability to catch the football, though, it was a matter for me of figuring out where to throw it to him. From his basketball background, he liked to front it. He could make the over-the-shoulder catches, but that's not ideally where he wanted the ball thrown. Once I learned that and saw how good he was, he created a whole new set of problems for defenses. I think Al Saunders gets the credit for figuring out the best way to utilize Tony.

Indeed, after a few adjustment seasons—which still accounted for Gonzalez averaging 869 yards and eight touchdowns—Gonzalez caught a career-best 102 passes for a career-best 1,258 yards in 2004.

Years before that, the Chiefs shrewdly traded up in the first round of the 1997 draft to select Gonzalez (13th overall) out of Cal, where he'd been a standout basketball player, too. During the next 17 seasons, Gonzalez, who often punctuated his touchdowns by dunking the football over the goal post, redefined the tight end position. He was the first in a long line of college basketball players-turned-tight ends—including Antonio Gates, Jimmy Graham, and Julius Thomas—who helped change the NFL game.

He went from another blocker who could occasionally catch to a bruising receiver. Gonzalez caught 100 extra balls every day in practice throughout his career. (His Hollywood looks belied a fierce work ethic.) He finished with 15,127 yards and 111 touchdowns on 1,325 regular-season catches (all NFL records for a tight end) and the 14-time Pro Bowl performer played in 270 regular-season games (190 for Kansas City).

In 2007 and '08, Gonzalez had two of his most productive seasons with more than 1,000 yards and nearly 100 receptions in each (99 for 1,172 in '07 and 96 for 1,058 in '08). But general manager Scott Pioli traded Gonzalez to Atlanta in April 2009 in exchange for a second-round draft pick in 2010 in what turned out to be a terrible trade for the Chiefs. (Pioli used that pick to select Javier Arenas, who spent three years with the Chiefs before being traded to the Falcons.) "It's somewhat bittersweet," Gonzalez told FoxSports.com at the time of the trade. "I love Kansas City. I grew up in Kansas City. The city means a lot to me. I got there when I turned 21. It will be sad to leave a city I love. But I'm looking forward to making a Super Bowl run in Atlanta every year for the next three or four years."

The Falcons never made it to the Super Bowl with Gonzalez, but he did finally win a playoff game during the 2012 season before the Falcons lost in the NFC Championship Game to the San Francisco 49ers. Gonzalez played five seasons in Atlanta, where he caught 409 passes for 4,187 yards. His diligent work ethic along with a commitment to a vegan diet helped account for his longevity, as he remained one of the best at his position throughout his 17-year career.

At the end of the 2013 season and at the age of 37, he retired. "It's time for me to go into the next stage of life just like everybody else," Gonzalez told reporters after his final game with Atlanta in December 2013. "Nobody's immune to this, and the way I've been able to go out on my own terms, it's a blessing. And like I said, I have no regrets."

To no one's surprise, Gonzalez was inducted into the Pro Football Hall of Fame in 2019.

10 Willie Lanier

The story might be one of the greatest in Chiefs history—even among the players of the 1969 team. And it's the moment that best sums up Willie Lanier's passion for football and his teammates.

During the fourth quarter of the AFL divisional playoff game against the defending Super Bowl champion New York Jets at Shea Stadium, the Chiefs held a 6–3 lead. After a pass interference call on Kansas City, Joe Namath and the Jets had the ball at the 1-yard line on first down. With his teeth clenched and tears—yes, tears—running down his face, Lanier, the intense middle linebacker, barked at the defensive unit: "They're not going to score! They're not going to score!"

On first down Namath handed off to Matt Snell, who gained half a yard. Then on second down, New York's Bill Mathis tried a similar play up the middle, but he was stopped for no gain. "Our guys started feeling better at that point, and we ratcheted things up," Lanier said.

On third down Namath attempted a pass, but Bobby Bell was in his face and disrupted Namath's throw. The Jets settled for a field goal. Just a few plays later, the Chiefs scored on a 19-yard pass play from Len Dawson to Gloster Richardson. Kansas City went on to win the game 13–6.

Of course, whenever Lanier is in Kansas City, he's remembered more for his 11-year Pro Football Hall of Fame career with the Chiefs from 1967–77 as a member of one of the game's best linebacker corps, including Bell and Jim Lynch. He's also known, for being part of Super Bowl IV, when the Chiefs' defense dominated Minnesota, forcing five turnovers and holding the Vikings to

Contact's Innovative Helmet

Willie Lanier became known as "Contact" during his rookie season of 1967 with the Chiefs. The moniker came from his aggressive play and the way he "liked" hitting offensive players. Part of the Lanier way of hitting, at least as a rookie, was to lead with his helmet.

In an early-season game against San Diego, however, Lanier's head hit the knee of a Chargers running back. He didn't lose consciousness or leave the game, but Lanier knew he had a concussion. The next week during a game against Houston, Lanier collapsed. "I was out for two hours," said Lanier, who had a subdural hematoma.

Thus began the impetus for Lanier to change his tackling style. His aggressiveness remained, but he no longer led with his head. In those moments when his head did get in the way, though, he had a unique helmet, which had a raised section a few inches wide from the top of the facemask to the base of the helmet. It looked as if his helmet had a Mohawk.

The design, which Lanier started to wear once he returned after the Houston game, was the creation of longtime equipment manager Bobby Yarborough. "When he returned to play, we switched him to a fluid-filled Gladiator helmet," Yarborough told helmethut.com. "I also customized a strip of center ridge padding on the exterior surface of the shell. I got this idea from the old padded MacGregor helmets who offered this as a standard product in their catalog. I cut a four-inch wide strip of shoulder pad type foam padding and glued it down the center ridge. I glued a second layer of three-inch padding on top. I covered the foam padding with tightly stretched wide red vinyl tape. I finally repainted the entire helmet with a dark scarlet spray paint, which I got from Riddell.

"You could hit the helmet with a baseball bat, and it would not hurt the player wearing it. The ironic part is that after his rookie-season injury, Willie learned not to tackle headfirst anymore…I told him the special helmet was just a security blanket for him. Willie admitted to me later in his career that he kept using the padded helmet primarily because it gave him a unique and menacing look."

That first padded helmet from Yarborough is on display at the Pro Football Hall of Fame.

67 rushing yards, in a 23–7 win. "We didn't really see Minnesota as being better than Oakland [which the Chiefs beat in the AFL championship]," said Lanier, who was enshrined in Canton in 1986. "And the Jets were the previous Super Bowl winner. It was one of those times that if [the Vikings] were going to be better than those teams in our eyes, they were going to have to prove it. They didn't."

When asked about great personal moments that may stand out, Lanier quickly deflects and points to the people. "The intensity of every moment is so full that I don't have a biggest moment," he said. "I think about the quality of Lamar Hunt and his founding the team and creating the opportunities for a lot of talented players. I think about the relationships that were created that time and continue today. And I think about the combination of Lamar, Jack Steadman, and Hank Stram in our success. We had quality front-office people, quality coaches, and quality players. Everyone was on the same page with the same mission and same desire for the ultimate outcome."

11 Allen, Montana, and the 1993 Season

An old quarterback beyond his prime and some washed-up Heisman Trophy winner—that was the thought of some around the NFL when the Chiefs signed quarterback Joe Montana and running back Marcus Allen before the 1993 season. After all, Montana was coming off elbow surgery and would be 37 years old during the season, and Allen had been spending time on the bench with the Los Angeles Raiders; some people assumed his career was finished. Instead, the duo gave Kansas City fans some extra excitement heading into the season and led the team to the conference championship game at Buffalo.

Unlike previous seasons when the Chiefs needed a spark, they were coming off a 1992 campaign that included cornerback Dale Carter being selected as the NFL's Defensive Rookie of the Year, a solid season by newly-acquired quarterback Dave Krieg, and a postseason berth after getting 10 wins. (San Diego shut out the Chiefs 17–0 in their AFC wild-card game, as the Chargers sacked Krieg seven times.)

But something funny happened along the way. The Chiefs caught wind that Montana might be available from the San Francisco 49ers. While Montana was injured, Steve Young became the league's MVP. So general manager Carl Peterson went to work on Montana and the 49ers, reaching a deal in April. The Chiefs agreed upon a three-year, $10 million contract with Montana and would send their first-round pick in the '93 draft in exchange for the legendary quarterback, safety David Whitmore, and a third-round pick in '94. (Incidentally, San Francisco used that 1993 pick to move down and draft former Kansas star and future Pro Bowl defensive lineman Dana Stubblefield.)

With the Montana deal done, the Chiefs focused on Allen, who was a free agent and had already been talking with Peterson. In June, thanks to the Montana signing, Allen agreed to three one-year contracts. "You'd have to be crazy not to take advantage of an opportunity to play with Joe Montana," Allen said at the time. "I want to go to the Super Bowl, and Kansas City does, too. Hopefully, I can help them get there."

With two future Hall of Fame players signed and a draft that included selecting another likely future Hall of Famer in guard Will Shields, the general consensus with Chiefs fans was Super Bowl or bust. And why not? Montana was a three-time Super Bowl MVP, and Allen had earned the distinction once.

Montana and Allen and the regular season didn't disappoint, starting with the first game. In the season opener at Tampa, Montana threw for 246 yards and three touchdowns with no interceptions, and Allen caught one of those touchdown passes while running for 79 yards on 16 carries, as the Chiefs cruised to a 27–3 win.

After a 30–0 loss at Houston in Week 2, the Chiefs lost only four more times during the regular season. Meanwhile, Montana and Allen each had Pro Bowl seasons. Montana, who missed five games due to various injuries, threw for 2,144 yards and 13 touchdowns.

Allen, who was used sparingly while the Chiefs figured out what he could do at 33 years old, ran for 764 yards and 12 touchdowns on 206 carries. "The Chiefs tried to monitor how much I played because they didn't know if I could last the entire season," Allen said. "Really, I could've played every down that season and felt better by the playoffs. I was the type of player who got better and stronger throughout a season, regardless of my age."

The Chiefs played host to Pittsburgh in an AFC wild-card game on January 8. Throughout most of the game, it looked as if the Steelers were going to end Kansas City's season prematurely. Pittsburgh, which never trailed in regulation, jumped out to a 17–7 lead in the first half. Montana was struggling on the 18-degree day. His first seven passes fell incomplete. Late in regulation, though, he warmed up, going 22-for-28 with 203 yards in the second half. With 1:43 left in the fourth and going for it on fourth down, Montana found Tim Barnett in the end zone for the 24–24 tie. Then, with 11:03 remaining in overtime, Nick Lowery, who missed a 43-yard attempt with 12 seconds left in regulation, nailed a 32-yard field goal that gave the Chiefs a rematch date at Houston, winners of its last 11 regular-season games, the next weekend.

Trailing 13–7 early in the fourth quarter of that game, Montana and Allen rallied the Chiefs for 21 points at the Astrodome. After

Montana threw two touchdown passes on a 299-yard day, Allen, who ran for 74, sealed the 28–20 win for Kansas City. "I was watching the game from the end zone," Peterson said. "We got down to the 21-yard line, and Joe took a snap, turned, and handed the ball to Marcus. When Joe turned around—before Marcus had even hit the line of scrimmage—he threw his arms up signaling touchdown. Then Marcus made about three moves and took it to the left corner of the end zone for the score. I asked Joe later [why he raised his arms so early]. He said, 'I saw the man who's got the best vision there is, and he took it.'"

And the Chiefs were headed to their first AFC Championship Game. There, in Buffalo, however, instead of Allen taking over for the Chiefs, it was Bills running back Thurman Thomas, who had 186 yards and three touchdowns as Buffalo won 30–13. Montana suffered a concussion early in the third quarter with the Chiefs trailing 20–6. Kansas City's lone touchdown of the game came from Allen, who capped a 90-yard drive with a 1-yard scoring run. It was Buffalo's fourth straight AFC championship.

Montana played one more year with the Chiefs before retiring. Allen, the NFL's Comeback Player of the Year in '93, played until the end of the 1997 season. Not bad for an old quarterback beyond his prime and some washed-up Heisman Trophy winner.

12 Kansas City, Here We Come

During the 1962 season, as the Dallas Texans were marching toward an 11–3 record and AFL Championship Game against in-state rival Houston, owner Lamar Hunt felt he needed to move to another city. For the fledgling American Football League team, it was growing difficult to compete for fan support with the NFL's Dallas Cowboys.

Since 1960 the Texans and the Cowboys wrangled for top billing in the city. For the most part, especially early, it looked like the fan support favored the Texans. While both teams played their home games at the Cotton Bowl in September 1960, the Cowboys drew 30,000 for a game against the Pittsburgh Steelers. The next day the Texans drew 42,000 for a game against the Los Angeles Chargers.

The next year, Hunt, who didn't mind a challenge, tried to get the Cowboys to play the Texans in an exhibition game. The Cowboys, who had gone 0–11–1 in 1960, declined. During that '62 season, though, in spite of their success on the field, the Texans were slipping in attendance. In their last three home games, they had attendance totals of 13,557 (vs. Oakland), 19,137 (vs. Denver), and 18,384 (vs. San Diego).

Kansas City, Missouri, mayor H. Roe Bartle was on a business trip in Atlanta when he caught wind that Hunt had been in Atlanta to look at facilities for a possible move. That's when Bartle, nicknamed "the Chief," put on the charm. He tried getting pro football in Kansas City at least two other times—both with the AFL. The first was when a Maryland businessman looked at putting a team in Kansas City, but the deal fell through. Then there was thought the Raiders would move to Kansas City from Oakland, but that fell through, too.

After Bartle and Hunt met in Dallas, Bartle invited Hunt to Kansas City for a visit. Hunt was concerned, however, that if anyone knew he was considering moving the team, it would be bad for the league and his Texans. Bartle guaranteed complete secrecy. Even when Hunt came to scout Kansas City as a possible location, only Bartle and his chauffeur knew Hunt was there. He flew to Kansas City under an assumed name, he checked in at the

Muehlebach Hotel under an assumed name, and when Bartle had to introduce him to someone, he called him "Mr. Lamar."

The same held true when Hunt's right-hand man on football matters, Jack Steadman, visited. He was introduced as "Jack X."

"Mayor Bartle would say I was an Internal Revenue Service agent in Kansas City investigating the expense accounts of some of the city's most prominent citizens," Steadman said. "We finally got the deal put together, but we didn't tell anyone. The Chamber of Commerce got the season-ticket campaign going, but all they knew is that they were selling season tickets for a football franchise. Nobody knew who. In 1963 you could do that. They didn't know your business unless you told them. I stayed in touch with my secretary when I came to Kansas City, but she didn't even know where I was."

By the end of the 1962 season, Hunt knew he was going to move the franchise—with Kansas City as the leading contender and New Orleans, Atlanta, and Miami well behind. But as the Texans prepared for their AFL title game against the Oilers on December 23, Hunt and Steadman kept the secret even from the players and coaches.

Thanks to two touchdowns by Abner Haynes, the Texans jumped out to a 17–0 lead. They *eventually* won the game 20–17 on a 25-yard field goal by Tommy Brooker…in the second overtime.

Less than two months after the city of Dallas had its first professional football championship, Hunt announced on February 8, 1963, that he was moving the Texans to Kansas City if the city sold 25,000 season tickets. Three months later on May 22—despite just 13,025 season tickets being sold—Hunt announced that he, indeed, was moving the franchise.

Although the move seemed great for Kansas City, the Texans players weren't so sure. Head coach Hank Stram had the unenviable task of convincing the players that moving north was a good thing. "We went through quite a difficult transition because we

"The Chief"

There's been a groundswell in recent years to change the names of sports teams with a Native American moniker. After the Washington Redskins changed their team name, there have been quiet grumblings about the Chiefs.

True, part of the Chiefs name comes from the Native American heritage in the area. But the name is really a nod toward Mayor H. Roe Bartle, who was nearing the end of his second and final term as mayor when he convinced Lamar Hunt to move the team from Dallas.

Bartle, by all accounts, was a gregarious and generous man—a giant of a man, figuratively and literally. According to former sports editor for *The Kansas City Star*, Joe McGuff, in his book, *Winning It All*, Bartle, who was 6'3", admits to weighing 320 pounds and probably goes well above that." Shortly before running for mayor, Bartle was giving approximately 700 speeches a year for as much as $500 apiece, which was high by 1950s standards.

He wasn't motivated by money, though, as much as he was public service. After serving in the Navy during World War I and then getting his law degree from the University of Chattanooga in 1921, the 20-year-old Bartle began to work with the Boy Scouts of America. He started as a scout executive in Wyoming, following a training session in Kansas City. The Boy Scouts, which were about 10 years old at the time, experienced tremendous growth under Bartle. During his two years in Wyoming, the state went from four troops to 50 troops. Through his work with the Boy Scouts, Bartle received the nickname "the Chief" because of his large size and leadership.

From 1925 to 1928, Bartle held a similar post in St. Joseph, Missouri, where his dad had moved a few years earlier. Then, in 1928 Bartle moved to Kansas City as the chief area executive, a post he held until 1955 when he ran for mayor. Bartle's term as mayor began in 1956, a year after the Philadelphia Athletics began play as Kansas City's first Major League Baseball team. His two four-year terms ended in 1963, shortly after the successful move of the Dallas Texans to Kansas City.

Bartle Hall, the major convention center in downtown Kansas City, Missouri, is named in honor of Bartle, who died on May 9, 1974.

were a Texas team," Stram said. "We signed players from Texas who wanted to be in Dallas. All of a sudden, we moved to Kansas City. It was traumatic because we had told our players that we would always be a Dallas team. When we decided to move, it ruffled the emotions of a lot of guys. However, once we got to Kansas City, it didn't take long to fall in love with the city and the people. We were always so appreciative of the support we got from the fans in Kansas City and how involved they were with our football team. They really responded to what we were doing. As we went along, we grew and developed not only as a football team, but also as a community. Growing as a community was very important for all of us involved in the transition."

The move gave many players, such as wide receiver Chris Burford, who had just purchased a new home in Dallas and was attending law school there, a new place to call home—even if they weren't thrilled in the beginning. "Going to Kansas City was a *big* surprise to the players," he said. "It was tough going from the Cotton Bowl to old Municipal Stadium, which was an old baseball park. The first year, we didn't have many people show up. In our first exhibition game, there were less than 10,000 people there (5,721), which was embarrassing."

Then there was the name. Hunt and Stram were dead-set on keeping the name Texans. The Kansas City Texans, they felt, evoked pride for the people of Texas. Steadman argued that the new fan base in Kansas City wouldn't appreciate the name. "I argued with Steadman for hours about the subject," Hunt said. "I was really set on calling the team the Texans. That's how firm I was on the subject...I tried to reason with Jack that if the Rams could go to Los Angeles and keep their name, why couldn't we move to Kansas City and keep our name. It's a completely illogical argument, but I was so wrapped up in the name at the time that it didn't seem that way. Jack said it would be a disaster and, of course, he was right."

The team changed its nickname to the Chiefs—largely in honor of Mayor Bartle—and, once settled, Hunt said he thought Chiefs was "the greatest nickname I have ever heard." Hunt then took it upon himself to design a new logo. After all, a solid outline of Texas might not fly well in Kansas City either.

Hunt began doodling on a legal pad and before long he drew an arrowhead with an interlocking KC. He had been a fan of how the San Francisco 49ers and a lot of baseball teams had interlocking letters. "I drew it up and I liked it," Hunt said. "I am sure I showed it to Jack Steadman and Hank [Stram]. But we didn't do anything more than that. Now teams do surveys of public opinion and get all this input and what would look good and what they should do."

With some minor modifications here and there, Hunt's logo has stood the test of time and is one of the most recognizable in American sports.

Once the team got going during that first season in Kansas City, the players—particularly those from Texas—realized their new home might be a little colder at times than Dallas. "The last three games [that first year], we played in 12 to 15 below zero," said E.J. Holub, a lifelong Texan. "That turf felt like concrete. The 1,000 fans there were either in bedrolls or drunk. After that we really got going."

Truth be told, in those final three games in 1963, all at home, the Chiefs averaged a little more than 14,000 fans. "The town changed over time," Burford said. "It became much more sophisticated about professional football. The fan base grew, and the fans got behind us. Then in 1966, which was a fabulous season, we landed in Kansas City after beating Buffalo in the AFL Championship Game, and the fans surged onto the runway. It was a very exciting time for us as players."

13 Buck Buchanan

Junious Buchanan was a great basketball player and football player at Parker High School in Birmingham, Alabama, during the 1950s. Truth be told, the roundball was his first love. The 6'7" Buchanan played football as a way to stay conditioned for hoops.

Without any scholarship offers in hand from his school for either sport, Grambling's legendary college football coach Eddie Robinson received a phone call one day from a man in Birmingham. "There's a football player here you need," the man said.

"Who?" Robinson asked.

"Junious Buchanan," the man said. "He's my nephew."

That story is one of the most fortuitous in Chiefs history because after an outstanding career at Grambling, including selection as an NAIA All-American in 1962, Junious "Buck" Buchanan was the first player selected in the 1963 American Football League Draft—by the Dallas Texans. Adding to the aura of the story, the Texans got that No. 1 pick in the only trade ever orchestrated by owner Lamar Hunt, when he sent quarterback Cotton Davidson to the Oakland Raiders. Even though the New York Giants of the established NFL also picked Buchanan, he signed with the Texans. "I signed with them because I considered it an honor to be the first player chosen by the league," Buchanan said. "I thought it was very significant to have that honor since I had played for a small black school. I was determined to prove that players from small schools could play in the big leagues."

And, boy, did he ever prove that.

From 1963–75 Buchanan used his incredible speed (10.2 in the 100), tenacity, and 6'7", 270-pound mountain of a body to dominate offensive linemen and quarterbacks from his defensive tackle position. "When you played Buck, you couldn't sleep the night before a game," said former Oakland Raiders Hall of Fame guard Gene Upshaw, whom Al Davis drafted in the first round in 1967 just to block Buchanan. "You don't imagine a guy 6'8", 300 pounds being so quick. You'd go to hit him, and it was like hitting a ghost."

With the addition of Buchanan and draft mate Bobby Bell, coach Hank Stram was getting the ingredients for his triple-stack defense, which used three linemen and four linebackers. (Today it's basically a 3-4 defense, but teams weren't employing it then.)

In the first quarter of Super Bowl I, Buchanan sacked Hall of Fame quarterback Bart Starr for a 10-yard loss, giving Buchanan the distinction of recording the first sack in Super Bowl history. Even though some felt the Chiefs were overmatched—almost intimidated—by Green Bay and the mighty NFL in that AFL-NFL Championship loss, Buchanan most certainly was not. "A lot of guys on our team might have had some type of fear, but I didn't," he said. "I had played against them [in the College All-Star Game] and I felt I knew their team. I guess I wasn't aware of the league thing because I knew a lot of the guys in the NFL and I thought I was just as good as they were."

Throughout his career Buchanan proved he was just as good as, if not better than, anyone else in pro football. For eight consecutive years, Buchanan went to either the AFL All-Star Game or (after the merger) the Pro Bowl. He was the player voted Chiefs MVP in 1967 and '69.

At the end of that 1969 season, Buchanan was a major part of the Chiefs' win in Super Bowl IV. In his triple-stack defense, Stram decided to switch between Buchanan and Curley Culp at the nose against Minnesota center Mick Tingelhoff instead of putting the 235-pound Tingelhoff against Willie Lanier. At that time in football, the center focused on a linebacker—not on someone the size of Buchanan. "There was never any doubt in my mind that we could play a good defensive game," Buchanan said. "The things the Vikings did we could control. We didn't think they could run on us. Not many teams run against our defense, and the Vikings don't have great speed. I thought we were bigger and stronger and I thought we had more speed than they did. We saw teams play Minnesota that tried to do things you just can't do against them. I think we had a good game plan."

By the time Buchanan retired in 1975, he had played in 182 career games, including 166 in a row. He became active in the Kansas City community, owning a construction business and an advertising agency. He was inducted into the Chiefs Hall of Fame in 1981 and then the Pro Football Hall of Fame in August 1990, not long after doctors discovered Buchanan had lung cancer.

Buchanan died July 16, 1992. He was 51. "The first time I met him, I was impressed with his awesome size, speed, and agility," Stram said, "but underneath it all, you came away impressed with a tremendous person, a great competitor, and a terrific leader. He loved what he represented, his family, and the Chiefs."

14 Hank Stram

Hank Stram, who was known as "the Mentor," began with the Chiefs organization in 1960—the first year of the American Football League —when the team was known as the Dallas Texans. For the next 15 years, he molded players, helped the organization move to Kansas City, and helped the team make a smooth merger to the NFL. Oh, and he won. A lot. With Stram at the helm, the franchise won three AFL titles and went to two Super Bowls, including the world championship in Super Bowl IV. Stram, whom the Chiefs inducted into the team's Hall of Fame in 1987, died on July 4, 2005 at the age of 82. The following is from one of the many interviews he did with Matt Fulks.

What comes to mind when you think about your time in Kansas City?

Hank Stram: It was a very special time in our lives. We enjoyed it tremendously. We were always so appreciative of the support we got from the fans of Kansas City and how involved they were with our football team. The fans really responded to what we were doing.

Not only were the fans wonderful, but we also had a great group of players. The whole idea behind a winning team is that you have to make a personal sacrifice necessary to get the job done. Our players were willing to make that sacrifice. I used to tell our team all the time, "Since you started playing football, people have called you a football player. But truly, you've never been a football player...you're young men who play football. So football is what you do; it's not what you are. You're going to be a man the rest of your life, but you won't be able to play football the rest of your life. Still, we'll always be a team for the rest of our lives." We had a great, closely knit family. There was a strong bond of fellowship, friendship, teamwork, and all those types of things.

Was that family bond a key to having such a successful run?

HS: I think a combination of things attributed to our team's success. People say that coaches win football games. That's not true—the players win the football games. A coach puts those players in a position where they can best express their talent and ability. Plus our players were great people. I have always felt that you win with good people who are willing to make every personal sacrifice to achieve what your team is out to achieve. In terms of attitude and discipline, our guys knew what was expected of them. Some people laughed about the fact that we had tailor-made suits for our traveling purposes. Wherever we went as a team, we wore those suits. We took a lot of pride in what we did and how we did it. I always told our team that no matter where we were or what we did, we were always going to be first class.

At our first meeting in Roswell, New Mexico, in 1960, we had about 150 players, and I told them to write down on a piece of paper that if and when the AFL ended, we were going to be the winningest team in the history of the American Football League. That was our organization's attitude. After the league's 10 years, guess what—we were the winningest team in the history of the American Football League.

Because of the David vs. Goliath perception for the AFL vs. the NFL in Super Bowl I, was the outcome overly disappointing?

HS: Any loss is a disappointing loss, especially that first AFL-NFL Championship Game (Super Bowl I). Going into the game, we really felt that we could beat the Green Bay Packers, but we were concerned about our defense. We were a much better team offensively than defensively at that time. Green Bay had a very good offensive team. Still, we felt that if we played up to our capacity offensively, that we would have a good chance to win the game. So, of course, when we didn't win the game, it was a huge disappointment for us and the league. That game did provide us with a lot of impetus that we wanted to make it back to that championship again, and if we did make it back, we would win.

What was the team's mind-set going into Super Bowl IV against Minnesota?

HS: Having played in that first championship game, we definitely knew what we had to do to beat Minnesota. So, the fact that we made it back and won so dramatically was an extra special occasion. We went into that game with a great amount of confidence. We knew the Vikings were a very good football team, but we felt the match-ups were in our favor because we had a very large football team, especially on the offensive and defensive lines. If you win two of the three areas—offense, defense, special teams—in a game, most of the time you'll win. We won in all three categories, which is something that rarely happens, especially in a Super Bowl. That's a day that will always linger in my mind's book of happy memories. We felt that we would make it back to the Super Bowl again after that win. Unfortunately, the rest is history.

15 The Longest Game

It's the bane of a kicker's life: you're expected to hit the game winners and haunted by the key misses.

In spite of being one of the Chiefs' main cogs throughout their successful early years, Hall of Fame kicker Jan Stenerud has carried around a personal demon for more than 40 years. During what's known as "the longest game," when the Chiefs lost to the Miami Dolphins in the playoffs on Christmas Day in 1971 at Municipal Stadium, the usually accurate Stenerud missed three field-goal attempts—a botched fake at the end of the second quarter, a miss at the end of regulation, and one that was blocked in the first overtime.

Although it's unfair to place the blame of that loss on Stenerud, it's a game that still bothers him. In fact, when asked whether his made field goals in Super Bowl IV or the misses against Miami stand out more to him personally, Stenerud didn't leave a lot of room for interpretation. "I spent 19 years in the league, I'm in the Hall of Fame, and every [gosh darn] time I talk to someone in

Kansas City, they keep hammering and hammering and hammering [that game]," Stenerud barked. "Thirty, 40, 50 years afterward [people] won't know I did anything else except miss those kicks. I'm not going to comment anymore on that."

"Yes, the normally mild-mannered Jan gets upset about that, although we never blamed him," Len Dawson said.

Maybe it's easy to see why Stenerud takes it personally and why he's reminded of it every year. It has been termed pro football's longest day: 82 minutes, 40 seconds, to be exact. And one of the best games in NFL history. For Kansas City fans, it's simply known as one of the most disappointing losses in franchise history—or the year that Santa left a huge lump of coal in the Chiefs' stockings. "I do remember that we didn't enjoy our Christmas Day dinner that year," offensive lineman Ed Budde said gruffly, more than 40 years after the Christmas Day game. "We really thought we were going to be in the Super Bowl again that year. Everyone thought that."

Even though they were starting to get a little long in the tooth at certain positions, the Chiefs were a great team—only two years removed from winning Super Bowl IV. They finished the regular season with a 10–3–1 record. On the other side, a relatively young Dolphins team was a season away from undefeated immortality.

In a game that featured 13 future Hall of Fame players, the Chiefs jumped ahead early with 10 unanswered points in the first quarter, the second score of which came on a short touchdown pass from Dawson to Ed Podolak, who was the star of the game.

Shortly before halftime while leading 10–7, Kansas City decided to try a fake field goal. Ideally, Bobby Bell, the long snapper at the time, would send the ball directly to Stenerud, who would attempt to run for a first down. Stenerud, evidently, sold it too well and faked out his own teammates. "When I looked back at Jan, he was looking down just like he'd do when he was ready to kick," Bell said. "As a snapper I always sent the ball back there like a bullet. I kept thinking, *Jan, let me know you're ready for this, let me know you're ready for this.* I didn't think he was ready, so I snapped it to Lenny."

Despite being the franchise quarterback, Dawson was the regular holder. "We had worked on that play," he said. "Miami blitzed everybody. All 11 people went, and Ed [Budde] and Mo Moorman were pulling out. That was one of three [kick attempts] that didn't go right that day."

Coach Hank Stram had indeed thought he found the ideal situation for his trick play. "In our preparation I decided to install a running play where the ball would be snapped directly to Jan, who was a lot faster than people thought, and he would run for at least a first down," Stram said. "The situation was perfect because the kick was well inside Jan's range. There was a ton of electricity on our sideline. I told Jan to just make sure that he lined up like he normally would and keep his head down toward his target, but the ball was going to come to him after Lenny called for the automatic. Since Lenny was surprised when the ball was snapped to him, there wasn't much he could do with it. As it turned out, there was complete daylight for Jan to run it in for a touchdown if we had run the play."

Instead, Stenerud hurried the kick, which misfired, and the Dolphins scored, tying the game at 10–10 on a field goal by Garo Yepremian before intermission.

Each team scored two touchdowns in the second half. After Miami tied the game at 24 with less than 90 seconds remaining in the fourth quarter, Podolak ran the kickoff back 78 yards to the Miami 22-yard line. The Chiefs moved the ball 7 yards before attempting a sure-to-be game-winning kick with 35 seconds left. Stenerud missed.

His woes continued. In the first overtime, the Chiefs had a chance to win the game on a 42-yard attempt, but Nick Buoniconti blocked it.

Eventually, in the second overtime, Yepremian ended the game with a 37-yard field goal. That 27–24 outcome was Miami's only lead of the day. "It was tough to lose that game, and we had opportunities. Not that they weren't a good football team, because they were very good, but that was our best team," Dawson said. "We were a better football team than the Miami Dolphins. I ran into Nick Buoniconti [in 2013], and he finally admitted we were a better football team. I was with him for 23 years on *Inside the NFL*, and he never admitted it then."

In a bittersweet effort, the Chiefs got a playoff-record 350 all-purpose yards from Podolak during the double-overtime game. But it wasn't enough for what might've been one of the best performances ever by a Chiefs player and on one of the greatest Chiefs teams ever. "Most of us, including those on the [Super Bowl IV] team, felt that the '71 team was better," said Podolak. "We finished the season very strong and felt that we could go all the way again. That game was the beginning of the dominance of the Miami Dolphins and the beginning of the fade of the Kansas City Chiefs."

Jim Kearney, who played for the Chiefs during 1967–75 without ever missing a game due to an injury, agreed with Podolak's statement. "That was our best team during my time in Kansas City," he said. "The Miami Dolphins won the Super Bowl that year, but we had a better team…I cannot remember driving home from that old stadium after that game. It's like a *Twilight Zone*. I guess it was denial."

The Chiefs didn't return to the playoffs until 1986. The Christmas Day game also was the team's final one at Municipal Stadium. They moved to Arrowhead the next season. "That was one of the bitterest losses for us. We had so many chances to win," Stram said. "It was tragic that we lost that game. We were a very good football team."

"I have that game recorded at home," Bell said, "but I've never watched it. I never want to see it again."

16 Tailgate at Arrowhead

The sounds, the smells, the crisp fall air—and licking barbecue sauce off your fingers at 9:30 on a Sunday morning. It's a rite of passage that every fan of football or food needs to experience: tailgating at Arrowhead.

It seems to make sense that the barbecue capital of the world would have one of the best tailgating experiences in professional sports. At least it seemed that way to Carl Peterson and one of the Chiefs marketing gurus at the time, Tim Connolly. Early in the Peterson-Marty Schottenheimer era, Connolly was hired to help transform the team's image and in turn attempt to increase season-ticket sales from 1988's modest number of 26,000. One of the ideas was to make Arrowhead a destination by encouraging tailgating. "It's part of a large playbook of operations to make the gameday experience more than a game," Connolly said in the book, *The Grand Barbecue*. "Tailgating has taken on a life of its own. It's almost a competitive event in itself. This is what Kansas City is known for."

The tailgating experience took on a life of its own and on a national scale on October 7, 1991, the night Kansas City hosted the Buffalo Bills on *Monday Night Football*. It was the first *Monday Night Football* game at Arrowhead since 1983, and the fans made sure the national audience (and the Bills) knew where they were. Exterior photos of Arrowhead before the game showed a midwestern colored sky with a smoke you could almost smell wafting up from the countless grills and cookers. Inside, the Chiefs cruised to a 33–6 win against the defending AFC champions. "That was a crazy night," said Chiefs Hall of Fame safety Deron Cherry. "The tailgating that night, the unbelievably loud crowd during the game changed the whole atmosphere at Arrowhead. That's the loudest I ever heard Arrowhead during my career. On top of that you had [ABC broadcasters] Dan Dierdorf and Frank Gifford talking about the tailgating and all the barbecue. That was the night Arrowhead got its heartbeat back."

Since that night Arrowhead has become known as one of the top places in the country to tailgate before a game with pregame delicacies ranging from hot dogs and bratwursts to prime rib and barbecue shrimp—and everything in between. All the while kids from age five to 75 are tossing footballs. It's almost a Mardi Gras atmosphere every time the Chiefs have a home game.

Many fans show up when the gates open three and a half hours before kickoff and pay the fee to park and be part of the festivities. And if you look closely, you might see current and former Chiefs players walking through the parking lot, talking with fans...and sampling food. "With the parking lot full like that and to see the smoke from the barbecues," former Chiefs safety Eric Berry said, "I'm getting hyped in the car just driving in. Unlike other stadiums you really step into Arrowhead and the experience of it when you pull into the parking lot."

17 So Close: The 2018 AFC Championship Game

A split inch and a coin flip. That's how close the Chiefs came to beating the blankety-blank New England Patriots in January 2019 and advancing to the Super Bowl, following a stellar MVP season for first-year starting quarterback Patrick Mahomes. Let's pause, though, and marvel at this one fact: Arrowhead Stadium hosted the AFC Championship Game for the first time ever. And it was the closest the Chiefs had been to the Super Bowl since playing for that right against the Buffalo Bills at the end of the 1993 season.

The 2018 Chiefs looked like a team of destiny with the league's best player making plays that only kids playing in the streets would attempt. Mahomes was surrounded throughout the season with perfect weapons for his arsenal: speedy Tyreek Hill, one of the game's best tight ends in Travis Kelce, and a young running back named Kareem Hunt. The Chiefs cruised through most of the first three months of the season. At least the offense cruised. Defensively, the team struggled—evident in their only two losses through November: 43–40 at New England and 54–51 at the Los Angeles Rams. In fact, the defense gave up at least 21 points in all but four regular-season games.

But then an off-the-field incident changed the course of the team for the rest of the season. On November 30, two days before the Chiefs' game at the Oakland Raiders, a video surfaced from February of Hunt shoving and kicking a woman at a Cleveland hotel during the offseason. The Chiefs wasted very little time in cutting Hunt. However, it wasn't necessarily because of the incident, per se. "Earlier this year, we were made aware of an incident involving running back Kareem Hunt," according to a statement released by the team. "At that time the National Football League and law enforcement initiated investigations into the issue. As part of our internal discussions with Kareem, several members of our management team spoke directly to him. Kareem was not truthful in those discussions. The video released today confirms that fact. We are releasing Kareem immediately."

The Chiefs beat Oakland that Sunday but then lost two of their four remaining games. But in spite of the mini-December slide, the Chiefs won the AFC West and finished with the conference's best record at 12–4. That meant all that separated the Chiefs from Super Bowl LIII were two wins at Arrowhead. The team's first postseason matchup was an all-too familiar playoff thorn, the

2018 MNF vs. Los Angeles Rams

One of Kansas City's losses in 2018 came on Monday November 19, against the Los Angeles Rams in what many call the "greatest regular-season NFL game ever." It definitely was an epic game. At least, for fans who like offense and weren't pulling for the Chiefs, as the Rams held on for a 54–51 win.

In hindsight, knowing the outcome didn't really hurt the Chiefs, it was a special game that included two 9–1 teams, two of the top quarterbacks in the NFL, two teams scoring more than 50 points (first time in NFL history), the Chiefs coming back from a 10-point deficit in the fourth quarter, and four lead changes in the final quarter. Frankly, many saw it as a potential Super Bowl LIII preview. Originally, the game was supposed to be played in Mexico City, but poor field conditions there forced it to the Los Angeles Coliseum, a place that hadn't hosted a *Monday Night Football* game since 1985. That only added to the mystique of the game.

One would think that when Patrick Mahomes throws for a career-high 478 yards and six touchdowns, the Chiefs would win. But he also had three interceptions, including one being a Pick-6 and two in the game's final two minutes. "It's always fun to play against real good teams," Mahomes said. "[But] it's the same as when we played New England. You can't make mistakes against great teams. You need to limit your mistakes but be aggressive."

Behind the arm of Jared Goff, who threw for 413 yards and four touchdowns with no interceptions, the Rams jumped out to a 13–0 lead in the first quarter. Two minutes later Mahomes hit Tyreek Hill for a 25-yard touchdown play. For the next two-plus quarters, the scoring went back and forth. Neither team went ahead by more than six and they played to a 23–23 tie at halftime.

Late in the third quarter with the Rams leading 33–30, Samson Ebukam intercepted Mahomes and ran it back 25 yards for a touchdown. Los Angeles took a 40–30 heading into the fourth quarter. (Think about that for a second: the score was 40–30. There were 35 points to be scored in the final 15 minutes.)

On their ensuing possession, the Chiefs started from their own 9 at the start of the fourth. Kansas City took just three plays before scoring on a 73-yard catch and run from Mahomes to Hill. The Chiefs' defense took that momentum and used it for a fumble recovery and touchdown by Allen Bailey a minute later to make it 44–40 for their first lead of the game. After each team traded touchdowns three times, putting the Rams ahead 54–51 with 1:49 remaining, Kansas City had two more chances to get in field-goal range for Harrison Butker, who missed a point-after attempt earlier in the game. With each opportunity, though, Los Angeles picked off Mahomes, including one at the Rams' 28 with 25 seconds left. "We can learn from this," coach Andy Reid said. "We can't give up 21 points on turnovers, have to take care of the football. We created some turnovers and points [but had] too many penalties. We'll heal up and get set to go for the stretch run."

Indianapolis Colts. Thankfully, this wasn't the same Chiefs team. On a snowy Saturday afternoon, Kansas City jumped ahead early on first-quarter touchdown runs by Hunt's replacement, Damien Williams, and Hill. The Chiefs, who had seen Mahomes become just the third quarterback in NFL history with at least 50 touchdown passes during the season, had a very un-Chiefs like scoring day with four rushing touchdowns and none in the air. It didn't matter as they went on to a 31–13 win. It snapped a six-game home playoff losing streak. "We wanted to light up the city," defensive tackle Chris Jones said. "We didn't want to take the road down memory lane."

Next up for the Chiefs were the Patriots, who were playing in their eighth consecutive AFC Championship Game. Still, many saw this as a possible changing of the AFC guard from Tom Brady and Rob Gronkowski to Mahomes and Kelce. From the outset it looked like that might not happen. New England got the ball first and ate up eight minutes and five seconds as Brady marched his team 80 yards for a 15-play touchdown drive. The score remained 7–0 until the Patriots crossed the goal line again with less than 30 seconds left in the half.

Kansas City's offense came alive in the second half, setting up a thrilling fourth quarter. Trailing 17–7, the Chiefs finished off a drive that started in the third quarter and scored nine seconds into the fourth to cut New England's lead to 17–14. The Chiefs took their first lead of the game after Daniel Sorensen picked off a Brady pass and returned it 24 yards to New England's 23. Two plays later, Williams, who scored three times, got a short pass from Mahomes and took it down the sideline for a 23-yard touchdown, making it 21–17. Each team scored again before the unfortunate and unforgettable final few minutes of regulation.

With Kansas City leading 28–24, Brady moved the Patriots into Chiefs territory with about a minute to play. With 54 seconds left, Brady threw a pass intended for Gronkowski, but it was intercepted by Charvarius Ward. That would've sealed the game. Not so fast. Kansas City's Dee Ford was called for offside. He was a fingertip too early.

The 41-year-old Brady took advantage of the opportunity. On the next play, Brady connected with Gronkowski for a 25-yard gain down to the Chiefs' 4-yard line. With 39 seconds left, Rex Burkhead ran in for a touchdown and another Patriots lead. That was plenty of time, though, for Mahomes to get the Chiefs in field-goal position, where Harrison Butker hit a 39-yarder that tied the game with eight seconds.

That forced overtime, where the rules dictate that if the team with the ball first scored a touchdown, the game was over. Guess what? New England won the toss, the Chiefs' defense looked like it did throughout the regular season, and the Patriots won on another run by Burkhead. "We put ourselves in position to win the game. That's what makes it so tough," coach Andy Reid said. "If it's a rout, you chalk it up to experience. But this one right here, where you're in it to win it, that's a tough deal. We gave ourselves every opportunity to do it, and they got us in overtime."

18 Jamaal Charles

If there's one game to describe Jamaal Charles and the type of back he's been for the Chiefs, look no further than December 15, 2013. The Chiefs were playing at Oakland with a chance to clinch a playoff spot for the first time since 2010 and only the second time since '06. Charles ran for 20 yards and one touchdown. Oh, and he happened to catch eight passes for 195 yards and four touchdowns.

The Chiefs manhandled the Raiders 56–31 during a game in which Charles became the only player in NFL history to record four receiving touchdowns and at least one rushing touchdown in the same game. "A big part of this team depends on me," said Charles after the game. "Once I'm healthy this offense can go a long way, and this team can go a long way."

Staying healthy has been a factor for Charles since the Chiefs selected him in the third round of the 2008 NFL Draft out of the University of Texas. He missed all but two games in the 2011 season because of a season-ending knee injury, he's missed a few games with sprains and strains, and he suffered a concussion on the Chiefs' first possession of the crushing 2013 wild-card loss to Indianapolis. All told, heading into the 2014 season, Charles has started 49 of the 80 games in which he's played for the team.

Charles went on to finish the 2013 season, his second as the team's main running back, with an AFC-leading 1,287 yards and a career-high 12 touchdowns. Even though he has spent most of his career splitting time with other running backs, 2013 was the fourth time in his career that he's rushed for at least 1,000 yards. Charles is the only running back in Chiefs history with that distinction, surpassing fellow Longhorn Priest Holmes, who had three 1,000-plus-yard seasons.

His numbers are historic. Among running backs with at least 1,000 career carries, Charles is the NFL's all-time career leader in rushing average through the 2013 season with 5.58 yards per carry, ranking ahead of Jim Brown (5.22), Barry Sanders (4.99), and Adrian Peterson (4.98).

Much of Charles' success is because of his blazing speed. A dedicated track athlete in college, he is one of the fastest players in the NFL. Among his accolades as a Longhorns track star, he finished in fourth place at the NCAA Indoor Championships in the 60-meter dash (6.65) and won the 100-meter dash (10.23) at the Big 12 Outdoor Championships.

Despite owning that jaw-dropping speed, Charles still has room to refine his game, "I saw progress all the way through the [2013] season, whether it was just subtleties in the run game or the blocking scheme, the route running," coach Andy Reid told CBS Sports in March 2014. "We were able to expand his package as we went. I think he'll just continue on."

That's why Chiefs fans are hoping the arrow(head) is pointing up for Charles, even though the dynamic star turns 28 during December of the 2014 season. After all, his part-time status for much of his career gives him a little less tread on his tires than the typical back his age. "For a running back, once I turn 30, I'm not in my prime anymore," he told *The Kansas City Star*, "but I want to overcome that and I hope I can be different and show everybody that I can continue to be the best back in the National Football League."

19 Martyball

Carl Peterson had been the Chiefs general manager for nearly a month when he received a call about his team's open head coaching job. It was Marty Schottenheimer, who was wrapping up an ugly breakup with the Cleveland Browns.

"Marty just told me the truth, that I might read that he got fired or pushed out or whatever," Peterson said in *Martyball!*, Schottenheimer's 2012 authorized biography, "but that he felt strongly about not losing control of hiring his staff and that he had to part ways with Art [Modell]. I understood that completely and asked him if he'd be interested in Kansas City. He said he'd love to meet with me."

Schottenheimer had a successful run with the Browns. After finishing .500 in each of his first two seasons, Schottenheimer's Browns won 12 games in 1986 and then 10 games in both '87 and '88. And the Browns went to the playoffs in four of those five years. With a crushing 38–33 loss at Denver in the '87 AFC Championship Game and the fact owner Art Modell insisted Schottenheimer make staff changes—specifically hire a new offensive coordinator and reassign his brother, Kurt—the head coach and owner parted ways following the 1988 season.

His conversation with Peterson would alter the Chiefs for the next decade. From 1989–98 the Chiefs went 101–58–1 under Schottenheimer, including double-digit win totals in four of his first five years, plus 13–3 seasons in 1995 and '97.

Schottenheimer, who always saw himself as more of a teacher than anything else, believed in the old football mantra that "defense wins championships," and that defensive focus—along with an emphasis on a punishing ground game—became the foundation for "Martyball." Schottenheimer started by hiring his former secondary coach in Cleveland, Bill Cowher, as the Chiefs defensive coordinator. "Like me, Bill was not a particularly gifted athlete, but he got the most he could out of his ability," Schottenheimer said in *Martyball!* "And I think he enjoyed coaching for the same reason I did—to teach and get the most out of his players."

Schottenheimer was far from a great player in six professional seasons—four with Buffalo and two with Boston—though he was an AFL All-Star for the Bills as a rookie in 1965. Schottenheimer, a linebacker, started 10 games.

When Schottenheimer took over in Kansas City, the Chiefs roster featured some solid players, including Deron Cherry, Dino Hackett, Albert Lewis, Kevin Porter, and Neil Smith, but Kansas City needed a lot more help. When training camp started that summer, there were 47 newly acquired players, including Derrick Thomas, the team's first-round draft pick that spring. Schottenheimer wasn't convinced his team, or at least that roster, could win more than eight games. He, however, actually had the makings of a pretty good team for his first season. "I knew we weren't the most talented team in the league by any stretch," Schottenheimer said. "But I was certain we were going to play hard and hopefully play smart."

For the most part during the decade, that's exactly what the Chiefs did under Schottenheimer: they played hard and they played smart. After going 8–7–1 and missing the playoffs that first season in 1989, the Chiefs turned things around in Year Two.

Perhaps none was as special or as electric during Schottenheimer's tenure as the 1993 campaign. That year—Schottenheimer's fifth with Kansas City—the Chiefs signed future Hall of Famers Joe Montana and Marcus Allen. For the first time since the 1971 season, the Chiefs had enough talent on both sides of the ball to reach the Super Bowl. In '93 they came pretty darn close as they

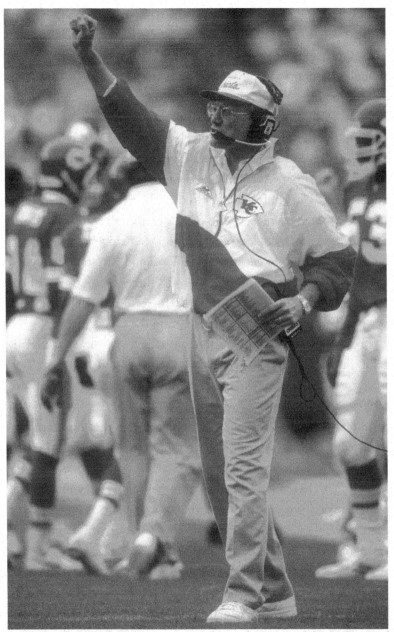

Chiefs head coach Marty Schottenheimer, who emphasized a conservative ground game and a punishing defense, calls out a play against the Miami Dolphins in 1993.

finished 11–5 and reached the AFC Championship Game against Buffalo, following thrilling comeback wins against Cowher's Pittsburgh Steelers and at Houston. Unlike those two games, though, Montana and the Chiefs couldn't engineer a comeback against the Bills.

On a cold day in Buffalo, Montana was knocked out of the game in the third quarter, and the Chiefs were knocked out of the season with a 30–13 loss. It would be one of the toughest losses in Schottenheimer's career. "There were other teams we had with better records," Schottenheimer said in *Martyball!* "But that team had Joe Montana. We were one step away from the Super Bowl and we had Joe Montana. Can you give me a scenario where you have a better opportunity to get to a Super Bowl and win it?"

The Chiefs went to the playoffs three more times under Schottenheimer. Heading into the 2014 season, though, the team has not won a playoff game since beating the Oilers in 1993.

Following the 1998 season in which an uncharacteristically sloppy Chiefs team lacked discipline and finished 7–9, failing to make the playoffs for only the second time since 1990, Schottenheimer stepped down. It was the first time in Schottenheimer's 15-year head coaching career that his team finished with a losing record. "The responsibility of the head coach very simply is this," Schottenheimer said at the end of the '98 season. "You have to create an environment in which your football team can perform and play and then you have to make sure that every week they are prepared to do that...Clearly it was our most disappointing [season] since we've been here."

Although Schottenheimer said during his press conference that it was "time to give someone else an opportunity to implement their plan," owner Lamar Hunt wasn't eager to do that. He twice tried to talk Schottenheimer into staying before the formal announcement. In spite of being tagged as "the coach who couldn't win the big one," Hunt considered Schottenheimer's decade "a golden era in Kansas City Chiefs football."

Schottenheimer eventually went on to coach Washington for one season (2001) and San Diego for five (2002–06), but he never duplicated the sustained success he had in Kansas City. During his decade with the Chiefs, he went to the postseason seven times. That's one more time than the organization reached the postseason in the 29 seasons before Schottenheimer and three more times than the Chiefs have gone in the 15-plus seasons since Schottenheimer's departure. Chiefs fans aren't the only ones left to regret Schottenheimer's departure and ask, "What if?" "I look back and wonder if I should have stuck it out and tried one more time to win a Super Bowl for Lamar," Schottenheimer said in *Martyball!* "I go back and forth in my mind if I did the right thing. Some days I think it was right, some days I have regret. It doesn't haunt me, but I do think about it. I sure do."

20 1962 AFL Championship

Have you heard the story about the Chiefs playing in pro football's longest game? Actually, this chapter isn't that one. It's about the longest *until* the Christmas Day clash between the Chiefs and the Miami Dolphins.

The American Football League in 1962 struggled to get much of a foothold against its big brother, the NFL. The Dallas Texans and Houston Oilers helped change that, though, with their exciting and lengthy AFL Championship Game on December 23, 1962. *What is it about the franchise's games on or around Christmas?*

Heading into 1962 the Texans had been average during their first two seasons. They were 14–14 after going 8–6 in 1960 and 6–8 in '61. Coach Hank Stram took a calculated risk, though, by signing his old quarterback from Purdue, Len Dawson, who had been a backup for five years in the NFL with Pittsburgh and Cleveland. He had attempted 45 total passes and threw for 204 yards and two touchdowns in those five seasons.

Dawson quickly supplanted Cotton Davidson as the Dallas quarterback and helped lead the Texans to an 11–3 record and AFL West championship while racking up 2,759 yards and 29 touchdowns on 189-for-310 passing.

Across the field at Houston's Jeppesen Stadium for the AFL championship, the Oilers were establishing a dynasty of sorts. They'd been in this spot each of the league's first two years and came in to this contest with an identical 11–3 record to the Texans.

With the Texans leading 3–0 after the first quarter, two touchdowns by Abner Haynes—one on a 28-yard pass play from Dawson and another on a 2-yard run—Dallas jumped out to a 17–0 lead at halftime.

In the second half, though, the ageless George Blanda, who was 35 at the time and would play until the age of 48 in 1975, guided the Oilers to a comeback. He hit Willard Dewveall for a 15-yard touchdown play and then kicked a 31-yard field goal before Charley Tolar tied the game on a 1-yard run.

The teams remained tied at 17 through the end of regulation, setting up one of the biggest blunders in Texans/Chiefs history. Preferring to let his defense try to make something happen and knowing that Blanda could use the strong wind to his advantage for a possible field goal, Stram sent Haynes to midfield for the overtime coin toss. The instructions seemed simple enough: if Dallas wins the toss, choose to have the wind at the Texans' backs, which meant having the stadium clock at their backs.

With television announcer Jack Buck holding a microphone at midfield, the referee instructed Haynes to make the call. He correctly picked heads. In a loud voice, Haynes said, "We'll kick to the clock."

Oops. That gaffe not only allowed Houston to begin overtime with the wind, but also the ball. Everyone was stunned. "I was sick," Jerry Mays said. "I was sure we had blown it."

The Texans, however, hadn't blown it. Neither team scored in the first overtime. During the second overtime, Dawson drove the Texans deep into Houston territory, and Tommy Brooker hit a 25-yard game-winning field goal. By the time Brooker hit the kick, the two teams had played the longest professional football game ever at 77 minutes, 54 seconds. More importantly, the exciting, double-overtime game helped the nation see that the AFL was a legitimate and fun league. "Sunday marked the day that the American Football League came to raging notice," wrote Shirley Povich, the famed columnist for *The Washington Post.* "With its title game between Houston and Dallas, it served up a suspense-choked thriller on coast-to-coast television that shattered the skeptics whose wont it had been to regard the AFL merely as the other pro league and perhaps not quite professional...At least two of the teams they turned up, Dallas and Houston, were major league in their performance and the game they played was undistinguishable from NFL football."

21 Deron Cherry

Okay, it's time for trivia. In what round was Chiefs Hall of Famer Deron Cherry drafted?

A. First
B. Second
C. Sixth
D. None of the above

A and B, surprisingly, aren't right. C probably threw some people off the trail. If you said D, you're right. But can you name the round in which the Chiefs drafted Cherry?

Actually, that's a trick question. Cherry wasn't drafted out of Rutgers. The biology major signed with the Chiefs as a free agent *punter.* "I had to beg [head coach] Marv Levy to let me try out at the safety position," said Cherry, who pretty much did it all during his time at Rutgers as a punter, quarterback, and cornerback.

That persistence, along with a strong work ethic and athletic ability, helps make Deron Cherry one of the greatest success stories in Chiefs history, if not in the history of the NFL. From 1981–91 Cherry established himself as one of the best defensive backs in the league with six consecutive trips to the Pro Bowl (1983–88). He led the Chiefs in interceptions six times and tackles four times and had six 100-tackle seasons.

Cherry's career gave Chiefs fans a stadium full of memories. There was the 1990 game against the Raiders, Cherry's first contest after knee surgery had kept him out for 10 months, and he forced Bo Jackson to fumble. There was the 1991 playoff game at

Arrowhead against the Raiders when Cherry intercepted quarterback Todd Marinovich twice. But one game that to some fans was Cherry's best came during the 1985 season in a downpour against the Seattle Seahawks. Cherry tied an NFL record with four interceptions. He probably could've had more. "I had my hands on nine balls that game," Cherry said. "I actually had [a hold of] number five, but my own guy, Lloyd Burruss, knocked the ball out of my hands. I tied an NFL record, but I had five other opportunities to make interceptions and didn't do it. Just catching one of those would've given me the record."

Porter's Dream

It might seem odd to walk up to a teammate and tell him that you had a dream about him the previous night. (Check that: it might be odd to have a dream about a teammate *period*.) But on the night of November 3, 1990, that's what happened to former Chiefs defensive back Kevin Porter.

His backfield mate and good friend, Deron Cherry, was ready to suit up the next day for his first game in 10 months, following knee surgery. Before the game against the Raiders, Porter told Cherry about the dream. On Cherry's first play of the game, he'd hit the ball carrier, who'd fumble the ball, and Cherry would recover it. Highly unlikely against the Raiders and Bo Jackson, who was playing in his second football game of the year following baseball season.

As it turned out, Cherry made his season debut during the second quarter. On his first rushing attempt of the day, Jackson, who could crash over defenders like a locomotive (and embarrass them in the process), found a hole. One player—Cherry—stood between Bo and six points.

Sure enough, there was a bone-jarring crash between the two—only it was Cherry delivering the blow. The head-on tackle forced Jackson to fumble the ball, and the Chiefs recovered. Not many people who saw the play will soon forget it. "The first person I saw after the play was Kevin Porter," Cherry said. "I ran over to give him a high-five, but he ran away like he had just seen a ghost."

Record or not, Cherry was a leader in one of the NFL's best defensive backfields with the likes of Burruss, Albert Lewis, Kevin Porter, and Kevin Ross. "As the quarterback of our defense—in the sense that I was calling the defensive plays on the field or making changes when their quarterback called an audible—I had to study and know what an offense would try to do," Cherry said. "I took pride in calling the right coverage on each play. That's a demanding job, but I think my teammates realized that and counted on me each week."

Since his playing career, Cherry has been just as successful as an entrepreneur and has helped with various charitable efforts in the Kansas City community. For nearly 20 years, he was part of the Jacksonville Jaguars ownership group, too—from before the team was announced in 1993 until Wayne Weaver sold the franchise in 2011.

It can be tough enough for most guys to transition from player to coach but from player to owner? "As a player I at least knew I could go out there and control some of the things going wrong on the field. As an owner you can't control anything on the field," Cherry said. "During my first game in the owner's box, I was ready to jump out of the window to get on the field."

In spite of his longtime ties to the Jaguars, Cherry is and will always be an important part of the Chiefs family and the Kansas City area. "It's an honor to have spent my entire playing career with the Chiefs," Cherry said. "This is a special organization in a wonderful city. There's not a better place in the country."

22 Carl Peterson Changes the Culture

In the final years of Carl Peterson's regime as the Chiefs' CEO/president/general manager, which ended after the 2008 season, it became easy to forget how he changed the mentality around Arrowhead. It's easy to forget how the Chiefs got old in a hurry after the Christmas Day game against Miami in 1971 and reached the postseason only once between then and 1990.

It's easy—and in some ways rightly so—to remember the ineptness of the 2000s. But it was Peterson who took the reigns of the organization and turned it around from 15 years of mediocrity at best. Peterson, along with coach Marty Schottenheimer, took a team that went 4–11 in 1987 and 4–11–1 in '88 and had made the playoffs just once in 17 years and turned it into one of the top organizations in the NFL.

The Chiefs won the AFC West title four times under Peterson and reached the AFC Championship Game in 1993. Peterson renewed enthusiasm for the team—and pride. Along the way Arrowhead Stadium became known as the loudest and best home field in the NFL, and home games became a destination, a must thing to do for any Kansas Citian. Though the mammoth stadium often was less than half-full during the '87 and '88 seasons, Peterson helped foster a special atmosphere at the Truman Sports Complex with an incredible streak of sell-outs and popularized one of the NFL's best tailgating scenes by capitalizing on the city's barbecue tradition.

Instead, to some the second of Peterson's two decades at the helm will bog down his legacy in Kansas City. There were some questionable first-round draft picks, coaching, and player moves.

Peterson brought in an aging coach (Dick Vermeil) and let the team get old beyond repair—similar to what happened in the 1970s. It's largely what eventually led the organization to the ineptness of the 2007 and '08 seasons under Herm Edwards, when the team won only six games, equaling its worst two-year stretch in the team's history. (The 1977 and '78 Chiefs won a combined six games.)

Certainly a fair criticism, but considering how he changed the culture and helped bring an excitement and experience that remains today, Chiefs fans should be thankful for Peterson. It was no small feat to take the Chiefs of the '70s and '80s and turn the entire organization into one of the NFL's best throughout the '90s. Since 2009 Peterson has been the chairman of USA Football, which is the independent, non-profit governing body of football at the youth and amateur levels.

The Chiefs were so bad for so long, what made you want to take the job in December 1988?

Carl Peterson: It began and ended with Lamar Hunt. I'd known him from league meetings when I was with the Eagles. He was a modest, kind, stay-in-the-background, almost egoless guy that I felt I would be comfortable working for. He gave me everything I needed to get the job done. When he first talked to me about the job, he had me come to Kansas City on three occasions to evaluate the organization from top to bottom. He had me stay on the Country Club Plaza under an assumed name. I would go to the game and sit in one of the many, many empty suites. I got a good feel for where the Chiefs were, what they were, their past, and where they may or may not be going in the future.

When he eventually asked if I'd take the job, I told him I would, but I said, "I'm going to ask you to do something that you won't be comfortable with. This organization is totally fractured; it's a total mess. If you want me to run the franchise, I need to do

President/general manager Carl Peterson, who reversed the losing ways of the Chiefs, sits behind head coach Marty Schottenheimer, one of his first major hires.

it from the top to the bottom. I think only one person can have authority to make those changes. I need to be the president, general manager, and CEO. It's a great deal to ask and I appreciate that you may not want to do it." Typical Lamar, he said, "Do you mind if I give that a little thought?" He called me within 24 hours and said he'd do it. We made arrangements for how it would be handled, and he said, "I'd like to have the respect of the Kansas City Chiefs return to the way it was so many years ago." I had to make a lot of changes and do so quickly. I will add that there was one place where we wouldn't be making changes. We had some focus groups to see what the fans thought. The overwhelming response from fans was: don't change Len Dawson and Bill Grigsby.

Your first Chiefs draft pick was Derrick Thomas, who went fourth overall in April 1989. What was it about D.T. that helped you guys bond so well?

CP: Derrick had such an engaging personality and a smile that could melt you from 100 miles away. He was a great college football player at Alabama…We were so thankful that he dropped to the fourth pick. When he got here, I told him that I needed him here as the first draft pick. I didn't want him living in Alabama or Miami or anywhere else. I told him I wanted him in Kansas City so he could become part of the fabric of the Kansas City Chiefs. "I want you seen and I want you doing things here," I told him. He smiled and said, "Carl, I'm your man."

Derrick's dad died when Derrick was about four, and I didn't have a son, so we became like a father and son. Besides being a great player on the field, he did so many things in the community that people didn't know about and will never know about. Of course, he started the Third and Long Foundation. When he died way too early in life, 25,000 people filed through Arrowhead for his viewing. There were 12,000 people at Kemper for his ceremony. He was a great person, even though he wasn't perfect. But he was the beginning for us changing the Chiefs.

The Chiefs went to the AFC championship under you and had three 13–3 seasons that ended in the playoffs. What was Lamar Hunt's reaction to those tough losses?

CP: My office at Arrowhead opened up to a big suite that held about 60 to 70 people and had an apartment upstairs where Lamar and his family stayed when they were in Kansas City. That was part of my office. After our third 13–3 season, which was in 2003, and loss with Dick Vermeil in that unbelievable shootout against Peyton Manning and Indianapolis, I was sitting at my desk after trying to console everybody else. By that time I was worn out and so disappointed. Lamar came into my office and said, "Carl, there will be those who say it was coaching. There will be those who say it was player personnel. There will be those who will say it was administration. And, yes, there will even be those who will say it was ownership. I choose to say it was bad luck. We'll get 'em next year." And he walked away. He could've chewed me out for 10 hours, and I would've taken it. But that's the type of person he was.

Do the Chiefs and Kansas City still mean a lot to you?
CP: (Former Raiders owner) Al Davis accused me of requiring anyone who came to Arrowhead to wear red. He accused me of starting Red Fridays, which actually the Red Coaters started. I never mentioned the word *red* to anyone. The fans helped it take on a life of its own. I am very pleased and personally proud of how much Lamar enjoyed that. They had such a great history before I arrived, but over years of bad football, the fans just eroded. It was horrible to see that stadium with 33,000 people in there. By the way, we increased it to 79,560 seats because Lamar wanted more people to see the Chiefs in person. He'd always say, "Carl, if the Dallas Cowboys can become America's team, the Kansas City Chiefs can become mid-America's team."

Our philosophy was all-inclusive. Everybody from Lamar to the fans were a part of it and contributed. We wanted everyone to take pride in what we were doing and how we were doing it. We wanted employees to come to practices and cheer the team. We wanted it to be like a family. In this business you're about people. As much as you want to win, ultimately it's about the people and the relationships that you make along the way. We had great times along the way and we made a lot of people happy. It was a special and fun run.

23 Birth and Death of the AFL

Lamar Hunt desperately wanted to own a football team. He was in his early 20s and already a millionaire thanks to his father, oil man H.L. Hunt. In fact, early in the American Football League's existence, when Lamar Hunt was losing nearly a million dollars a year, a reporter asked H.L. how long Lamar could keep that up. "Oh, maybe 150 years," H.L. quipped.

With his desire and nearly unlimited cash flow, Lamar Hunt contacted the NFL about granting him an expansion club in his hometown of Dallas. The NFL denied the request but told him that the Chicago Cardinals could be for sale. Owner Walter Wolfner offered to make Hunt a minority owner at 20 percent. That wasn't good enough for Hunt, so he passed.

In 1959 after the NFL and the Cardinals had essentially shut the door on Hunt, the dreamer in him stepped up. He wondered, *Why wouldn't a second league work? Baseball had its American and National Leagues. Why not football?* That's all Hunt needed. He got the names of some of the other people who had contacted Wolfner about the Cardinals and asked if they would be interested in forming a new league.

K.S. "Bud" Adams of Houston jumped at the opportunity. Two other groups—Bob Howsam in Denver and Max Winter and Bill Boyer in Minnesota—also agreed. Not long after, Hunt also added Barron Hilton in Los Angeles and Harry Wismer in New York to the group to form the six-team American Football League. By the end of that year and before the teams drafted players, the league added franchises in Buffalo and Boston, thanks to Ralph Wilson and Billy Sullivan, respectively. This group became known as "The Foolish Club."

Naming of the Super Bowl

With the AFL-NFL merger agreed upon in June 1966, the committee, which consisted of commissioner Pete Rozelle—AFL representatives—Lamar Hunt, Ralph Wilson (Buffalo), Billy Sullivan (Boston Patriots) and—NFL representatives—Tex Schramm (Dallas), Carroll Rosenbloom (Baltimore Colts), and Dan Reeves (Los Angeles Rams), started ironing out details for the championship game.

After Hunt asked about the championship game, one of the men wasn't sure if they were talking about the individual league championships or the newly formed championship game between the AFL and NFL. Hunt responded, "You know, the last game. The final game. The Super Bowl."

As the story, which has been told countless times, goes, each of the Hunt children at the time had a Super Ball from Wham-O. Daughter Sharron, who was six years old then, played with hers constantly. "She and Lamar Jr. always were talking about the Super Ball," Hunt said. "I don't remember consciously thinking, *Gee, this is going to be a good name for the game*."

And that's a good thing because when he first mentioned "Super Bowl" during the committee meeting, he received a less than warm response. And to Hunt's defense, that wasn't his intention. "Nobody ever said let's make that the name of the game," he said. "Far from it. We all agreed it was far too corny to be the name of the new title game."

As time went on, though, the name began to stick and ultimately won out—almost because there weren't better options. Rozelle, who was a former sports information director at the University of San Francisco and public relations director of the Los Angeles Rams, knew the big game needed a moniker. And eventually, after rejecting names such as "World Series of Football" (too close to baseball) and "Pro Bowl" (the NFL was using that name already), Rozelle acquiesced and started using the term "Super Bowl" with the third championship game, which was played between the Jets and Colts. The first two games, which we now know as Super Bowls I and II, were originally called "The AFL-NFL World Championship Game."

Shortly before the initial November 22 draft, however, things almost unraveled for the new league. The Minnesota group pulled out, accepting an offer for a National Football League expansion team. (At the end of January 1960, the AFL awarded the franchise designated for Minnesota to an Oakland group headed by Chet Soda and Wayne Valley.) Then the NFL came to Hunt about that expansion team that he had wanted to put in Dallas. Hunt returned the favor the NFL had extended to him in 1958—he turned them down. "[The AFL] was so important to me," Hunt said. "I had a

Several of the original AFL owners pose in October of 1959. From left to right in the front row are: Bob Howsam (Denver), Max Winter (Minnesota), Lamar Hunt (Dallas), and Bud Adams (Houston). From to left to right in the back row are: Barron Hilton (Los Angeles), Ralph Wilson (Buffalo), and Harry Wismer (New York). (AP Images)

lot of money in it, a lot invested in it. Emotionally, I spent a lot of time, effort, and energy on it...[quitting] wouldn't have been the right thing to do."

Thus began the new league in which Hunt's Dallas Texans enjoyed relative success during their first two years, finishing second each season in the four-team West division. Then in 1962 the Texans put together an 11–3 campaign and reached the AFL Championship Game against in-state rival Houston.

As one might expect, the two leagues didn't co-exist smoothly. The AFL needed to prove itself, while the NFL did all it could to make sure the new league failed. The animosity between the two leagues brought about battles over signing the top college players. Two of the biggest—Otis Taylor and Gale Sayers—involved the Chiefs in the 1965 draft.

The Chiefs and the Chicago Bears both drafted Sayers in the first round. Since Sayers was born in Wichita, Kansas, grew up in Omaha, Nebraska, and was a two-time All-American at the University of Kansas, everyone assumed the "Kansas Comet" would end up with the Chiefs.

Not so fast.

"We determined, whatever it took, he was the one man we had to have," said legendary Bears coach George Halas. And they got him, even though the Chiefs offered Sayers $27,500 a year, which was more than the Bears' offer of $25,000.

"I really felt that if Lamar and the Chiefs had offered me $50,000 a year for three years, I probably would have gone to the Kansas City Chiefs," Sayers said. "I thought that being new in the football business, they wanted to get the best players so they could keep their league together. It seemed like the Bears and Chiefs were in cahoots because I really thought the Kansas City offer would be $40,000 to $50,000 a year. I really felt for me to better myself as a football player, I had to play against the best, and that was in the NFL."

As these "signing wars" continued to escalate, as well as players' salaries, owners in both leagues felt the two leagues needed to merge. There had been discussions by various owners in both leagues but never with any type of resolution. Finally, in April 1966 Dallas Cowboys owner Tex Schramm—with NFL commissioner Pete Rozelle's blessing—contacted Lamar Hunt. The two men met in the parking lot of Dallas' Love Field airport.

Later that spring Hunt and Schramm came to terms for each of their leagues. The AFL would give the NFL a $20 million indemnity payment paid over time. Pete Rozelle would be the commissioner of the new league. And the NFL, which originally wanted to dissolve the weaker AFL franchises or at least move the New York Jets and Oakland Raiders to other markets because they shared cities with current NFL teams, decided to take all of the AFL teams and leave them in their established cities. (The NFL did give most of the indemnity payment, however, to the New York Giants and San Francisco 49ers.)

On June 6, 1966, Hunt, Schramm, and Rozelle announced at a press conference in New York City that the two leagues were merging, beginning with the 1970 season. Appropriately, perhaps, in the final championship game before the merger, the Chiefs beat the NFL's Minnesota Vikings 23–7 in Super Bowl IV. As a proud Lamar Hunt received the championship trophy after the game, he told CBS' Frank Gifford: "It's pretty fantastic. It's a beautiful trophy and it really is a satisfying conclusion to the 10 years of the American Football League. I want to say especially a thanks to the people of Kansas City. This trophy really belongs to them as well as the organization. This team is Kansas City's."

24 Raider Haters

From their early days—after they got rid of their original name, Señors—the Raiders had a reputation around the league. They played dirty. They were intimidating. They were renegades, scoundrels. To Chiefs fans, who may prefer words that cannot be printed, they're simply the "hated Raiders."

Emblematic of the Raiders' play, Ben Davidson, a fearless defensive end during 1964–71, helped start one of the most infamous moments in the rivalry when he speared Chiefs quarterback Len Dawson. "We had a mystique," Davidson said. "In Kansas City, for instance, the fans would yell things at us constantly. So, at the same time, we'd stand up, turn around, and stare at people. They wouldn't say anything after that. But that was part of our mystique."

"We didn't let anything bother us," said Hall of Fame linebacker Ted Hendricks, who played in every game during his 15-year NFL career. "If someone got a penalty or something happened during the game that turned things around, we stuck together and tried harder to make up for the difference. We always felt we were in games. In fact, we never lost a game; we just ran out of time."

There have been countless "classic" match-ups between the two teams, dating back to the early American Football League days. At the time, the Texans and the Raiders (or Señors, if you prefer) were two of the top teams in the league, which is how the rivalry started. Tom Flores, best known as a player, coach, and now broadcaster for the Raiders, actually played part of the 1969 Super Bowl IV season as a backup quarterback for Kansas City. He says that when he joined the Chiefs there wasn't a sense of joining the "enemy."

For most of the players in the early AFL, there was camaraderie because of the league's uphill battle against the NFL. Flores,
someone who has seen the rivalry from both sides, says it wasn't
necessarily built on disgust as much as reverence. "The AFL in
those days had only eight teams, so you got to know players and
teams pretty well," Flores said. "There was a tremendous amount
of talent on the field when the Raiders and the Texans/Chiefs
played. Just look at the 1969 Super Bowl Chiefs and the playoff
Raiders. Some of the game's best players were on those two teams:
Lenny Dawson, Jim Tyrer, Mo Moorman, Freddie Arbanas, Buck
Buchanan, Willie Lanier, Bobby Bell, on and on for the Chiefs.
The Raiders had Gene Upshaw, Art Shell, Daryle Lamonica, Billy
Cannon, Fred Biletnikoff. Each team was practically an All-Star
team. There was a lot of respect between the players of the two
teams."

With all due respect to Flores, fans on both sides will say the
rivalry hit full steam in 1970 with the Otis Taylor-Davidson don-
nybrook. It hasn't slowed down since.

Even though there have been lean years for both organizations
during the rivalry, one team's seeming superiority in a particular
year is thrown out for the Chiefs and Raiders. The Chiefs hold a
67–53–2 all-time lead. Kansas City has the longest winning streak
in the series at nine games during 2003–07 with the Raiders' longest
streak of seven games happening during the hapless years for the
Chiefs 1975–78. Even the most lopsided wins are nearly identical.
In 1964 the Chiefs recorded their widest margin of victory with
a 42–7 win. Four years later in 1968, the Raiders recorded their
biggest win, 41–6 against the Chiefs.

For players on both sides, it's a date to circle on the schedule
each season. "Arrowhead has always been a fun place to play for
the Raiders, win or lose. I came into the league in 1972, and in
the early days there'd be a helicopter flying over the stadium,"
said four-time All-Pro Raiders receiver Cliff Branch, "Al Davis

swore Hank Stram was up spying on us. Then, we went into Kansas City in 1975 undefeated. At the time the Chiefs had that horse, Warpaint, that would run around the field after every touchdown. Kansas City ran a big score on us that day 42–10. A couple days later, we were getting ready to watch the film, and John Madden came in and said, 'We damn near killed their horse!'"

The names of the players have changed, and the first names of the owners, (Mark) Davis and (Clark) Hunt have as well, but Chiefs-Raiders remains one of the most contentious rivalries in the NFL. "We'd always get excited about playing them, whether it was at home or out there. Of course, it was always fun to go out there because it was Halloween regardless of the time of year," said former Chiefs running back Priest Holmes. "When the Chiefs and the Raiders play, you know it's going to be a fight even if one team is the best in the league with the top offense and the other is struggling. It doesn't matter. That's a rivalry that was around long before me and will continue for years to come."

25 Travis Kelce: The Loose End

At one point Chiefs tight end Travis Kelce used one of the bedrooms in his Kansas City apartment as a walk-in closet. Watch Kelce during a game, talk with him at a charity event, or follow him on social media, and there won't be any shock that one of his bedrooms doubles as a closet. There are larger-than-life personalities, and then there's Kelce, who might be the loosest tight end in the NFL. He has a unique clothing style. He's not afraid to show off his dance moves on or off the field. He's not afraid to take a microphone on national TV and yell to Chiefs fans that, "You gotta fight for your right to party!" Oh, and he had a short-lived reality TV dating show. And he's doing all of that while flashing his million-dollar smile. "I wouldn't even say I'm really good at dancing. I'd just say I'm not shy to movement," Kelce told *GQ*. "At a young age, people would laugh at me moving. None of it looked like it should have been called a dance move. But it was just me being goofy."

Kelce's flamboyancy—combined with immaturity—came out at ill-timed moments on the field, especially early in his career after the Chiefs selected him in the third round of the 2013 NFL Draft. He drew unsportsmanlike flags in three consecutive games. He's been flagged for punching a football into an opponent's jock, for excessive celebrating, and for, well, throwing a flag. That one against the Jacksonville Jaguars got him ejected because he was already flagged and chose to throw his own flag at the official. It's not the first time Kelce's been a nimrod. During his collegiate career at Cincinnati, where he was playing with older brother, Jason, Travis failed a drug test before the Sugar Bowl in New Orleans. He was kicked off the team and lost his scholarship. He stayed in school and worked odd jobs to pay the tuition until Jason and some teammates talked the coaches into reinstating Travis.

The Chiefs drafted Travis in 2013. Jason, a center, had played for Andy Reid with the Philadelphia Eagles. Before selecting Travis in the third round, the story goes that Reid called him and said, "Are you going to f--- this up? I have the next pick and I wanna know if you're gonna be the player I need you to be, or if you're gonna keep being this young punk who doesn't listen to anybody." After Travis promised to behave, he handed the phone to Jason, who talked with Reid for a couple moments. Reid—likely with a smirk—said that's not exactly how the conversation went down. "You have to understand that I knew Travis before we took him,"

Reid said. "I had his brother [with the Eagles], and he came to visit his brother all of the time. I didn't ask if he was going to screw it up or tell him that he was going to screw it up. I just said that, 'You know how I operate, and welcome aboard, and that I'm probably not going to be the easiest on you.' He said, 'I got it.'"

However it happened, the Chiefs selected Kelce four years after trading their previous great tight end, Tony Gonzalez. And even though there have been the frustrating moments, like the penalties and the occasional dropped passes, Kelce became the best tight end in the NFL.

In 2018 he recorded 1,336 receiving yards, setting a single-season record for tight ends in Chiefs history. He followed that up with 1,229 in 2019. He recorded more than 1,000 yards receiving in 2016 and '17, too, becoming the first tight end in NFL history with four consecutive 1,000-yard receiving seasons. Along the way, particularly in the 2018 and '19 seasons, Kelce seemed to change. He still had a blast on the field, but he wasn't as quick to do something boneheaded. "He has grown up tremendously," Reid said. "The talent was always there; it has always been there. He is very gifted. He has a great feel. He loves playing the game… It was just a matter of growing up, having the responsibility that he had here, and understanding that and handling that. I think he has done phenomenal with it."

26 Eat Kansas City Barbecue

As any Kansas Citian will tell you, we have the best barbecue in the country. For us natives, that's not really up for discussion. What is debatable, however, is which Kansas City restaurant has the best barbecue in the city. "I don't care where you go in Kansas City. You're going to find good barbecue," said Chiefs Hall of Fame safety Deron Cherry. "My office is in the middle of a triangle with Arthur Bryant's, Jack Stack, and Gates, so those are three great ones. Then you have Oklahoma Joe's [now called Joe's Kansas City Bar-B-Que] and LC's not far away. Really, there's not a bad barbecue place in town."

Barbecue and football are simply an intertwined part of the fabric—and history—of the city, dating back to the Chiefs' original days. "At the old stadium, we had Arthur Bryant's down the street, Ollie Gates has excellent barbecue, and then there's Oklahoma Joe's territory around town," said Hall of Fame quarterback and broadcaster Len Dawson. "There are so many good ones around town in addition to those three."

The following are various barbecue joints to hit up on the way to Arrowhead Stadium. They're perfect for tailgating, taking back to the house, or eating in. To help you further decide which tasty meal to eat while rooting on your team, we have included the recommendations of several Chiefs, though Cherry, Dawson, and Trent Green didn't have a favorite. "There are too many to mention," Green said.

Restaurants are listed in mouth-watering alphabetical order:

Arthur Bryant's Barbecue
Locations: 17th & Brooklyn Avenue, the Legends, Ameristar Casino
Specialties: beef sandwich, ribs, baked beans
Favorite of: Chris Burford, Ted McKnight, Mark McMillian

Bee Cee's Authentic Barbecue
Location: 12560 Quivira in Overland Park
Specialties: rib tips, ribs, smoked chicken wings, pulled pork
Favorite of: Shawn Barber

Fiorella's Jack Stack
Locations: Martin City, Country Club Plaza, Freight House District, Overland Park
Specialties: Poor Russ sandwich, Martin City Mayor sandwich, hickory pit beans, cheesy corn
Favorite of: Brad Cottam, Priest Holmes, Rudy Niswanger

Barbecue is part of the fabric of Kansas City Chiefs football, as demonstrated by fans tailgating before Opening Day at Arrowhead Stadium in 2012.
(AP Images)

Gates Bar-B-Q (home of the famous "Hi, may I help you?")
Locations: six around Kansas City
Specialties: ribs, Gates fries, sandwiches, Yammer pie
Favorite of: Kimble Anders, Curtis McClinton

Hayward's Pit Bar B Que
Location: College and Antioch in Overland Park
Specialties: smoked sausage platter, burnt ends, Ol' Fashioned BBQ Sammich, french fries, onion rings
Favorite of: Nick Lowery, Will Shields. Lowery, who now lives in Arizona, said: "I loved in order: KC Masterpiece, Bobby Bell's, Hayward's, Gates!" (KC Masterpiece and Bobby Bell's are no longer open.)

LC's Barbecue
Location: 5800 Blue Parkway in Kansas City, Missouri
Closed Sundays except for Chiefs and Royals home games
Specialties: ribs, huge beef sandwich, french fries, cobbler
Favorite of: Mark Collins, Bill Maas. Collins, who still lives in the Kansas City area, said: "Hands down the best barbecue in the city! Stopped there every Tuesday [our day off]. Still the best!"

Joe's Kansas City Bar-B-Que
Locations: Kansas City, Kansas; Olathe; Leawood
Specialties: pulled pork sandwich, Z-Man sandwich, red beans and rice
Favorite of: Eric Berry, Mark Vlasic, Casey Wiegmann

Zarda Bar-B-Q
Locations: Blue Springs, Lenexa
Specialties: burnt end or pulled pork sandwich, Billy's "Ton of BBQ" sandwich
Favorite of: Will Shields

27 Marcus Allen

Despite an incredible 11 years with the Raiders, much of Marcus Allen's time in L.A. was spent feuding with team owner Al Davis. One factor was a contract dispute, but the acrimony reached its apex in 1992 when Allen said Davis "told me he was going to get me" during a taped interview during the halftime of *Monday Night Football*. "He's tried to ruin the latter part of my career, tried to devalue me," Allen said. "He's trying to stop me from going to the Hall of Fame. They don't want me to play."

Despite the reduction in his playing time through the years, Allen knew he could be productive for another team. So, in 1993 at the age of 33, Allen sought another team. He landed with the Raiders' most hated rival, Kansas City. "Lamar Hunt is not a boastful person, but I know he was extremely excited to sign Marcus Allen," Chiefs president and general manager Carl Peterson said. "Getting him away from the Raiders made it even more of a pleasure. If you can get a quality player from a division opponent, it's like getting two players because you've diminished them and helped yourself. Marcus definitely helped us reach the playoffs during his time here."

The Chiefs wanted two or three good years out of Allen. They got five. During that time, Allen went over the 10,000 yards rushing and 5,000 yards receiving marks. Coincidentally, he did it against the Raiders. "Fate works in a funny way sometimes," Allen said with a smirk.

Destiny can't be controlled, but Allen was put on an upward trajectory in part due to his strong upbringing. He grew up in San Diego with four brothers and one sister in a close-knit family. Their parents, "Red" and Gwen, were always there, always supportive.

"Absenteeism in our parents is something we certainly didn't have to worry about," Allen said. "They were always there for us. They were always there for *each* of us."

That support is a large reason, Allen says, he reached his goals throughout a brilliant 16-year NFL career. "My parents instilled in us the belief that we could do anything we wanted to do," said Allen, who was introduced at his Pro Football Hall of Fame induction ceremony by his dad. "Despite the circumstances if we believed in something and worked hard enough, we could accomplish anything. I took those words and created possibilities for myself."

Allen's belief in himself and the support spilled over into him accomplishing anything—and seemingly everything. Besides being the first collegiate player with more than 2,000 yards rushing in a season, Allen won the Heisman Trophy at the University of Southern California in 1982. The Los Angeles Raiders drafted him in the first round of the 1982 draft. He won the Rookie of the Year award. He was the MVP of Super Bowl XVIII, when he rushed for 191 yards and two touchdowns. He was the NFL's MVP in 1985, when he ran for 1,759 yards.

During his 16-year career—11 with the Raiders and five with the Chiefs—Allen became the first player in NFL history with more than 10,000 yards rushing and 5,000 receiving (12,243 and 5,411). Indeed, he did it all. He ran. He caught passes. He blocked. He even passed on occasion. "He always seemed to know where to go with the football," Peterson said. "He knew when to jump over the top to get the first down or the touchdown, he knew when to slither through, when to get small—if you will—because he was a real student of the game. He knew not only every one of our offensive linemen's blocking assignments against every defensive front, but he knew what the defensive front was going to do in every goal-line, short-yardage situation."

"Sometimes Marcus would react to shadows in practice," said Tom Flores, the Raiders head coach from 1979–87. "He'd make

Allen Isn't the Only Defector

Fate does have a way of working out sometimes. Marcus Allen proved that when he scored the 100th touchdown of his career against his old team, the hated Raiders. After 11 years with the then-Los Angeles Raiders, Allen came to Kansas City for five productive seasons.

"It was always very weird to play against those guys [the Raiders] because I practiced with so many of them, and I knew them so well," Allen said. "It was almost like playing against your brother. You want to beat your brother, but you never want to hurt them. You never want to do anything that is going to embarrass them, and that's how it was with me when we played the Raiders."

Although the most gifted and the only member of the Pro Football Hall of Fame to play for both the Chiefs and the Raiders, Allen hasn't been the only one who played for both organizations.

The following is an alphabetical list of some of the players who have played for both teams:

	Years with Chiefs/Texans	Years with Raiders
Marcus Allen	1993–97	1982–92
Billy Cannon	1970	1964–69
Clem Daniels	1960	1961–67
Cotton Davidson	1960–62	1962–68
Tom Flores	1969	1960–66
Rich Gannon	1995–98	1999–2004
Dave Grayson	1961–64	1965–70
Albert Lewis	1983–93	1994–98
John Matuszak	1974–75	1976–81
Chester McGlockton*	1998–2000	1992–97
Andre Rison	1997–99	2000
Stanford Routt	2012	2005–11
Vance Walker	2014**	2013
Harvey Williams	1991–93	1994–98
Fred Williamson	1965–67	1961–64

* McGlockton, evidently, had no shame. He went from the Chiefs to the Broncos. He's the only player whose three consecutive teams were bitter AFC West rivals: Raiders, Chiefs, Broncos.
** Walker signed with Kansas City in March 2014.

a move only because he caught a glimpse of a shadow. He was so instinctive. He also had great patience, which I think comes from his great vision."

When the Raiders drafted Allen with the No. 10 pick in 1982, they were hoping that he wouldn't be the typical Heisman flop. In fact he was the third running back taken that year behind Darrin Nelson (Minnesota, seventh) and Gerald Riggs (Atlanta, ninth). "When you get a guy like Marcus as a rookie, you don't know if he's going to be as good as he was in college," Flores said. "I didn't think we'd miss with him. And we didn't. He never let us down. In fact, coaching Marcus was like driving a Mercedes. He set the tone for practice and he set the tone in the game."

Allen always stepped up when his teams needed him most. His teams won the AFC West in seven of Allen's 16 seasons—1982, '83, '85, and '90 with the Raiders and 1993, '95, and '97 with the Chiefs. He used football's biggest stage for one of his greatest performances, when he rushed for 191 yards and two touchdowns in the Raiders' 38–9 win against Washington during Super Bowl XVIII, his second pro season. Seventy-four of those yards came on one of the greatest runs in Super Bowl history, as he was selected as the game's MVP. "I daydreamed about being one of the greatest players who ever played the game," he said. "I visualized that one day I would be standing on that stage in Canton."

In 2003 Allen realized his dream of the Pro Football Hall of Fame. "It's very humbling and frightening to think that out of all the kids that ever put on a pair of football cleats or the kids that played in high school or college and even in the NFL, you've been selected for the Hall of Fame," he said. "In my mind this is not Marcus Allen going into the Hall of Fame; it's the Allen family standing there being represented. I am forever grateful for their support."

In doing so, Allen became the first player to represent the Chiefs *and* the Raiders as a Hall of Fame inductee, but he chose to have his Hall of Fame ring ceremony in Kansas City. "I embraced both teams that I played for, but I thought Kansas City would be a better place to have the ring ceremony," he said. "The fans' support in Kansas City was immeasurable. All I wanted when I signed was an environment where I'd be given a chance to play. Having the states of Kansas and Missouri—all the Chiefs fans—embrace me was icing on the cake."

28 Hall of Fame Snub

Otis Taylor was an outstanding receiver, one of the best during his era. And yet, surprisingly, he has never even been a finalist for the Pro Football Hall of Fame.

The reasoning for Taylor's omission is not perspicuous. From 1965----75, Taylor thrilled Kansas City Chiefs fans with his acrobatic catches and old-school toughness. During his time with the Chiefs, Taylor caught 410 passes for 7,306 yards and 57 touchdowns. (Those were team records until Tony Gonzalez broke them during 1997–2008.) Additionally, the two-time Pro Bowler had 19 100-yard games throughout his career. Taylor's 17.82 yards per catch average is second on the Chiefs to Carlos Carson, who averaged 18.12 during 1980--89.

Although it's tough to compare playing eras in terms of individual performance, most Chiefs fans make the comparison between Taylor and former Pittsburgh Steelers great Lynn Swann, a 2001 Hall of Fame inductee.

Playing nine seasons for the Steelers, Swann, who played in three Pro Bowls, hauled in 336 receptions for 5,462 yards and 51 touchdowns. Swann and Taylor both were on multiple Super Bowl teams. Taylor's best performance was in Super Bowl IV, when he made six receptions for 81 yards and one touchdown. In Super Bowl X, Swann caught four passes for 161 yards and garnered Most Valuable Player honors. Truth be told, Swann played on better teams than Taylor.

In fairness, compare Taylor to other receivers currently in the Hall. On a much more pass-happy squad, Charlie Joiner had 750 catches for 12,146 yards (16.19 yards average) and 65 touchdowns, playing most of his career in San Diego and the "Air Coryell" system. Paul Warfield, who was inducted in 1983 along with former Chief Bobby Bell, had 427 receptions for 8,565 yards (20.06 average) and 85 touchdowns. Fred Biletnikoff, class of 1988, caught 589 passes for 8,974 yards (15.24 average) and 76 touchdowns. And, finally, 2002 inductee John Stallworth—cousin of former Kansas basketball great Bud Stallworth—had 537 receptions for 8,723 yards (16.24 average) and 63 touchdowns…in 14 seasons for the same Pittsburgh teams that featured Swann.

Taylor was the prototype for the bigger, faster, stronger receivers in pro football. Coming out of Prairie View A&M, Taylor was in the neighborhood of 6'3", 220 pounds with outstanding speed and athletic ability. With the size to play tight end, Taylor was bigger than most professional receivers at that time, and not many defensive backs could cover him.

The Chiefs selected Taylor in the fourth round of the 1965 AFL Draft, but getting Taylor wasn't completely smooth. It was more fitting of a spy novel than a pro football draft. At the time before the merger, the AFL and NFL each held a draft. With the incredible competition for players, teams and leagues would do everything they could to make sure their draft picks couldn't sign with the other league.

The game of hide-and-seek with Taylor might've been one of the best by the NFL. Taylor and several other players in the '65 draft were invited by the Dallas Cowboys and the NFL to a party in Dallas. According to Taylor, "the gathering was actually an NFL tactic to keep me and the others away from the AFL. The plan was simple. The Cowboys would keep me 'hidden' until after the AFL's draft that upcoming Saturday and then they would sign me to an NFL contract instead."

As for the "hidden" part, the NFL kept players in various hotels and motels with NFL representatives keeping a close eye on the players, guarding their rooms, and even monitoring phone calls.

Had it not been for the Chiefs keeping watch on Taylor and using a former newspaper reporter, Lloyd Wells, as a scout, the NFL's plan might've worked. Lamar Hunt's secretary contacted Wells and told him that Taylor left school and was on his way to Dallas. Wells began pounding the pavement and working leads to find Taylor. Eventually, Wells got a phone number for one of Taylor's female friends in Dallas, who told him that Taylor was at the Continental Motel in Richardson, Texas.

Posing as a writer for *Ebony* magazine, Wells was able to get to Taylor, whom he had known for several years. Wells convinced Taylor to leave, but they'd have to do it later. "I finally called him at three o'clock in the morning, and Lloyd was there to pick me up by 3:30 AM," Taylor said. "I climbed out of the motel window when I left the room. The front door was still guarded by the NFL's babysitting custodian. Lloyd drove us to the Fort Worth airport—he didn't think it would be safe at the Dallas airport—and we flew to Kansas City."

The Chiefs drafted Taylor in the fourth round, and he signed for $15,000 with a $15,000 signing bonus and a brand-spanking-new red Thunderbird. Thus began a wonderful pro career.

Even though most people in the Kansas City area vividly remember Taylor's spectacular 46-yard touchdown reception against the Minnesota Vikings in Super Bowl IV, there are so many other plays and instances that define Taylor, including his spectacular one-handed catches, especially the one for a touchdown against the Washington Redskins. (Former Chiefs will tell you that Taylor used to work on one-handed catches during practice.)

Was Taylor a first-ballot Hall of Fame player? Probably not. There is no denying, however, that he was a catalyst on those early championship Chiefs teams. Seven players from those Kansas City teams—Bobby Bell, Willie Lanier, Len Dawson, Buck Buchanan, Jan Stenerud, Emmitt Thomas, and Curley Culp—are enshrined in Canton, Ohio.

Otis Taylor should be next. "Otis Taylor is supposed to be in the Hall of Fame in Canton," said Jim Kearney, a Chiefs defensive back from 1967–75. "He should be there right now. In the 1969 season, could we have made the Super Bowl without him? Maybe, but it wouldn't have been easy. I have films of Otis catching the ball one-handed and another time when he caught a pass behind him. We were raised together in Houston. We played against each other in high school and we played together at Prairie View. He might not have had the catching numbers that Biletnikoff had, but he won a lot of games for us. How could you leave off Otis Taylor? It's an injustice. I don't care how they cut it—he should be there."

29 Montana's Magical Night at Mile High

In what many consider to be one of the greatest games in *Monday Night Football* history, Hall of Famer Joe Montana finished with 393 yards and three touchdowns on 34-of-54 passing, outdueling fellow Hall of Famer John Elway, who completed 18-of-29 passes for 263 yards and two touchdowns on a chilly mid-October night in 1994.

"It was the best regular-season game I can remember," said legendary broadcaster Al Michaels, who has been the "voice" of *Monday Night Football* (and now *Sunday Night Football*) for more than 25 years, in 2013. "That was one of those games where the next day at the airport, it's all anybody could talk about. It was one of those, 'Did you see that game last night?' conversations."

The Chiefs got off to a terrific start that season, winning their first three games. It was only the third time in franchise history—and first since 1966—that the team won its first three regular-season games. Adding to that excitement, the Chiefs had played in the '93 AFC Championship Game against Buffalo. With Joe Montana under center, this was going to be *the* year.

Without much warning, Kansas City lost its next two. The Chiefs were shut out at home 16–0 by the Los Angeles Rams, as Montana threw three interceptions. After a bye week, they lost by two touchdowns, 20–6, at San Diego. In those two losses, the Chiefs failed to score a touchdown, which was a stark contrast to the 84 points they scored in their first three games.

"There's always concern when you don't get into the end zone," Montana said at the time. "We'll find a way."

Chiefs fans were hoping and praying that Montana was right—and right in a hurry because up next was a Monday night match at Mile High Stadium against John Elway and the Broncos. Kansas City hadn't won in Denver since the strike-shortened season of 1982, including defeats on five game-winning drives by Elway, and coach Marty Schottenheimer hadn't won at Mile High in seven attempts (five with the Chiefs and two with Cleveland).

To make matters worse for Kansas City, Montana was questionable for the game because of a bruised hip, and future Hall of Fame linebacker Derrick Thomas was going to be benched for the first quarter because he'd been late to three team meetings that week. (Schottenheimer, as much as he hated doing it, was going to suspend Thomas for the entire game until general manager Carl

Peterson met with Thomas and then talked Schottenheimer into the first-quarter suspension.)

Defense wasn't the issue, though, in the early part of the game against Denver. Kansas City's scoring woes continued as the Chiefs went another quarter without scoring a touchdown or any other points for that matter. Thankfully, Denver, which went into the game with a 1–4 record, didn't score either. That only set up a fantastic three quarters.

In the second quarter, Denver's Dan Williams intercepted a Montana pass at the Chiefs 21-yard line. Three plays later Leonard Russell gave the Broncos a lead on a 12-yard run. The Chiefs tied the game at 7 when Marcus Allen scored the 116th touchdown of his career on a seven-yard run with 6:57 left in the half. (That touchdown tied Allen with former Kansas Jayhawk John Riggins for fourth all time on the NFL career list.) Then, with 1:12 remaining in the second quarter and Denver leading 14–7, Montana found J.J. Birden for a 6-yard touchdown play. It was a nine-play, 62-yard drive for the Chiefs—and a foreshadowing of what would happen two quarters later.

Each team got a touchdown in the third quarter, thanks to the arms of their Hall of Fame quarterbacks. Early in the third, Montana connected with offensive lineman (and tight end eligible) Joe Valerio on a 4-yard score, and then Jerry Evans caught an Elway pass for a 20-yard touchdown late in the quarter.

With the game tied at 21 in the fourth quarter, kicker Lin Elliott, who had missed a 27-yard attempt earlier in the period, gave the Chiefs a 24–21 lead on a 19-yard field goal with 4:08 left—*way* too much time for Elway. "The years I was there, I think every single time we were leading against Denver," said Birden, who played for the Chiefs from 1990–94, "and every single time, Elway drove down, and we lost."

Elway pulled an Elway and moved the Broncos to the Chiefs' side of the 50. On the next play, Tracy Simien forced Shannon

John Hell-way

Kansas City fans could've loved John Elway. That is, if he'd signed with the Royals. In 1979 the Royals selected Elway, a high schooler, in the 18th round of the MLB amateur draft. (Incidentally, they selected another future Hall of Fame quarterback, Dan Marino, in the fourth round that year.) Instead, Elway went the football route. And he proved that he didn't like Kansas City.

Actually, on the contrary, for the torment he caused Chiefs fans during his 16-year career, he probably loved Kansas City. "John Elway's one of the best competitors we ever faced," said Neil Smith, who won two Super Bowls with Elway and Denver after leaving the Chiefs. "He rose our games to a level as players that we never thought we'd reach. We knew that if we didn't show up, he would, and that would be the difference."

Elway went 18–12 against the Chiefs. Those 18 wins were the most he had against any NFL team. Seven of those 18 wins were of the *Oh, crap, here comes Elway again*, comeback variety, including at least one in five consecutive seasons.

One seemed to sting a little more than the others. On October 4, 1992, Kansas City led 19–6 late in the fourth quarter at Mile High Stadium. But the Chiefs' record dropped to 3–2 after Elway threw two touchdown passes in the final two minutes to defeat the Chiefs 20–19. It was the Kansas City's 10th consecutive loss at Denver. That was the week, as many Chiefs fans might remember, that coach Marty Schottenheimer, who was 1–8 against Denver, joked that he might stay home and let his assistants coach this one. Afterward, he tried shaking off what he'd just seen. "There's a lot more to their team than Elway," he said. "There's a flow of energy. It changed when the Broncos got possession. Once they got into position, they capitalized."

Elway retired after the 1998 season. *Hallelujah!* "I didn't try to hurt [Elway], but I put the pain on him whenever I could," Smith said of his Chiefs days. "I hated playing him. He was always the difference-maker in the game. He was a thorn in your foot. He was a nightmare that kept coming back."

Sharpe to fumble after a 7-yard play with 2:45 to play. With one of the game's best quarterbacks in Montana and one of the game's best running backs in Allen, the Chiefs were ready to celebrate. But on the Chiefs' first play, Ted Washington stripped Allen of the ball on a play up the middle, and Denver's Karl Mecklenburg recovered at the Kansas City 39.

Six plays later with 1:29 remaining, Elway scored on a 4-yard draw play, giving the Broncos a 28–24 lead. Scoring a touchdown in 89 seconds would be hard to pull off for normal quarterbacks. But it was Montana, who was anything but an "average Joe." "We felt we had a pretty good chance," Montana said. "We knew they'd concede a certain part of the field to us, so we could throw underneath. We did that and kept moving."

Montana drove the Chiefs 75 yards on 7-of-8 passing, including a couple of runs by Allen. "It was a very confident huddle," Allen said. "Nobody was panicking. Joe was as cool and calm as always, just very business-like."

With 13 seconds left and the Chiefs at the Denver 5, Kansas City called its final timeout. The Chiefs decided to run "X-corner," which called for the fullback to follow the tight end, and then they'd split near the goal line. Montana did his best to calm his guys in the huddle. "He said, 'Okay, we got X-corner. Everybody relax, don't worry. If it's not there, I know where to go. Just do your job. Just do your job, I got this,'" Birden said. "You could look in his eyes, and this guy knows what he's doing."

As it turned out, it wasn't there. Tight end Tracy Greene wasn't open. Neither was Kimble Anders. But, of course, Montana did know what to do. He found his third read, Willie Davis, who caught Montana's perfect pass at the pylon and squeaked in for a touchdown. "I always say that if we throw that pass 10 times to Willie, he drops it nine times," Schottenheimer said in his authorized biography, *Martyball!* "But he caught that one."

With eight seconds left and the Chiefs up 31–28, it exorcized many Mile High demons while giving football fans one of the greatest Monday Night games in history. "To have Montana, to have Elway," Michaels said, "it turned out to be Joe's last year in the NFL and it was just spectacular. It was like a great heavyweight fight where it's this guy against that guy and very rarely does it live up to the hype, but Montana-Elway did on every level."

30 Neil Smith

He was excited to get the phone call. His dreams of reaching the NFL were about to come to fruition. Sure, as one of the top players coming out Nebraska, Neil Smith knew someone would pick him in 1988. That's why he was in New York already. But to actually get the call the night before was special. "I got a call from [Raiders owner] Al Davis," Smith said. "He told me that I was going in the second spot to the Raiders. I was going to be their No. 1 pick. Of course, I called everybody."

But things didn't go as planned for the Raiders. The Chiefs, who had the third pick after finishing 4–11 in 1987, instead trumped the Raiders by including their second-round (29th overall) pick and traded with the Lions for that second pick. Kansas City selected Smith. "I was stunned," Smith said. "I know I had a look of disbelief on my face. I accepted it, though, because I didn't want to be one of those guys to say, 'Trade me.'

"The Chiefs told me I was going to play a key part in their success. Kevin Ross, Deron Cherry, Albert Lewis, and Lloyd Burruss were already here in the defensive backfield. Then Marty Schottenheimer came in after my first year, and things really started changing. It went on and on from there. Derrick Thomas and Dale Carter were drafted. We became a team that was one of the greatest in the 1990s. [Defensive coordinator] Bill Cowher made us feel like it didn't matter, that we'd take on any 11 any year, and we'll beat you anywhere. We had that feeling of trusting in him and ourselves. That's really what football is. It's whether you can handle your job and then see how good you can be at your position."

As a defensive end, Smith was one of the best in his era. During a 13-year NFL career, nine years of which were spent with the Chiefs, Smith was a six-time Pro Bowler, the Chiefs' MVP in 1992, and the NFL sacks leader in 1993 with 15. He had 86½ sacks with the Chiefs along with 29 forced fumbles and five blocked field goals. Teaming with Thomas, the two made up one of the most terrorizing pass-rushing duos in NFL history.

Smith was an integral part of the Chiefs team that went into Denver on a Monday night in 1994 and beat the Broncos 31–28 in dramatic fashion. "The thing I remember the most is that going in, we knew we could put [11] years of losing in Denver behind us," he said. "We had in our minds that we were going to put that feeling out of our system."

And, boy, did they ever. Trailing 28–24 quarterback Joe Montana marched the Chiefs down the field in the final one minute, 29 seconds. Then with eight seconds left, he found wide receiver Willie Davis, who made an acrobatic move near the right sideline and scored the game-winning touchdown. "Our sideline was electric," Smith said. "You would've thought we just won the Super Bowl. But we got rid of that Denver mystique."

But three years later after that 1994 season, Smith signed a free-agent contract with the rival Broncos. Many Kansas City fans saw it as high treason. For Smith it was a chance to be one of the final pieces to help Denver capture a Super Bowl ring. "Money wasn't the factor," he says, "and I didn't want to get back at the Chiefs for anything. I just wanted to play in a Super Bowl."

He did, winning both appearances. "To win it back-to-back added something to my career that was missing," said Smith, whose career ended in 2000 after one season with the San Diego Chargers. "I just thank God that he granted my wish."

But if Smith had all of his prayers answered, he would've won a ring in Kansas City. It's something he still thinks about to this day. "The biggest thing I wanted to do in my career was win a Super Bowl for Kansas City and Lamar Hunt," said Smith, who was inducted into the Chiefs Hall of Fame in 2006. "I just wanted to raise that trophy up for Lamar and give him that championship feeling again."

So between AFC West rivals—Denver and Kansas City— where does Smith's allegiance rest? "Look, the feelings I have for Denver can't be taken away," he said. "But I still bleed Chiefs red."

31 Priest Holmes

The Chiefs were a scoring juggernaut in 2003 with an offense that featured Trent Green, Tony Gonzalez, Eddie Kennison, Dante Hall, and running back Priest Holmes. That season Holmes racked up an NFL single-season-record 27 rushing touchdowns. On December 28 Holmes scored his final two touchdowns of the year against Chicago. With the first—No. 26 on the year—he passed Dallas' Emmitt Smith for the single-season rushing touchdown record. The second gave him the single-season record for total touchdowns, passing Marshall Faulk, and he passed Chiefs legend Otis Taylor for most touchdowns (61) in team history. (Two years after Holmes set the NFL standard, Seattle's Shaun Alexander ran for 28 touchdowns.) When Holmes retired after the 2007 season, following a brief, one-year comeback, he left with the

Chiefs record for touchdowns in a career (83), most rushing touch-downs in a career (76), and most rushing yards in a career (6,070).

You started your NFL career with the Baltimore Ravens, got injured, and lost your starting job. Were you revitalized when you came to Kansas City in 2001?

Priest Holmes: When you have somebody who believes in you, that takes off the shackles that can hold some players back. When a guy's unsure of his role, it can be like Kryptonite. He's not able to focus on being a great athlete. For me it was an opportunity that coach Dick Vermeil gave me, and I was really excited.

What draws you to the game of chess?

PH: I'm an avid chess player. Like most people I sat back and watched uncles play it and learned that way. Then you start playing. It was one of the things that helped me be a better football player because as a running back, as in chess, you have to be three or four moves ahead.

You're extremely humble and don't like to talk about personal accomplishments, but is there an award or a stat from your career that you're most proud of?

PH: The first year I was with the Chiefs, I was able to lead the league in rushing. Curtis Martin had been ahead of me, and on the last day of the season, our games were at the same time. He had an off day with 50 yards, and I finished with 117. Near the end of the game, Coach came over to me and said, "You just need about 10 more yards. You need to get in there." *(Author's Note: Holmes ended the season with 1,555 yards to Martin's 1,513.)* That's an example of how the coaches pushed us because they wanted us to be success-ful. Even the linemen pushed me, which led to a time I misspoke. I received my first Pro Bowl nomination that season. When the coaches told me, I shouted, "Everybody's going with me!" It ended up being a great opportunity to take the linemen and their wives or significant others and members of the coaching staff to Hawaii to thank them.

What kind of camaraderie did you guys have on the offensive side?

PH: We had great guys in Trent Green, Tony Gonzalez, Tony Richardson, Jason Dunn, and an offensive line with guys like Will Shields and Casey Wiegmann. One of the things we enjoyed most was when coach Dick Vermeil and his wife, Carol, would invite us over to their house, as a unit and get to know each other outside the lines. When you have a chance to do that and learn more about a guy's family and what makes him tick away from the lines, that's what makes the NFL so great.

Having battled through several injuries, what was it like for you to play running back in the NFL?

PH: On a Sunday, when you know you're getting ready to play, that's the most exciting time. Your blood is boiling, and you're ready to go. You know that you have to make every play turn out as beautiful as it was practiced. If you do, come first downs, touchdowns, and excitement from 70,000 people jumping up and down and cheering. That's what's exciting. After the game ends, all of that fades away, and then your body starts to say, *Priest, you're an idiot for running into a wall time after time! How many times are you going to run into a wall?* The body is a phenomenal machine. If you train it and work on it, day in and day out, it'll give back to you what you deposit. At the same time, as we beat up our bodies and the pain sets in, it takes until Thursday before your body starts to wake up and come around. You still have to practice, of course. Sometimes it's not until Saturday morning that your body comes back to the place it needs to be.

**You were undrafted; suffered career-threatening knee, hip, and
spinal injuries; and are under 5'10". Are you ever amazed at
how successfully your career turned out?**

PH: When you look at the odds, it's not supposed to happen, but
I feel I took every opportunity and played to the best of my ability.
For the guys who have watched me, I hope I've left a legacy that
shows—regardless of your size, regardless of what's said—you can
accomplish all the goals you set forth.

32 Tom Condon

It wouldn't be a stretch to call Tom Condon the NFL's most powerful man. After all, *Sports Illustrated* ranked super-agent Condon
as the most influential agent in all of sports. But if it had not been
for one unfortunate moment in his playing career, Condon may
not have become an agent.

The Chiefs got a lot more out of Condon than they expected.
That's how it is with 10th-round picks who give a team a solid 11
years. The Chiefs selected Condon out of Boston College, where he
had been a walk-on, in the 1974 draft.

After playing in 14 games as a rookie at right guard, Condon
started in the first nine games of the 1975 season. During that
ninth game, however, at Pittsburgh, Condon went down with a
knee injury, ending his season. It was around that time that he
started thinking about life after football. He had a good idea that
he'd pursue a law degree at some point, just like his father, Thomas
Condon Sr.

The injury sped up the process. "My father told me, 'Son,
this football looks like a tough deal. I think you'd better go back

to school,'" Condon told *USA TODAY.* "I figured that regardless of what else happened, I'd always have a job with my dad…I was hedging my bets."

So, in 1977 while still playing for the Chiefs, Condon enrolled at the University of Baltimore School of Law. Eventually, after getting married, Condon worked out an arrangement to take classes at both Baltimore and UMKC and he completed his law degree in 1981.

After starting all but one of the Chiefs' games in 1976, Condon, who was the Chiefs' player rep and later the president of the NFL Players Association, started every game for the Chiefs for the next six seasons. By the time his career in Kansas City ended after the '84 season, Condon had started 131 games and played in 147 (14th at the time for the Chiefs).

Through his work with the NFLPA, Condon began representing players. His first client was teammate Art Still, who had been in the league for 10 years, in 1988. "It was almost happenstance," Condon told the University of Baltimore alumni magazine about becoming an agent. "I had dealt with so many of the players' clubs [that] I had veteran players ask me to represent them."

Since that time Condon has become one of the top agents in the NFL, representing some of the top players in the league—first with IMG and now with Creative Artists Agency. Among his 80 or so clients are the Manning brothers, Drew Brees, Tony Romo, Adrian Peterson, and Matt Ryan.

Another longtime client is Chiefs legend Tony Gonzalez. "For me and my career, he was exactly what I was wanting," Gonzalez, who changed agents from Leigh Steinberg to Condon, told the Baltimore alumni magazine. "I wanted someone who could help on and off the field with marketing and my foundation. He's the best agent in the NFL."

33 Eric Berry

Heading into the 2010 NFL Draft, the Chiefs needed help. Although several positions needed upgrades after a 4–12 season in 2009, they certainly needed an impact player in the defensive backfield. So with their first pick in 2010, they selected Eric Berry out of the University of Tennessee. Berry made an immediate impact at strong safety with 126 tackles, two sacks, four interceptions (including a Pick-6), and one forced fumble en route to becoming a Pro Bowl starter. He became the first rookie Pro Bowl selection from the Chiefs since Derrick Thomas in 1989. After missing nearly every game of the 2011 season with a knee injury, Berry established himself as one of the top defensive backs in the NFL in 2012 and '13. Following the 2013 season, in which he had three interceptions, two touchdowns, and two forced fumbles, he was selected to his third Pro Bowl.

Shockingly, though, a year later, in November 2014, Berry was diagnosed with Hodgkin's lymphoma. The American Cancer Society estimates that nearly 1.8 million Americans will face cancer, and more than 600,000 people will die from some type of the disease this year. But we don't expect Berry—or any other professional athlete in his prime to be that person. As expected, however, Berry fought. As he'd say later, "It was a battle every day." There were days that he cried. Like the morning he sat at the breakfast table with his dad near his home in Atlanta and cried for about 30 minutes. Or when he worked out, which he continued to do as much as possible during treatment. He was crying, he said, not only because of the emotion of making it through the workout, but also because workouts that had been so easy a few months earlier—something as simple as doing five pushups—were a chore. And, of course, there were times when he fought going to sleep at night, not knowing whether he'd wake up.

Meanwhile in Kansas City, Chiefs fans were pulling hard for Berry. His No. 29 jersey was popping up more often than usual. And fans started wearing T-shirts with his 29 on the back and "Berry Strong" on the front. Even NFL coach Bruce Arians, who was with the Arizona Cardinals at the time, and many of the Cardinals were wearing EB T-shirts when the Chiefs and Cardinals played.

Berry made it back to the field in time for the 2015 opener. During a press conference, he said something that cancer survivors often say. "I was just happy to make that journey with everyone who was close to me," he said. "Going through that with the people you're going through it with, you don't think about material things. You're thinking about the experiences you have with the people close to you. At the end of the day, that's all that matters. Making it through that journey, even though it was difficult, have been some of my best memories out of that whole process. I wouldn't change it for anything in the world. I was thankful to go through it with the people around me."

Getting back to being game ready was another chore, but Berry had two more Pro Bowl years, 2015 and '16, and he was selected as the NFL's Comeback Player of the Year in '15. Statistically, 2016 was one of his best, as he tied career highs with four interceptions and two touchdowns while recording 62 tackles.

His best game of 2016—and the most special for anyone watching—came on December 4 in his hometown of Atlanta. Most of his family and friends, who made up his support crew, attended. Berry made it even more worthwhile for them, as he returned an interception 37 yards for a touchdown late in the first half and ran over to hand his mom the ball in the stands. And then with 4:30 left in the game and Atlanta going ahead 28–27 on a touchdown, Berry picked off Matt Ryan's pass on a two-point conversion attempt and returned it for two points for the Chiefs. Kansas City went on to win the game by that two-point margin, 29–28. "I shed a few tears before the game, I shed a few during the game, I shed a few after," Berry said. "I was just thankful for the opportunity. I take pride in a lot of things that people take for granted so I just cherish it and make the most of it."

34 Trading for Joe Montana

With the arrival of general manager Carl Peterson and head coach Marty Schottenheimer before the 1989 season, the Chiefs franchise started showing signs of resurgence—on the field and with fan support. And that fervor in Kansas City—and around the country—may have reached an all-time high in 1993. That season the Chiefs were able to trade for future Hall of Fame quarterback Joe Montana, one of the most decorated quarterbacks in NFL history, and sign future Hall of Fame running back Marcus Allen. The following is Peterson's story of how he was able to acquire Montana.

"In 1992 after we lost in the playoffs to San Diego, Marty and I sat down, as we did after every season, and looked at our needs. Even though we had a fine quarterback in Dave Krieg, we decided that we needed a quarterback. As we discussed it, we knew that the San Francisco 49ers were going to get rid of either Steve Young or Joe Montana. Joe was the legend, but they weren't likely to get rid of Young, who was young and obviously very talented. They had to move one of them. I really thought that Joe had a couple years left in him. One of our player personnel guys at the time, Lynn Stiles, had been on the 49ers staff, and he knew Joe inside and out. He

Acquired in one of the biggest Chiefs trades ever, quarterback Joe Montana rolls out of the pocket (with Marcus Allen, another major acquisition, in the background) during the 1994 playoff victory against the Houston Oilers.
(AP Images)

said, 'If you can get Joe, he could be our answer on the offensive side.'

"I began calls with my old friend Carmen Policy of the 49ers. To this day we have a great relationship. As we talked about it, I felt he'd get rid of Joe, but I had to trade—which I didn't want to do—a first-round draft pick because those are like gold. We had discussions with Joe, who didn't have a no-trade clause in his contract, but he'd certainly have a say in where he went. I did have to give up a first-round pick for him, but when I knew I could get the deal done for Joe, I called Marcus Allen, who we'd already started talking about signing. Unrestricted free agency was beginning, and Marcus couldn't wait to get away from the clutches of Mr. Al Davis. When I told Marcus that we were getting Joe, he said, 'Wow, Joe Montana. That cinches it for me for two reasons. One, I've always wanted to play with Joe Montana, and two, Carl, I get to play against Al Davis twice a year, and we're going to beat them every time.' Right then I felt I got two Hall of Fame players for that first-round draft choice.

"The signing of those guys—but especially Joe—took not only the Midwest by storm, but also the country. Plus, people didn't know why those guys would want to come to the Kansas City Chiefs, but we had season-ticket holders in 48 states. The only other two were Vermont and Alaska. Our merchandise sales shot to third in the NFL. People from all over the country became Chiefs fans. We even had Sacramento and San Jose radio stations become part of our radio network because people wanted to hear about Joe and Marcus and the Kansas City Chiefs.

"We were already very good on defense, but Joe and Marcus took us to another level on the offensive side. Once we got into games, other players did not want to disappoint Joe and Marcus. Offensive linemen would've cut off their arms to keep people from touching Joe. The defensive guys, instead of going to the bench to rest, would stand on the sideline and watch Joe perform. Joe was uncanny, even at 37 years old, in leading the team. You always felt and believed at Arrowhead—which people nicknamed "Terrorhead"—that you'd win that day. I still believe to this day that if Joe hadn't been slammed on the frozen turf in Buffalo in the third quarter of the AFC Championship Game, we would've gone to the Super Bowl that year. Those were a fun two years that took the Chiefs to a new level. Without bragging about it, I know Lamar and his wife Norma were thrilled with the notoriety of the Chiefs."

35 Abner Haynes: The Team's First Superstar

As Abner Haynes began to stand out as a high school football player in the 1950s, envisioning the possibility of a pro career, he had a major dilemma. "Football was a conflict because the important day in our church is Sunday," Haynes said. "I could not figure out how I was going to function on Sunday. My dad kept saying that I had to be at church on Sunday."

His dad's insistence is easy to understand, as he was Bishop F.L. Haynes of the Church of God in Christ in Texas, and Abner himself had been leaning toward a career in the ministry. "Church was our life," Haynes said. "I was raised to take the church another step further."

Luckily for Chiefs fans, Haynes was able to play on Sundays and with his dad's blessing. "My dad and I were talking about my future one day, and he said, 'God needs more than preachers. You can help and do the same thing in the community and within football that you could do as a minister,'" said Haynes, who played for the Dallas Texans/Kansas City Chiefs from 1960 to 1964. "I couldn't believe my ears!"

Haynes, whose No. 28 the Chiefs retired, quickly became the franchise's first superstar. He held five club records as recently as 2003. In 2013 Jamaal Charles tied Haynes' final two team marks: most touchdowns in a game (five) and most points in a game (30). The latter was set against the Raiders in 1961, which is notable because Charles tied the mark against the Raiders, too. Haynes also was selected as the American Football League's first Player of the Year in 1960.

But he isn't quick to talk about his playing days. He'd rather talk about bridging the racial issues he's faced throughout his life. "I ain't half the man that my dad was, but I'm still trying to help where I can," said Haynes, who retired from football in 1967 after stints with the Denver Broncos, Miami Dolphins, and the New York Jets. "I'm living to teach people. If people would just shoot straight, a lot of our problems could be solved. We need to live together in this world. Not just in this country but in this world."

Besides the years he spent as an executive with Zales Jewelers right after retirement, Haynes has remained focused on people. His biggest venture has been with an organization he started called Abner Haynes Heroes of Football. The group is a network of former players helping one another and society. "We really want the older players to have a vehicle to feel good about themselves," said Haynes. "There's plenty of life left after football. There are plenty of ways that we can contribute to a community."

From high school, through being the first black player at North Texas, through his pro career of the unstable 1950s and 60s, Haynes has been a trailblazer in race relations. He endured everything from not being allowed to stay in the North Texas dorms to people threatening his life.

Instead of being bitter, however, he has tried to practice what his dad preached. "His emphasis to us was integration and education and making stands, being a part of the community and contributing something," Haynes said. "Through so many scary moments...I learned how to trust God and put things in his hands."

36 The Norwegian Ski Jumper

For his 19 years of pro football service, Jan Stenerud became known as one of the NFL's most prolific kickers.

Two years before his NFL career started, though, Stenerud, who was from Fetsund, Norway, had never played American football. A three-time Big Sky champion, he was attending Montana State on a ski jumping scholarship.

During his junior year of college, Stenerud took a break from running stadium steps for ski practice and kicked some field goals with some buddies of his who were on the football team. His first attempt, toe first, was a bust. Then, however, Stenerud, who was a stud European football player in Norway, tried a couple "soccer-style" kicks. Forty yards...perfect. He moved back to midfield. Sixty yards...perfect—with room to spare.

The basketball coach, Roger Craft—father of former K-State basketball player Les Craft—saw Stenerud's booming kicks and immediately told the football coach, Jim Sweeney. The spring before Stenerud's senior year, he tried out and made the football squad. "It was kind of silly," Stenerud said. "One day I was in school on a ski scholarship; the next I was on the football team. And I didn't know anything about football. Nothing."

The rest, of course, is history. The Chiefs picked him in the third round of the 1966 American Football League Futures Draft.

Stenerud wasn't the first NFL kicker to employ a soccer style, but he was the first to do it with such consistency and accuracy.

During his 13 years with the Chiefs, Stenerud hit 279 of his 436 field-goal attempts and scored 1,231 points. In 1991 he was rewarded as the first pure place-kicker to be inducted into the Pro Football Hall of Fame.

He also made his mark in Super Bowl IV when he connected on three field goals against the Vikings, including a 48-yarder, which was a longtime Super Bowl record. "There was such a commotion in the warm-ups," he said. "They let so many camera people on the field even then. My only thought was to bear down for three hours, and don't let anything distract me. That went through my mind the whole game."

Stenerud, who never missed an NFL game due to injury or illness, finished his 263-game career with the Green Bay Packers (1980–83) and Minnesota Vikings (1984–85). Following his playing career, he went to work for HNTB, an engineering, architecture, and planning firm. Until the mid-1990s, Stenerud, who says he "will always be" a Chiefs fan, lived in the Kansas City area, where he still visits frequently for both work and to see old friends, including many of his Chiefs teammates. But he doesn't dwell on his Pro Football Hall of Fame career unless someone asks him about it. "[I don't think about it] as much as you would think," Stenerud said. "You just don't sit in a rocking chair and think about it."

Kansas City fans have seen several instances of great athletes who became local icons by being in the right place at the right time. Chiefs Hall of Famer Deron Cherry signed with the Chiefs as a free-agent punter before becoming one of the best defensive backs in team history. Royals Hall of Famer Frank White was working as a sheet-metal clerk when he was "discovered" for the Royals Baseball Academy.

But possibly the luckiest of them all is Jan Stenerud. "That could be the right term," he said. "Opportunity knocked, and I was ready. [I was] very fortunate the way it worked out."

37 Dick Vermeil

To some at the time, Dick Vermeil was seen as the Chiefs savior, the coach who would lead Kansas City to the Super Bowl. Under Vermeil during 2001–05, the Chiefs developed into one of the game's most potent offenses but reached the postseason just one time—2003—when they lost in the AFC divisional playoffs to Indianapolis. Although Vermeil has been out of the spotlight since retiring from the Chiefs, he's been doing anything but slowing down, working on charitable endeavors as a corporate/motivational speaker and expanding the Vermeil Wines label.

When you think back to time here in Kansas City, what comes to mind?

Dick Vermeil: The first thing that comes to mind is the Hunt family. They were special and they'll always be special. I miss them. I really do. I think about working for Carl Peterson. We're very close and friends since we were both young guys. And I think about the experience of coaching in Kansas City—the people, who were understanding, patient, warm, loyal. Really, in terms of fans and being sympathetic and understanding and appreciative, you can't beat 'em.

So, you had a good time in Kansas City?

DV: Oh, yeah. To be able to coach guys like Willie Roaf at the end of his career, and Will Shields for five years, and Tony Gonzalez, Tony Richardson, Priest Holmes, Eric Hicks, and working with the coaches that I worked with here. It was a great, great experience with great people. The only thing we didn't do here is win a world championship. We were a good football team but not good enough. That's the way it goes. I feel, in a way, that I came here to help Carl Peterson to put a Lombardi Trophy in Lamar Hunt's hands and I didn't get it done. That's the only negative.

Do you ever regret that?

DV: No, I don't regret coming here. I probably should've come here in 1989 [when Peterson became the general manager].

But do you regret not winning the title?

DV: Yeah, I regret it. I'd like to go back and try it all again, but I'm too old.

What was it like to coach Trent Green?

DV: I have a special relationship with Trent Green. He is a very special human being and was a very special player for us. He's the best first-round pick I think most people could ever trade for. We gave up a first-round pick for him, and boy, did he produce in every way.

What was it like to work with Lamar Hunt?

DV: He was so humble, so authentic. He was wealthy enough to be whatever he wanted to be and he chose to be awfully nice. [Vermeil smiles.] We've all been around people who had money but chose to be arrogant. Lamar and the entire Hunt family were so good to the Vermeils. I will always appreciate that relationship.

38 2012–13: What a Turnaround

The NFL is set up so teams shouldn't flounder at the bottom of their respective division for long. When a team has a bad year—say it finishes with a 2–14 record in the AFC West—it'll get a high draft pick and a favorable schedule the next season. Only the Chiefs haven't been able to take advantage of that system during recent years of mediocrity. That is, until 2013. With a new general manager, head coach, and capable quarterback, the Chiefs gave fans renewed optimism in 2013.

Even before the Chiefs played their first game with Andy Reid as head coach, they had an intangible: camaraderie. And that made a huge difference. "It was a combination of several things," said Pro Bowl safety Eric Berry. "I think the biggest thing that helped us was chemistry. We had a new coach and a new quarterback, of course, but we didn't miss a beat when they came in. We were ready and had good chemistry, even if it didn't show on our record in 2012. That helped us in the transition."

Although the core of players including Derrick Johnson, Tamba Hali, Justin Houston, Jamaal Charles, and Berry was in place, new general manager John Dorsey and head coach Andy Reid picked up other key players. With the first selection in the NFL draft, the Chiefs picked tackle Eric Fisher, who had a slow start but at times looked like a top pick. And they signed several free agents, including Donnie Avery, Mike DeVito, Marcus Cooper, and Sean McGrath.

The franchise, which has had such trouble finding quarterbacks, also found a steadying presence when the Chiefs traded for Alex Smith, who threw for 3,313 yards, 23 touchdowns, and seven interceptions in 2013.

Whatever the reason, it all worked to the tune of a 9–0 start in 2013. Among the nine wins, which tied a franchise-best start, was a win at Arrowhead over the Dallas Cowboys, a Thursday night victory against Reid's former team, the Philadelphia Eagles, and a sound 24–7 beating of the Oakland Raiders. During the stretch the Chiefs defense did not allow more than 17 points, and only the Tennessee Titans and Cleveland Browns scored 17 points. The 1977 Atlanta Falcons were the only other team to accomplish that feat through its first nine games. Perhaps more amazing there were 20 times during their first nine games when the Chiefs' opponent had the ball to tie or take the lead in the fourth quarter, but Kansas City's defense gave up only three points.

After a bye week, though, the Chiefs, particularly a defense led by their once ferocious pass rush, began to look vulnerable. In three straight weeks they lost to the Denver Broncos twice and a heartbreaker—a fourth-quarter defensive breakdown—against the San Diego Chargers. Kansas City rebounded with back-to-back blowouts against the Washington Redskins (45–10) and Oakland (56–31) before limping into the playoffs with key injuries and two losses that closed out the regular season.

That's when the Chiefs suffered their toughest and most shocking loss of the season. Playing an AFC wild-card game at Indianapolis, the Chiefs jumped out to a 38–10 lead early in the third quarter. They were bound for their first postseason win in 20 years. Then, Colts quarterback Andrew Luck improbably raised his team from the dead, and Indy went on to end Kansas City's season with a 45–44 win against a Chiefs team, which lost several key players to injury.

As stunning and disappointing as that loss was, however, the Chiefs gave fans a reason to be excited and optimistic once again.

39 Jack Steadman

This might come as a shock to many sports fans, but when it comes to pro sports in Kansas City, there's one name that needs to be remembered right along with the top executives: Jack Steadman.

Since the time he arrived with the Dallas Texans in 1963 until his retirement as vice chairman of the board for the Chiefs in 2007, Steadman did as much for sports and entertainment in Kansas City as any other front-office person. With Lamar Hunt keeping his residence in Dallas, Steadman became an extension of Hunt in Kansas City.

Steadman oversaw the Chiefs' move to Kansas City in 1963 from Dallas. The Truman Sports Complex? An idea Steadman started hatching in 1964. And he was deeply involved in the American Football League's merger with the NFL in 1970. The Chiefs' three AFL championships and two Super Bowl trips, including their win in Super Bow IV? All on Steadman's watch.

Of course, it wasn't always good. There were the team's wretched 1970s and '80s, excluding the five seasons that Marv Levy spent as the head coach from 1978–82. That is, until Steadman regrettably fired Levy after the strike-shortened 1982 campaign. "I kept getting advice that Marv had lost the team, and we had to make a change," Steadman said. "I listened to that advice…I should never have judged what other people were telling me or what other people were telling me during a strike year. In firing Marv we hired John Mackovic, which was a bigger mistake. History shows that's correct. Had Marv stayed here, we would not have encountered the problems we had here in the 1980s. That's the biggest mistake I made, and I've learned from it."

Steadman righted those wrongs by changing the structure of the organization and bringing in Carl Peterson, who built the Chiefs into a consistent winner, to run the team.

Steadman's undertakings, however, weren't limited to the Chiefs. Theme parks Worlds of Fun and Oceans of Fun? You guessed it. Also Steadman's ideas. "I thought we were in the entertainment business, so I thought we should open an amusement park to get people to Kansas City," he said humbly.

Steadman is a former chairman for the Heart of America United Way and former president of the Chamber of Commerce of Greater Kansas City. (In 1988 the chamber selected Steadman as "Kansas Citian of the Year.") And he's been involved with the American Royal Association and the Starlight Theatre Association. "I have a strong Christian background and I believe we're put on this Earth for a purpose," said Steadman, who began working for Hunt Oil Company right after he graduated from Southern Methodist University in 1950. "I believe much of my life has been preordained. I accept my failures and enjoy my successes, but the philosophy has always been that my job was to represent Lamar and the Chiefs in this community the best that I could."

Although Steadman considered retiring in the early 2000s, he stayed with the Chiefs long enough to oversee the team's involvement with the Arrowhead Stadium renovation funding and to secure leases that would keep the Chiefs in Kansas City for the foreseeable future.

Once the referendum passed in 2006, he sat down with Lamar and Clark Hunt and said he felt it was time to step down. In October of that year, plans were set for Steadman to do just that at the end of the season. When Lamar Hunt passed away in December, Steadman thought briefly about postponing his retirement party to help Clark through the transition. Instead, he stuck with the original plan. "I'm very comfortable that Clark will do a great job and be a great owner," Steadman said shortly after retiring. "It's a good time for me to move on and let the young guys take over."

In the days after his retirement, Steadman said his biggest legacy will be the Truman Sports Complex—not just for what it's meant for sports in Kansas City, but also for how other cities followed suit and stopped building the cookie-cutter two-sport stadiums. That said, how does he hope Chiefs fans—and all Kansas Citians for that matter—remember him? "As an honest, hardworking businessman who dedicated his life to getting things accomplished in [the Hunt family] businesses and in the community," he said. "I've been very fortunate. It's been a blessing."

40 The Detroit Connection

Fred, Ed, and Ed. It could've been the three brothers on Bob Newhart's show in the 1980s. *I'm Fred. This is my brother Ed, and this is my other brother Ed.* Instead, they were three important components to the Chiefs success during the early Super Bowl years.

Besides being key members of the Chiefs and being drafted within a four-year span (and each having similar names), Fred Arbanas, Ed Budde, and Ed Lothamer share another connection. All three went to Michigan State and all three were from Detroit. The fact that all three grew up in Detroit was a coincidence. The fact that all three came to the Chiefs from Michigan State was not.

It all started with Arbanas, who was selected by the NFL's St. Louis Cardinals in the second round of the 1961 draft and the more offensive-minded Dallas Texans of the AFL in the seventh round that year. He went on to become one of the team's most popular players. During his nine-year career with the Texans-Chiefs from

1962–70, Arbanas solidified himself as one of the best tight ends in pro football. He caught 198 passes for 3,101 yards and 34 touchdowns in 118 games. A five-time All-AFL performer, even the season after he lost the sight in his left eye due to an attack by a stranger in December 1964, Arbanas played the rest of his career

Like Father, Like Son

Brad Budde had a famous last name—at least to football fans in the early 1970s—but he wasn't living off that. Budde, who played at Kansas City's Rockhurst High School, started all four years at the University of Southern California from 1976-–79, finished second in the Outland Trophy voting, and was selected as an All-American his senior year, the same year that he was picked as USC's Offensive Player of the Year.

After USC, Budde became an answer to a trivia question when the Chiefs drafted him No. 1 in 1980. The Chiefs drafted Brad's dad, Ed, in the first round in 1963, thus making them the first father-son to be drafted in the first round by the same team. But Brad says he never felt the need to live up to Ed's remarkable 14-year career. "I wanted to make my dad proud, but that's mostly a father-son thing and not trying to live up to what he accomplished," Brad Budde said. "Other than that I didn't feel any extra pressure. My parents brought me up as Brad the human being and not the machine of what I could do on the field. Being a person was the priority."

Brad Budde learned football from the best, observing the great, stable Chiefs teams of the late 1960s and early '70s. Unfortunately, his Chiefs weren't his father's Chiefs.

During his seven years, Brad played for two head coaches and five offensive line coaches. And whereas Ed Budde's Chiefs contended each year for championships, Brad's Chiefs reached the playoffs just once in 1986 before losing to the New York Jets.

"Being around Hall of Famer players and a Hall of Fame coach like Hank Stram, you learn what excellence is all about," Brad Budde said. "It's sad that [with] the good leadership of the coaches I had [that we] never had a chance to shine. Without consistent leadership you can't win. To me it was disappointing because we had talent, but we didn't have a system long enough to catch fire."

blind in that eye. The Pro Football Hall of Fame selected Arbanas in 1970 for the all-time AFL team.

Just because Arbanas was here, it didn't make the Texans-Chiefs a sure thing for Budde. Had there not been an interesting twist, he likely would've gone to his hometown Detroit Lions. Budde, who still talks with his upper Midwest accent, believed the Lions were going to draft him in 1963 with the 12th pick. The Lions even had a representative with Budde on draft day at Michigan State. Shortly after the draft started, the Lions scout received a phone call. He hung up and turned to Budde. "I'm sorry," he said, "I hope you'll join the NFL [instead of the AFL], but the Philadelphia Eagles have just drafted you."

The Eagles picked Budde fourth. However, in the AFL draft, the Texans, who had two first-round picks, selected Buck Buchanan first and then Budde. "With the AFL I saw exciting football with more passing and more running," said Budde, who played guard for the Chiefs during 1963–76. "Plus, Fred Arbanas, who was two years ahead of me at Michigan State, was already with the team. He was probably the main reason I signed with the Chiefs."

Having Arbanas and Budde in Kansas City factored into the decision of Lothamer, who was also selected by the Baltimore Colts in 1964. "I talked with Lamar [Hunt] and decided—mainly since Ed and Fred were here—that I'd sign with the Chiefs," Lothamer said. The tackle played for the Chiefs until 1969, retired, and then rejoined the team for 1971–72 after coach Hank Stram talked Lothamer out of retirement.

Arbanas and Budde are in the Chiefs Hall of Fame. Arbanas became the fourth member of the Chiefs Hall of Fame when the team inducted him in 1973. Budde was inducted in 1984.

41 Trent Green

Quarterback Trent Green played 15 years in the NFL, was a two-time Pro Bowl selection, and threw the ball more than 16 miles (or 28,475 career yards). Each of those facts alone is impressive enough. More so, however, when you backtrack. San Diego selected Green in the eighth round of the 1993 NFL Draft out of Indiana. After spending that season buried on San Diego's depth chart and the next year with the BC Lions of the Canadian Football League, Green signed with Washington in 1995. Five seasons after being drafted, Green played in one game in 1997. Green was Washington's starter in 1998 before signing with his hometown St. Louis Rams coached by Dick Vermeil, in 1999. Green had a great start to the preseason before San Diego's Rodney Harrison plowed into his knee and ended his season. Off injured reserve in 2000, Green replaced an injured Kurt Warner—his replacement in '99— and showed he was so back to form that Vermeil, as Chiefs head coach, traded for 31-year-old Green before the 2001 season.

During the next six seasons, Green became one of the most pro-lific quarterbacks in Chiefs' history. By the end of the 2006 season, Green was first on the Chiefs' all-time list for consecutive starts for a quarterback (81), career passer rating (87.3), career completion percentage (61.94), passing yards in a season (4,591), most career 300-yard games (24), most 300-yard games in a season (eight in 2004), and longest pass completion (99 yards to Marc Boerigter in 2002). He's second to Len Dawson in career starts (88 to Dawson's 158) and career passing yards (21,459 to Dawson's 28,507). He became only the fourth quarterback in NFL history to have three consecutive seasons with at least 4,000 yards, joining Dan Fouts, Dan Marino, and Peyton Manning. Not too shabby for an eighth-round draft pick who didn't get his first career start until he was 28.

You had such a special relationship with head coach Dick Vermeil. How did he help you?

Trent Green: He's a unique individual and someone who I value greatly. His perspective on things is amazing. His leadership skills—and I don't know what he was like in the UCLA and Philadelphia Eagles years—are about relationships, making everybody feel valued. Whether you're the grounds crew, the secretaries, the trainers, the players, the media people, whoever, he had a unique ability to make everybody feel invested. That's his team-building and his leadership. I learned a lot from him through that. I had a lot of similar views, but he expanded that even more. He also taught me a lot about dealing with different motivators. If a reporter wrote or said something negative about Coach, he'd let it go. He would be in a press conference or an interview the next day with the guy who just bashed him in the media and he'd move forward as if everything was great. I went through some of that negative press my first year here, and he'd say, "You can't control what they do; you control only what you do. They have a job to do, so don't get upset with them whether it's fair or unfair. Life's too short to let it affect you." He had a unique perspective on that aspect of this business. Some of that comes with his age at that time, I'm sure, but that helped me a lot.

How would you describe Priest Holmes?

TG: Obviously he's unbelievably gifted from a physical standpoint. He had this quiet approach. He wasn't a big talker. When he did talk, people listened. He wasn't a verbal guy. Throughout the course of a week, he had his moments, but he was pretty quiet. A lot of that was because he was internally driven. On Saturdays—our walk-through day for a Sunday game—after going over everything and the guys all left, Priest would stay out there and mentally go through the reps. Visualization was big for him. Certain running backs are good at certain things, but Priest had an incredible combination of patience, vision, and speed. He had the ability to be patient and let the linemen develop the play. Some guys just want to go, go, go, and they end up hitting a hole too quickly and running into a wall. Priest had incredible vision. Maybe the play was to go in one gap, but if the play developed in a different spot, he usually saw that and could make a cut to go a different direction. As part of that vision, Priest was good between the tackles, but he made a name for himself out in space. Our linemen were so athletic that they could help Priest get out in space. And, of course, tied in with getting outside the tackles, Priest had speed, which we saw often. Some guys have patience and vision but not speed and vice versa. Priest had all three.

How would you describe Carl Peterson?
TG: I like Carl. We still talk today. Everybody thinks that because of the way things went down in 2007 that we don't like each other. That's not the case. I understand the business side of football. Carl had a job to do and he did it. Sure, I was disappointed, but I don't blame Carl. I thought he was good at what he did. It was disappointing, I'm sure, for him that we didn't win more championships and playoff games, but I think he genuinely cared about the people and this organization. He had a fondness for Lamar Hunt and the Hunt family that I think still exists today—even with things ending for him the way they did. For what he was able to do for this city, I don't think he gets enough credit. I wasn't here when he first came in, but I understand there was a dormant NFL scene in Kansas City. He turned that around. People might not have liked some of the things he said or some of the decisions he made, but when you're wearing a lot of hats, like he did, sometimes you're going to get all the credit or all the blame. I think he should get more credit.

How would you describe Lamar Hunt?

TG: Lamar was one of the most unique people I've ever met in my life. I really wish I had had more time to get to know him better. I wish that I had known our time was limited before he got sick. I would've loved to have talked to him more about leadership and his philosophy on certain aspects of life—similar to the conversations I have with Coach Vermeil. Lamar had a unique ability to relate to a lot of different types of people. For a guy coming from where he came, able to accomplish what he accomplished—whether you're talking football, soccer, basketball, or tennis—he had such an interesting outlook on things. The way he treated people the same was incredible. You can talk to anyone in the Chiefs organization who knew him, and they all loved him. I've even had fans tell me Lamar Hunt stories. I had one fan tell me about how he was in Europe to watch the World Cup, and he saw Lamar riding on a train from one World Cup site to another. The fan said Lamar was sitting by himself, trying to figure out a map. That's just who he was. You never would've guessed he was a millionaire. He was modest and humble.

What is the Trent Green Family Foundation?

TG: The Trent Green Family Foundation is our foundation that we started in 1999, when I was with the Rams. It goes through the Greater Kansas City Community Foundation instead of being a 501c3. Every cent that comes in goes toward grants. Right now we focus on helping Children's Mercy Hospital, Ronald McDonald House Charities, the YMCA and we recently started a reading program with Phoenix Family, which serves underprivileged families in the Kansas City and the surrounding area. We started a program through them called HIKE (Help Instill the Key to Education), which is trying to increase reading proficiency levels for kids. Statistics have shown how important reading is to helping kids succeed in high school and staying off the streets and away from gangs, drugs, and so on. Our goal is to get kids reading proficiently by third or fourth grade. We started in 2013 and we've opened three reading centers. In the first six months of the first center being open, 108 kids had gone through the program, and more than half had increased their reading level by a grade level. That doesn't mean they're reading at their grade level yet, but in six months, half have jumped a grade level. Through the YMCA we opened a Trent Green Family Foundation Field, which is a Challenger football and soccer field in the northland. Part of that process included building a Challenger playground. The majority of our work through the foundation is right here in the Kansas City area.

42 Dying as a Hero

What is it that makes someone do what is necessary to become a hero? Why would a major league umpire chase down a mugger in Texas? Ask former ump and Kansas City native Steve Palermo, who has gone through years of hell, rehabilitating from a bullet that hit his spinal cord area after the assailant shot him.

Why would an NFL player leave a multimillion dollar career behind to join the Army Rangers during a time of war? Pat Tillman did that and lost his life fighting for our country.

And why in the world would a promising NFL running back, who didn't know how to swim, jump into a Louisiana pond to try to save three boys he didn't even know? Two years after being selected as the AFC Rookie of the Year, Joe Delaney did just that in June 1983. "One of the things that comes to mind immediately was his unselfishness," said Billy Jackson, a former University of

Alabama running back, who, like Delaney, was drafted by the Chiefs in 1981. "He was always thinking of others before himself. That was off the field and on it."

Even though no other Chiefs player has worn Delaney's No. 37 since—it's not officially retired—the team *finally* recognized Delaney in 2004 with induction into the organization's Hall of Fame and Ring of Honor.

Delaney may have played just two seasons for the Chiefs, but this honor was long overdue. As a rookie starter in 1981, Delaney rushed for 1,121 yards. Included in that total was a 193-yard rushing performance against the Houston Oilers. In the strike-shortened 1982 season, which wiped out seven games, Delaney still mustered 380 yards.

Then on June 29, 1983, while relaxing in a park in Monroe, Louisiana, Delaney heard the pleas of three boys. Instinctively, he hopped up, ran to the muddy water, and jumped in. On his way a little boy asked if Delaney could swim. "I can't swim good," he said, "but I've got to save those kids. If I don't come up, get somebody."

Instead of trying to get someone else to do it since he was scared of water above his waist, Delaney jumped in, trying to save three strangers who also couldn't swim. No amount of running ability or quickness or speed or agility mattered at that moment. In some ways Delaney was successful. One of the boys was able to get back to safety. However, the other two—and Delaney himself—drowned.

A few weeks later, on July 13, 1983, President Ronald Reagan posthumously awarded Delaney the Presidential Citizen's Medal. The next year the NCAA selected Delaney, who rushed for a school-record 3,047 yards at Northwestern State (Louisiana), as the recipient of the NCAA Award of Valor.

Delaney, who also has been enshrined in the College Football Hall of Fame, did what he felt he had to do. He didn't sit in the park and calculate the reasons for or against going to the water. Heroes don't think; they act. And Delaney acted unselfishly. "In the South we call people like Joe a 'good ole country boy.' I was a country boy, so we had that bond immediately," Jackson said. "I remember every week when the rookies had to bring in doughnuts. Joe never let me bring the doughnuts. He had already gone by Winchell's and picked out this great variety. We had only five running backs, but Joe would bring in two boxes of doughnuts. That's the type of guy he was, unselfish and fun. We had some great times together."

43 The Playoff-Crushing Colts

Lin Elliott. Peyton Manning. Andrew Luck. Those are just a few of the names that conjure wretched postseason memories for Chiefs fans. From their first postseason appearance in 1962 through the 2013 season, the Dallas Texans/Kansas City Chiefs have played in 23 postseason games. Four of those games were against the Indianapolis Colts, which is more than the Chiefs have played any single opponent in the playoffs. And each of those four games resulted in a crushing end to Kansas City's season.

1995 AFC Divisional Playoff: January 7, 1996
Colts 10, Chiefs 7
The Chiefs went 13–3 in 1995, won the AFC West, and held home-field advantage for the playoffs. Those achievements alone are somewhat surprising, considering the preseason predictions. "Most experts had us picked sixth out of five teams in our division,"

said former Chiefs defensive lineman Pellom McDaniels. Instead the Chiefs worked hard and proved the "experts" wrong.

Unfortunately the dream season came to an abrupt end in a divisional playoff loss at home against the Colts. Besides a 13-win season, the Chiefs had weather on their side against the dome-dwelling Colts, as bitterly cold winds swept through Arrowhead and gave the 11-degree temps wind chills around 9-below. Perhaps the cold weather affected both the Kansas City quarterback and kicker most. Steve Bono threw three picks, and kicker Lin Elliott missed field-goal attempts from 35, 39, and 42 yards. The name Lin Elliott still conjures up bad memories for Chiefs fans. "To his credit, after the game Lin Elliott took every question in front of his locker, and there were *a lot* of questions," said longtime Kansas City TV sports anchor Dave Stewart. "In fact we were in the second wave of reporters, and he sat there and ate all of it. He's definitely a hot-button player fans will always despise."

"I spent a week in my basement after that game," McDaniels said. "After the way we played all season, I could not believe we lost by a field goal."

2003 AFC Divisional Playoff: January 11, 2004
Colts 38, Chiefs 31
During a game in which neither team punted—only the third time in NFL postseason history that's happened—there were only five penalties and one turnover between the NFL's top two scoring offenses. For the Chiefs it came down to two unfortunate offensive plays on essentially back-to-back possessions and not getting at least one key defensive stop.

Near the end of the first half, it appeared as though the Chiefs had cut into Indy's 21–10 lead when Tony Gonzalez's 27-yard touchdown catch was called back because of offensive pass interference. Morten Andersen ended up missing the 31-yard field goal attempt. "That was a corner route, and the referees said Tony pushed off with his left arm," quarterback Trent Green said. "Well, the guy that was covering him had hurt his shoulder the week before. Did he push off? Yes. Was the defender hanging on to him? Yes. Tony was trying to get the guy's arm off of him…If you see a close-up of the play, you can see that he winces because of the shoulder pain. To the officials it looks like Tony pushed him hard. Granted, it's a lot to ask an official to know the injury report of that guy's shoulder, but that was a big part of his reaction and the call."

The Chiefs had the ball at the start of the second half and again seemed to be headed for a touchdown when Priest Holmes, who ran for 176 yards in the game, fumbled on the Colts' 22-yard line at the end of a 48-yard run. Indy recovered. "Those are two possessions when we should've scored," Green said. "Offensively, we look at that and know we should've scored. Defensively, we couldn't get stops. That's what makes that game so frustrating."

2006 AFC Wild-Card: January 6, 2007
Colts 23, Chiefs 8
Kansas City's offense couldn't get it going in the RCA Dome and avenge a loss from three years earlier. Even though the Chiefs barely snuck in the playoffs as a wild-card team playing the AFC South division winner and favored Colts, many thought the Chiefs had a great chance to pull off the upset. The Colts' Achilles' heel was their run defense, which ranked last in the NFL and allowed 173 rushing yards per game during the regular season. Meanwhile, Chiefs running back Larry Johnson finished with 1,789 yards as the NFL's second-leading rusher.

The Colts, however, held Johnson to a season-low 32 yards on 13 carries and the Chiefs to 44 rushing yards, seven first downs, and 126 total yards—all Colts franchise playoff records. The Chiefs needed almost 41 minutes to record a first down.

Adam Vinatieri hit three field goals in the first half, giving the Colts a 9–0 lead at halftime, but then Indianapolis marched down the field for a touchdown midway through the third quarter for a 16–0 lead.

Even though Kansas City's defense picked off Peyton Manning three times, the Chiefs offense could not capitalize.

2013 AFC Wild-Card: January 4, 2014
Colts 45, Chiefs 44

This will go down as one of the most stunning losses in Chiefs history. The 11-win Chiefs dominated—manhandled—the Colts at Lucas Oil Stadium. It was bound to be the team's first postseason win in almost 11 years—since January 16, 1994 at Houston. Behind 378 passing yards, four touchdowns, and no interceptions for Chiefs quarterback Alex Smith, Kansas City went up 31–10 at halftime and then added to that minutes into the third quarter when Smith hit Knile Davis for a 10-yard touchdown. At that point with the Chiefs leading 38–10, according to ESPN Stats & Information, Indianapolis had a 0.9 percent chance of winning.

But against a Chiefs defense that looked like it was playing not to lose, Colts quarterback Andrew Luck came alive. He threw three of his four touchdown passes in the second half, and amassed 443 yards in the air for the game, including a game-winning 64-yard touchdown pass to T.Y. Hilton. Meanwhile, the Chiefs were littered with injuries, including a concussion that sidelined running back Jamaal Charles early in the game.

That loss gave the Chiefs eight consecutive postseason defeats, which ties them with the Detroit Lions for the longest playoff losing streak. "That loss stuck with us," said Chiefs safety Eric Berry, who forced a fumble that Luck improbably recovered and ran in for a touchdown in the fourth quarter, during the offseason. "It simply comes down to finishing. That sums up that loss. When your offense puts up that many points, you cannot give the lead up like that. I put that on myself and our side of the ball. Especially on the secondary, we put a lot of pressure on ourselves to be accountable.

We feel that we need to be the strong part of the defense. We just want to hold up our end of the bargain."

44 Visit the Pro Football Hall of Fame

For Chiefs fans who want to travel a little to pay homage to former players and coaches, a trip to the Pro Football Hall of Fame is a must.

Located in Canton, Ohio, about 777 miles east of Arrowhead Stadium, the Pro Football Hall of Fame is an informative museum that's a combination of history preservation and modern-day interactive experiences. The Hall of Fame opened as a 19,000-square foot museum in 1963. Through several renovations and expansions, including a two-year, $27-million project that ended in 2013, the building is now an 118,000-square foot tribute to all of the greats of professional football. "Coming to the Hall of Fame is always a very unique experience," Chiefs legend and Hall of Fame member Willie Lanier said for a video shortly after the latest remodel, "especially now that all the renovation has been done and completed."

Although Canton might seem like an odd spot to place the Hall of Fame, there actually is a good reason it's there. Canton is the birthplace of the American Professional Football Association, which became the NFL. In 1959 the Canton newspaper led the charge for the construction of a professional football hall of fame, stating, of course, that the most "logical" spot was in Canton. The National Football League agreed and awarded the Hall of Fame to Canton in 1962. The city began a fund-raising campaign that brought in more than $378,000. It broke ground in August 1962, and 13 months later the Pro Football Hall of Fame was open to the public.

A Hall of Chiefs

As of the 2019 enshrinement, 13 men who spent the majority of their careers with the Chiefs are in the Pro Football Hall of Fame.

Name—Induction Year
Lamar Hunt—1972
Bobby Bell—1983
Willie Lanier—1986
Len Dawson—1987
Buck Buchanan—1990
Jan Stenerud—1991
Hank Stram—2003
Emmitt Thomas—2008
Derrick Thomas—2009
Curley Culp—2013
Will Shields—2015
Tony Gonzalez—2019
Johnny Robinson—2019

As of the 2019 enshrinement, 10 men who spent part of their careers with the Chiefs are in the Pro Football Hall of Fame.

Name—Induction Year
Mike Webster—1997
Joe Montana—2000
Marv Levy—2001
Marcus Allen—2003
Warren Moon—2006
Willie Roaf—2012
Bill Polian—2015
Morten Andersen—2017
Bobby Beathard—2018
Ty Law—2019

Besides the bronze busts of 23 people with Chiefs ties, among the Chiefs-related artifacts you may find:

- Ed Budde's helmet
- Lanier's unusual helmet
- Gloves and cleats worn by Tony Gonzalez
- Will Shields' 2004 Pro Bowl jersey
- Football signed by Len Dawson, commemorating his MVP performance in Super Bowl IV
- Football that Priest Holmes carried into the end zone against the Chicago Bears for his record-setting 27th rushing touchdown in 2003

The Hall of Fame is open year-round except for Thanksgiving and Christmas. As of 2020 admission for adults was $28, seniors (65 and older) $24, children (six–12 years old) $21, and younger than six are free. The museum opens at 9:00 AM and closes at 8:00 PM during the summer (Memorial Day weekend through Labor Day) and 5:00 PM during the fall and winter. For more information visit www.profootballhof.com.

45 Montana vs. Young

It might be one of the most famous photographs in Chiefs history. Hall of Fame running back Marcus Allen busts through the defense and scores a touchdown, while guard Will Shields blocks on Allen's right side.

Study the photograph for a few more seconds, and two things pop out: in the background, with arms raised as if he's touching the clouds, is No. 19 for Kansas City, quarterback Joe Montana. It was Montana's signature celebration, but the other noticeable thing that helps explain Montana's overt enthusiasm—Kansas City's opponent on that sunny and presumably warm day was San Francisco, the team that had traded Montana in for a flashy newer model in Steve Young. "[Montana] said the game was nothing special, but we sensed it was," Chiefs wide receiver Willie Davis said. "When we saw him do that and jump in the air, we knew it was."

Montana displayed similar emotion late in the final quarter when he connected with Allen on a 38-yard pass play that practically sealed Kansas City's 24–17 win in their second game of the 1994 season, one that owner Lamar Hunt called the "game of the century."

Appropriately nicknamed "Joe Cool," Montana downplayed the game all week. He wouldn't let on to his coaches, teammates, or the media that this game, his first against the team that was considered *his* for 13 seasons and that he led to four Super Bowl wins (and received the MVP award after three of those victories) meant a little more. "Obviously, you knew that deep down Joe wanted to beat the 49ers," Marty Schottenheimer said in his biography, *Martyball!* "That's only human nature. But he never brought it up in front of the team during practice that week and he wasn't nervous. I just think he wanted to make sure there was no distraction, as hard as that was, for the other guys on the team."

Although Montana tried to downplay it, it was anything but business as usual at One Arrowhead Drive. The Chiefs public relations department, which normally received 30 to 40 total credential requests, fielded 200 requests—for photo and video credentials alone.

The game itself didn't disappoint. In front of 79,907 (the largest crowd at Arrowhead Stadium since its first season in 1972) Montana was his typically accurate and not flashy self. He threw for 203 yards on 19-of-31 passing with two touchdowns and no interceptions. His understudy with the 49ers, Steve Young, threw for 288 yards and one touchdown, but he was picked off twice.

In spite of the hype of Montana vs. Young, it was the Chiefs defense that put on a show—and played the key role in the victory. Besides the two interceptions, Kansas City's defense sacked Young four times (including three by Derrick Thomas, who also forced a fumble and picked up a safety that cut the 49ers lead to 14–9) and left the new 49ers quarterback with multiple wounds, bruises, a bum leg, and in such pain and exhaustion that Young vomited over the bench late in the game. "You know we got a lot of mobility over on defense," Thomas said after the game. "We got guys that can really pursue. We just ran and ran and ran and ran and kept running. I mean, that's the only way you defense [Young]."

The Chiefs took an early lead when Montana dumped a 1-yard pass to tackle-eligible Joe Valerio. The 49ers took a 14–7 lead in the second quarter on a touchdown pass from Young and a run by Marc Logan. But with Thomas' safety and then a third-quarter touchdown play from Montana to tight end Keith Cash, the Chiefs took a lead they wouldn't relinquish. Allen's 4-yard touchdown run in that famous photograph gave the Chiefs a commanding 24–14 lead late in the third quarter.

In the locker room after the game, Montana, relaxed as ever, passed around hamburgers that someone brought for him. "Guys like Neil [Smith], these were the guys putting the pressure on," he said. "I wasn't watching Steve all that much out there, but I knew he was under a lot of pressure, and what it meant to me was, *Hey, those are the guys who are getting us the ball back*...I'm glad it's all over."

46 Three Wise Men: Reid, Dorsey, and Smith

The three wise men came from the East bearing gifts of gold, frankincense, and myrrh. Well, actually, they came from Philadelphia, Green Bay, and San Francisco bearing gifts of coaching acumen, franchise building, and a live arm. Indeed, when Andy Reid, John Dorsey, and Alex Smith came to Kansas City, Chiefs fans highly anticipated the 2013 season.

The organization was coming off four years of inconsistency on the field with a paranoid, controlling general manager running the front office. The Chiefs had become the New England Patriots 2.0, minus the winning, good coach, and MVP quarterback. At no time during Scott Pioli's reign was that magnified more than in the 2012 season, when the Chiefs went 2–14 under head coach Romeo Crennel and quarterback Matt Cassel. (A plane even flew over Arrowhead Stadium while dragging a banner that said: "WE DESERVE BETTER! FIRE PIOLI — BENCH CASSEL.")

In an attempt to make sure not all Chiefs fans were polarized by Pioli, Crennel, and bad football, owner Clark Hunt led the search to find Crennel's replacement after the '12 season. (Of course, that meant that Pioli's days likely were numbered.) As luck would have it, Reid had been pushed out of Philadelphia after years of *just* playoff football for the Eagles. Under Reid the Eagles went to the playoffs in nine of 14 years. Such success would be welcome in Kansas City, considering the Chiefs had been to the playoffs only three times since 1997.

In early January 2013, Hunt had his man, and the dominoes began falling. Within an hour of the Chiefs announcing that Pioli had been fired—and only four days after the Eagles fired Reid—reports surfaced that the team reached an agreement with Reid. It became official on January 5, when the Chiefs tweeted a photo of Reid and Hunt signing the contract.

A week later, on January 12, the Chiefs hired their new general manager John Dorsey, a longtime Green Bay Packers personnel guru whose wife had Kansas City roots. Dorsey and Reid worked together when Reid was an assistant coach at Green Bay during 1992–98.

"John's outstanding track record as a talent evaluator and his experience helping to build a successful organization make him an ideal choice for our next general manager," Hunt said in a statement released by the Chiefs. "He is a respected player personnel executive and a person of high integrity who I believe will work very well with Coach Reid. I'm excited to have both John and Andy on board to build our football team."

From left to right: general manager John Dorsey, quarterback Alex Smith, and head coach Andy Reid helped lead the turnaround of the Chiefs in 2013. (AP Images)

The next block in that building process, many assumed, would be addressing the quarterback situation. During the two-win 2012 season, the Chiefs benched their $63-million signal-caller Cassel and went with Brady Quinn. For the first time in the team's history, the Chiefs had the first pick in the upcoming draft, which would be perfect if there was a stud quarterback coming out. Only problem: there weren't any can't-miss quarterbacks in the draft.

So, the Chiefs targeted Smith, who'd lost his starting job in San Francisco to Colin Kaepernick. On March 12, the first day of the NFL's new year, the Chiefs announced a trade with the 49ers for Smith. In return for Smith, the first overall pick in the 2005 NFL Draft, San Francisco received Kansas City's second-round picks in 2013 and 2014. In Smith, though, the Chiefs had a quarterback whose previous two seasons were far better than the parade of Cassel, Quinn, Kyle Orton, and Tyler Palko. Smith went 19–5–1 during those two years, while the Chiefs went 9–23. Smith's completion percentage was higher, 64.3 to 57.7, as was his touchdown-to-interception ratio of 30–10 compared to 21–38.

"I love his competitive nature," Dorsey said of Smith. "I love his leadership, his ability to be one of the teammates. He makes smart decisions. He doesn't turn the ball over. He's athletic. Guys believe in him. In today's football that's one of the first components you need, a quarterback who can lead your team."

With the Chiefs' three wise men of 2013, the team was in good hands. En route to going 11–5 and reaching the playoffs that season, the Chiefs became the first team in NFL history to start a season 8–0 after having the worst record in the league. "As we've gone along, the guys are starting to believe in the constant message we're saying: it's going to take everybody involved in this whole process to reach the goal of getting into the playoffs," Dorsey said. "We've accomplished the first goal, but by no means are we satisfied."

Under Dorsey's direction the Chiefs had the fourth best winning percentage in the NFL from 2013 to 2016 with records of 11–5, 9–7, 11–5, and 12–4. They trailed only the New England Patriots, Denver Broncos, and Seattle Seahawks in those four years. However, behind the scenes things weren't going as smoothly. In somewhat of a surprising move at the time, the Chiefs fired Dorsey in June 2017. Dorsey went to Cleveland in the same capacity, but the Browns weren't as successful. Dorsey and the Browns mutually parted ways after the 2019 regular season.

47 Tour Arrowhead

For any self-respecting Chiefs fan, one of the ultimate experiences is to tour Arrowhead Stadium. The Chiefs offer various tour options throughout the year, including one on gamedays.

Public Guided Tour
Lasting approximately 90 minutes, the Public Guided Tour ("Sea of Red" Tour) takes fans to the Scout Investments Club Level, the press box, the locker room, and the Chiefs Hall of Honor. The tour includes stepping next to the field. (Touching the actual playing field surface is prohibited.) Exact stops for the Public Guided Tour, which is not available on gameday, vary based on availability of certain areas throughout Arrowhead. Public Guided Tours are $30. "The best part of the Sea of Red Tour for me was getting to see all the parts of the stadium that fans don't usually have access to on gameday," said longtime fan Zach Sewell. "Not only did we get to see the suites and broadcast booths in the club-level sections, but we were able to walk where the players enter and exit the field

and see how those two entrances are connected by the hallway that leads to the locker room. The tour is full of tidbits of knowledge for the interested NFL fan. We got to see the press room from Andy Reid's perspective with each of us standing behind the podium where he takes questions after each home game. The tour is worth the money to get a feel for what the gameday atmosphere is like on the players' side."

Other Arrowhead "Tours"

Arrowhead Stadium has been the site of a lot more than Chiefs football throughout its 40-plus years. There have been other football games—the 1974 AFC-NFC Pro Bowl; the Big 12 Championship; the "Border War" between KU and MU from 2007–11; Pittsburg State and Northwest Missouri State contests; K-State and Iowa State in 2009 and '10, to name a few—and "other" football games, including a World Cup qualifying match, various exhibition soccer matches, as well as serving as home to the Kansas City Wizards (now Sporting Kansas City). Arrowhead, though, has been a perfect venue for concerts and other non-sporting events. Since it opened in 1972, Arrowhead has played host to more than 100 non-football and non-Wizards events. Here are some of the noteworthy ones:

1973—Elton John
1975—Rolling Stones
1976—Earth, Wind & Fire
1977—Peter Frampton
1978—Willie Nelson
1984—Michael Jackson
1988—Pink Floyd
1992—U2
1993—Paul McCartney
1996—Promise Keepers convention
2001—George Strait
2004—Billy Graham Crusade
2012—Kenny Chesney and Tim McGraw
2015—Rolling Stones
2017—U2

Guided Private Tour

For fans wanting to take a group—or for an intimate tour for your family or for a few friends—a guided private tour might be an option. Each tour is 90 minutes long and includes the press box, Hall of Honor, club level, Chiefs locker room, and one of the sidelines. Private tours for groups of 11-plus are $25 per person and go up from there for smaller groups.

Gameday Tour

For the ultimate Chiefs fan experience, there's the Gameday Tour, which, as the name suggests, takes place on the day of Chiefs home games. This tour includes the press box, the Hall of Honor, plus one of the sidelines. The Gameday Tour costs $150 to $300.

For information about all of the Arrowhead Stadium tours, visit www.goarrowhead.com or call 816-920-4547.

48 Attend Training Camp

By the end of summer, after going to countless Royals and T-Bones baseball games, not to mention numerous summer camps (or school) for the kids, fans start sensing the start of football season. Chiefs fans who want to experience an up-close feel of that year's squad need to head to Missouri Western State University in St. Joseph, Missouri, for training camp.

Running from late July until the middle of August, training camp allows fans a chance to watch the team for free as it prepares for the upcoming season. Check the full schedule for exact times and dates, but the Chiefs practice most days, beginning early in the morning (before the heat kicks in). After practices several players hang out and sign autographs. Generally, there will be two practice sessions during each training camp when the entire team signs autographs. Most of the outdoor practices are free. Parking, however, costs a whopping $5 as of 2019. (If only Arrowhead Stadium's parking was the same price, right?)

Missouri Western is located approximately an hour north of Arrowhead and 45 minutes north of Kansas City International Airport. Various websites can help plan your trip, including kcchiefs.com, stjomo.com, and gogriffons.com.

While you're in St. Joseph, be sure to check out the area's historical sites. After all, St. Joe was the starting point for the Pony Express, a middle point for Lewis and Clark, and the ending point for outlaw Jesse James.

After the Chiefs moved from Dallas to Kansas City in the early days of the franchise, the team held training camp during 1963–90 at William Jewell College in Liberty, Missouri. When Carl Peterson became the president and general manager, he moved it to River Falls, Wisconsin, where it stayed for 20 years before moving to St. Joseph in 2010. "Given the increased year-round interest in the Chiefs," owner Clark Hunt said, "it was important to our family to conduct camp closer to our fans in mid-America."

It's been a great move for both sides. The fans in the Kansas City metro—as well as surrounding states such as Iowa and Nebraska—can attend camp more easily. And the players appreciate the larger crowds and the fans' love at training camp. "Oh, man, that's a great feeling," safety Eric Berry said. "Our fans are the greatest. It could be pouring down rain or a heat index of 115, but fans still pack the place. Sometimes it's tough for players to get up for practices, the energy isn't there, but then the fans are out there yelling for the team even during our stretches. That motivates us through practice. Their energy rubs off on us, and we end up having a good practice. Obviously not every practice is great, but you can feel the energy from the fans, and that's a huge help."

49 1966 AFL Championship

The Chiefs needed something big to happen in 1966. They hadn't been to the AFL Championship Game since their last season in Dallas and they hadn't won more than seven games during any of their first three years in Kansas City.

Coach Hank Stram, for one, felt good about the direction of the team. The Chiefs drafted Aaron Brown, a defensive end out of Minnesota, in the first round that year, and he'd be joining an improving defense with the likes of Bobby Bell, Buck Buchanan, Walt Corey, Sherrill Headrick, E.J. Holub, and Jerry Mays. And their last draft pick was 1965 Heisman Trophy winner Mike Garrett, a running back out of the University of Southern California. He would be part of a Chiefs offense that had 65 different formations in their arsenal, all out of the tight-I, and they'd reveal about 24 per game. "I thought we were on the verge of being a very good football team," Stram said. "I was concerned, however, about certain areas of our team. We had some defensive problems, and I was concerned about the quality of some of our replacements."

There was another reason Stram wanted to be excited for the 1966 season. The team that won the AFL championship that year would face the NFL winner in what we now know as Super Bowl I. Along with that came a pretty good payday. Players on the losing team in the AFL championship would each receive about $3,500. Players who won the AFL that year would get a minimum of

$10,500 per player ($6,500 for winning the AFL and either $7,500 or $15,000 apiece for the Super Bowl, depending on whether they won).

The Chiefs ended up having the best season in franchise history to that point, finishing the regular season with an 11–2–1 record. Adding to the excitement, they were playing in front of bigger crowds at Municipal Stadium. They consistently drew more than 30,000 at home and on the road. Only twice during the season did they play in front of fewer than 25,000: September 25 at Boston (22,641) and December 11 at Miami (17,881).

In spite of having the best record in the AFL, the Chiefs traveled to Buffalo for the league championship game. The Bills, defending AFL champs, finished the regular season with a 9–4–1 record.

Before the team left for Buffalo, there was a luncheon in their honor at the Muehlebach Hotel. More than 1,200 people showed up to wish the team good luck. Lamar Hunt made a brief speech, announcing that Stram was getting a five-year extension and sharing a dream he had. "I even had my first Super Bowl dream the other night," he said. "I seldom dream, but I remember enough about this dream to know I was in the [Los Angeles] Coliseum. I can't remember what was going on or any of the details, but I could see the Chiefs coming out on the field. I guess the important part is that we were there."

On a frigid January 1 day in Buffalo, the Chiefs made sure their owner's dream came to fruition. And they did so early. On the opening kick, Jerrell Wilson recovered a Buffalo fumble at the Bills 31-yard line. Three plays later Kansas City struck first when Len Dawson connected with tight end Fred Arbanas for a 29-yard touchdown play.

Buffalo and its strong offense, led by quarterback Jack Kemp, tied the game late in the first quarter on a 69-yard touchdown pass

Buck Buchanan, a 6'7", 270-pound defensive lineman, stands on the sideline during the Chiefs' 31–7 win against the Buffalo Bills, a gritty playoff victory that sent Kansas City to the first AFL-NFL Championship Game.

play to Elbert Dubenion. That would be Buffalo's only score of the day.

The same couldn't be said for Dawson and the Chiefs. In the second quarter, Dawson found one of his favorite targets, Otis Taylor, for a 29-yard touchdown play. Then, shortly before the half with the Bills at the Kansas City 11, Johnny Robinson picked off a Kemp pass and returned it 72 yards, setting up a 32-yard field goal by kicker Mike Mercer. "I knew Robinson was there, but I thought I could get the ball through," Kemp said. "I had a lot on it, but he just made a fine play."

That 17–7 lead was more than Kansas City needed, but the Chiefs added two more touchdowns in the fourth quarter on touchdown runs by Garrett—a 1-yarder and an 18-yard jaunt. Though Dawson was sacked seven times, the Chiefs defense intercepted Kemp twice and recovered two fumbles while holding the Bills to only 40 yards on the ground during the 31–7 victory.

The Chiefs were AFL champions again. Unlike their '62 title, though, this time they'd be representing the league their owner started in the first AFL-NFL Championship Game.

50 Arrowhead's First Playoff Game

Although low key and one of the nicest guys you'd want to meet off the field, Deron Cherry was an intense competitor who hated to lose on the field. So when Los Angeles Raiders rookie quarterback Todd Marinovich smoked the Chiefs for 243 yards and three touchdowns—without getting picked off—in his NFL regular-season debut, Cherry, a Chiefs Hall of Fame safety, took it personally. "We hadn't seen him before that game and, of course, as a No. 1

draft pick, all the talk going into the game was about him," said Cherry. "Take nothing away. He had a big game, but he shouldn't have had that kind of game against our defense."

"That game" was the last regular-season contest of 1991: a December 22 game at the Los Angeles Memorial Coliseum. Going into the game both teams were 9–6. Both teams were going to the playoffs. And, in a bizarre twist, the winner would have home-field advantage in the next week's AFC wild-card game—against the loser.

In spite of Marinovich's big game, a player 15 years older, Kansas City quarterback Steve DeBerg, had an equally strong day. DeBerg threw for 277 yards, two touchdowns, and no interceptions in Kansas City's 27–21 win.

That victory brought great implications to wild-card weekend. That would mark the first playoff game ever played at Arrowhead Stadium, which had opened 19 seasons earlier, and it would be the final game at Arrowhead Stadium for Cherry, who was retiring after the season.

Oh yeah, and there was that Marinovich punk, who got the start over Jay Schroeder, who had been injured late in the season. "When we came back to Kansas City, I told Marty [Schottenheimer], 'Let me get a week to study this kid on film and then put me in a robber situation and let me read his eyes,'" said Cherry, who'd be playing the role of what the Chiefs considered "lurker" or "robber." "Once I studied the film, I realized that he was staring down his receivers like most rookie quarterbacks do. I thought if we disguised our coverage and I was opposite his throwing hand, he was going to turn and stare down his receivers, and we'd have some opportunities to pick some balls off. Sure enough, that's what happened."

On Marinovich's first pass of the playoff game, a third-down play at a cold but electric Arrowhead Stadium, Cherry was there for the interception. On the Raiders' next offensive series, Cherry again picked off Marinovich. During the Chiefs 10–6 win that day, in addition to his two picks, Cherry led the team in tackles with seven. Marinovich threw four interceptions that day, was sacked twice, fumbled, and managed only 140 yards in the air. "Cherry came down and had a great scheme," Marinovich said. "He comes down the middle and picks which side to read and either doubles the receiver or the tight end."

Marinovich never lived up to the hype after that first game against Kansas City. The next year he played in seven games, threw only five touchdowns, and recorded nine interceptions. He didn't play another NFL season.

The Chiefs' 1991 season ended the following Sunday, January 5, with a 37–14 loss at Buffalo.

But the excitement for that one weekend and the first post-season win at Arrowhead Stadium—Kansas City's first playoff win since Super Bowl IV—was a nice way to cap the 1991 season. "With that being my last game at Arrowhead," Cherry said, "it wasn't a bad way to go out."

51 Watch the X-Factor

Ladies and gentlemen, you are watching something that has never happened before in the National Football League—seven returns for a touchdown in 10 games...Incredible!

—Kevin Harlan, CBS Sports

Those words from former "voice" of the Chiefs Kevin Harlan probably weren't heard by the Chiefs fans who were screaming out of frustration—and then excitement—as Dante Hall broke free against the Denver Broncos during the fourth quarter of their game at Arrowhead in the 2003 season. Hall's 93-yard punt return, which seemingly broke the ankles of most of Denver's special teams players as he zigged and zagged inside the Chiefs 10 before breaking free on the outside, tied the game at 23 with the subsequent point-after giving Kansas City the decisive 24–23 lead. Oh, and that return, as Harlan pointed out, was Hall's seventh kick or punt return for a touchdown in 10 games, going back to the 2002 season.

Out of Hall's 11 returns for touchdowns between 2002–06 for the Chiefs, the one against Denver—which was his fourth in four games—is perhaps the most memorable. Besides giving the Chiefs a win against a rival and helping the team reach a 5–0 start for the first time in franchise history, the return seemed to be the most unlikely. Hall caught the ball cleanly, backtracked toward the end zone, went toward one sideline, realized he wasn't getting anywhere, and backtracked again. "I thought, *Oh, I've got to get out of this jam*," Hall told reporters after the game. "The first part of that return was not smart at all," Hall said. "I caught it maybe on the 8, then I retreated back to the 5, then the 2. I got dumber and dumber and dumber."

But suddenly his special teams mates cleared a seam down the other sideline. In an interview for kcchiefs.com, Hall said he knew when he cut back to his left that he had made the right decision. "The crowd had the best bird's-eye view, so listen to them and you can hear the roar," said the 5'8", 187-pound Hall. "The minute I broke left I knew that was the correct way to go because the crowd was going crazy."

Because of plays like this, Hall was known as the "human joystick" and the "X-Factor." "He's a human highlight reel," Chiefs defensive end Eric Hicks said. "He's like Michael Jordan. It's ridiculous. The play he made, really nobody was blocked on the initial part of the play. My God, I've never seen anything like that in my life."

Really, no one in NFL history had seen anything like Hall's stretch of games.

Thanks to YouTube, however, most of Hall's returns—including Kevin Harlan's call on CBS—can be relived. Four of Hall's 11 touchdown returns came during 2004–06, but here are the seven in the 10-week stretch that easily can be found online.

- December 1, 2002—90-yard punt return against the Arizona Cardinals
- December 8, 2002—88-yard kickoff return *and* 86-yard punt return against the St. Louis Rams
- September 14, 2003—100-yard kickoff return against the Pittsburgh Steelers
- September 21, 2003—73-yard punt return at the Houston Texans
- September 28, 2003—97-yard kickoff return at the Baltimore Ravens
- October 5, 2003—93-yard punt return against the Broncos

"Dante was such a unique player," said quarterback Trent Green. "He was a running back at Texas A&M but converted to receiver and return guy here. The way he could change direction, he doesn't have normal ankles, but he also isn't a big guy, so you have to watch how much he's used. It was fun on offense to figure out different ways to use him. Our offense was based on match-ups, and a lot of times he gave us the best match-ups because I knew the defender wouldn't be able to cover him. Give Al Saunders and the other offensive coaches credit because Dante's skill set was unbelievable, amazing—whatever superlative you want to use to describe it. Few guys in league history have been like Dante Hall."

52 2003 Offensive Line

The Chiefs' offensive numbers in 2003 were quite gaudy. Quarterback Trent Green and company led the NFL in total points (484), and they were second in total yards (5,910 to Minnesota's 6,294) and passing yards (3,981 to Indianapolis' 4,179). That was a year after they led the league in points (467) and were fourth in the league in total yards with 6,000.

Although it's easy to point to Green or running back Priest Holmes as a reason the Chiefs were so good offensively, ask one of those players, and they'll point to the five guys in front of them—the offensive line. "I came to the Kansas City Chiefs in 2001, and the exciting thing about that is that when I got here," Holmes said, "there was an offensive line here that you could tell was going to give us years of success and great opportunity."

That offensive line included left tackle Willie Roaf, left guard Brian Waters, center Casey Wiegmann, right guard Will Shields, and right tackle John Tait. In 2002 and '03, Roaf and Shields were Pro Bowlers. "When you have consistency in front of you, you can go in there with more confidence," Holmes said. "When you're doing your work as a running back and you know what the defense will throw at you, it makes your work easier when you know what the guys in front of you can and will do."

Roaf opened holes for Holmes and protected Green's blind side. He spent the first nine years of his 13-year career with the New Orleans Saints before joining the Chiefs prior to the 2002 season. During his five years with the Chiefs, Roaf started 58 games. He was inducted into the Pro Football Hall of Fame in 2012.

Waters joined the Chiefs in 2000. After starting just eight games during his first two seasons in Kansas City, Waters, who entered the NFL as an undrafted free-agent tight end with the Dallas Cowboys, was becoming one of the NFL's top left guards in 2002. From that season through 2010, Waters started every remaining game he played for the Chiefs (141), was a five-time Pro Bowl selection, and won the NFL's prestigious Walter Payton Man

Homegrown Chief

Not many professional athletes get an opportunity to play for their hometown team, especially when that's the Chiefs. The most recent and one of the most intriguing is Ryan Lilja, who signed (for a second time) with the Chiefs prior to the 2010 season. Lilja went to high school at Shawnee Mission Northwest before playing two years at Coffeyville (Kansas) Junior College and two years at Kansas State. He then signed with the Dick Vermeil-led Chiefs for the team's practice squad.

In September 2004 the Indianapolis Colts snared Lilja, signing him to their active roster. He ended up playing with the Colts for five seasons, during which time he won a Super Bowl ring blocking for a pretty good quarterback in Peyton Manning. "Manning is one of those dudes who's a perfectionist and he tries nonstop, day in and day out, to perfect his craft in every aspect. Nobody outworks him," Lilja said. "It was cool to be in the huddle with him. They treated me just like anybody else and held me accountable just like anybody else. [Head coach and former Chiefs assistant] Tony Dungy is one of the finest individuals I've ever been around. It was an honor to play for him."

When Lilja became a free agent after the 2009 season, several teams were interested in signing him, but one stood out: his hometown and original NFL team, the Chiefs. He spent three seasons—from 2010–12—with Kansas City. "As I was talking to people I trusted who were advising me, they kept pointing out that it's rare for guys to have an opportunity to play for their hometown team. I can't name any of my buddies with the Colts who did that. As I thought about that possibility, I got really excited," he said. "I didn't think I'd ever be in a position to come back and play for the Chiefs... I've been a Chiefs fan my entire life, and my family is still here, so signing with the Chiefs was a no-brainer for me."

Running back Priest Holmes (31) stares at the great blockers who cleared the way for him: (from left to right) Willie Roaf, Brian Waters, Casey Wiegmann, Will Shields, and John Tait.

of the Year award in 2009. He should get serious Hall of Fame consideration.

Then there's Wiegmann, who was one of the most underappreciated offensive linemen during his 15-year NFL career with the New York Jets (only three games), Chicago Bears, the Chiefs, and Denver Broncos. He also holds a streak that likely won't be broken anytime soon. From September 2001 through the 2011 season, Wiegmann started 175 straight games and, more impressively, had a streak of more than 11,000 consecutive snaps at center.

"Casey was undervalued probably because of his size," Green said of the 6'2" and 285-pound Wiegmann. "But he's so smart and was such an incredible technician. Plus he was quick. He could beat guys bigger than him. Because of the linemen around him, he never got the credit he deserved. I was glad to see him have a Pro Bowl year with Denver [in 2008], but he should've gotten that recognition with us. I guess we couldn't send our whole offensive line."

Shields, whom the Chiefs selected out of Nebraska in the third round in 1993 to help protect Joe Montana, set a couple consistency marks with the Chiefs that aren't likely to be broken. After not starting the first game of his rookie season, Shields went on to start 223 straight games—all for the Chiefs. That easily tops the team list for most games started (Tony Gonzalez is second at 174), most consecutive games started (Emmitt Thomas is second at 144), most games played (224) and is tied for second in most seasons with the Chiefs (14—Jerrell Wilson tops the list at 15). Shields, who was a Hall of Fame finalist in 2012, '13, and '14, should be enshrined soon.

Tait, the Chiefs' first-round pick in 1999, spent the first half of his NFL career with the Chiefs and the other half, beginning in 2004, with Chicago. After starting only three games during his rookie year, Tait started 136 games after that with the Chiefs and the Bears. During his 10-year career, Tait was used at both left tackle and right tackle.

Tait effectively protected Green, who, as quarterback, knew which buttons to push with each of his linemen and how to lead them. "To find ways to communicate with guys was intriguing to me," Green said. "I wasn't a scream and cuss-a-guy-out quarterback. That's worked for guys, but my thought was that it'd be better to encourage them. Granted, as some of the guys will tell you, I could give a look if I didn't like something they did; Brian used to joke about that. I just tried to keep the guys relaxed, especially in big moments, but I could get fired up and really push them. A quarterback didn't have to say much to Will or Casey, but I would go to those guys and have them get the other linemen going. Brian was a little more intense than the other guys so he liked the confrontation part of it. I could push his buttons a certain way. Willie was more relaxed and joking, but his button was with pride. So, if I needed to get him going, I could challenge his pride. That was a special group. I'd do anything for those guys."

53 Nick Lowery

Fans always have a love-hate relationship with their teams' kickers. That's certainly been the case in Kansas City. One of the most beloved, however, was Nick Lowery, who was with the organization from 1980–93. When he retired he was tied for second for number of seasons but first in games played (212), consecutive games played (188), career points (1,466), and points in a season (139) in Chiefs history. He also held the NFL record for most seasons with 100 or more points (11). After living in the Kansas City area following his career, Lowery eventually moved to Arizona, where he's been heavily involved in various community projects mainly geared toward children. The Chiefs (finally) inducted him into the team's Hall of Fame in 2009.

What kept you going and how did you think you were going to make an NFL team after getting cut so many times?
Nick Lowery: I'm not sure I was convinced I could, but I was convinced it was worth a shot. When you're an athlete and you go through being cut, you might shed a tear or two, but then you realize, "Hey, I'm still alive." Then you dust yourself off and decide what you're going to do next. We all deal with rejections in life. The rejection is very raw in sports, so how do you deal with it? For me No. 1 it was about making sure I focused more to be a better kicker. I was much different two years later.

How close were you to giving up on football and trying a different career?

NL: Well, I almost made it with New England and then the New Orleans Saints and San Diego. Every time I kept getting closer until I finally gave up. That would've been the end of the story. I had a job with the Senate Commerce Committee with Senator Bob Packwood. But a senate job on a committee is much more stable than you think because it doesn't matter who the senator is. On the Saturday of the wild-card games in 1979, I got a call from (then-general manager of the Chiefs) Jim Schaaf. He apologized for not calling me sooner but said he had back surgery. He then went on to tell me how the Chiefs value special teams, and they wanted to give me a chance. I told him thanks, but I wanted to pursue this senate job. And I hung up. That was the end of the story.

It was one of those moments of truth in life that I decided I needed to give it one more try. When I hung up, I didn't know why I didn't at least find out what they had to offer. I talked to my mentor about it. This is where mentors come in. He persuaded me that I'd always wonder about it. So I started trying to track down Jim Schaaf, who I'd never heard of before and I didn't know how to spell his name. I started calling hospitals and an hour later I finally found him at Research Hospital. They flew me to Kansas City the next week and they offered me a $2,500 bonus, which is pennies today. To me it was more than anyone else offered. I'm glad I gave it one more try.

Was it difficult replacing a Hall of Famer in Jan Stenerud?

NL: It wasn't tough, but needless to say, Jan didn't exactly like me the first couple years. We've since become good friends. In fact, a story I like to tell is from when I had my radio show on Sirius, and Jan was on with Morten Anderson. We were talking about pressure and how we perform under pressure. The conversation evolved to the Christmas Day game against Miami [when Stenerud missed

Dustin Colquitt

With the Chiefs winning Super Bowl LIV, brothers Travis and Jason Kelce now each have Super Bowl rings. But with the win, there's another Chiefs player, whose family has more than two rings. Fittingly, that's former Chiefs punter Dustin Colquitt, whose dad and brother each had rings already. Colquitt was released in the spring of 2020, but at the time of Super Bowl LIV, Colquitt was the longest-tenured member of the Chiefs. Kansas City selected him in the third round of the 2005 NFL Draft. So, he was selected when Dick Vermeil was the coach and then played for Herm Edwards, Todd Haley, and Romeo Crennel before Andy Reid.

The reason Colquitt lasted so long is simple: he's good. Really, really good. Through the Super Bowl LIV season, Colquitt, who was 37 at the time, had 462 punts inside the 20-yard line, which was third all time in NFL history. Three times in his career, he had the longest punt in the NFL for that season, and his longest was 81 yards in 2007. In 2006 his net average of 39.3 yards per punt led the NFL. He's in the top 10 in NFL history with more than 50,000 yards.

It also doesn't hurt to have good genes. Dustin's dad, Craig, won two Super Bowl rings with the Pittsburgh Steelers in the 1970s. His younger brother, Britton, won a ring with the Denver Broncos.

Although punters and kickers often have the longest careers—especially when they're as good as Colquitt—a few years may have been added to Colquitt's career with the addition of Patrick Mahomes. Frankly, although he's still needed, he wasn't used as often during Mahomes' first two seasons as the team's starter. In 2017 Colquitt punted 65 times. In 2018 and '19 that dropped to 45 and 48, respectively. That's a far cry from 2009 when his leg was used a career-high 96 times. In fact, Colquitt, who's also the holder on kicks, started making sure that he had the gloves that he wears for PATs in his jersey at all times. "There's more times when we're running to do an extra point than there are to punt, which is unbelievable to think about," Colquitt said. "It wasn't until Patrick got here that I started keeping my gloves in my jersey so I'm not running around looking for my stuff."

One great thing about Colquitt staying with the Chiefs for so long is that it's been great for the Kansas City community. Dustin and his wife, Christia, have been active with various charities. In addition to starting the Colquitt for Kids Foundation, Colquitt is involved with TeamSmile, Athletes in Action, and Fellowship of Christian Athletes. "I have learned the fastest way to make our NFL communities a better place to live, work, and play is to spend time with the people who make this a special place," Colquitt said."

some crucial kicks], and Jan talked about it for a while. Afterward he told me, "That's the first time I've talked about that, probably ever." That meant a lot to me because he's beaten himself up for a long time.

How did you set it up so that Muhammad Ali could visit the Royals during 2009 spring training?

NL: It's been a wonderful blessing for me to get to know Muhammad and his family. My friend, Dr. Andrew Jacobs, and I were at a Dodgers-Royals spring training game with [Royals general manager] Dayton Moore. When I mentioned the possibility, he was completely behind the idea.

The Royals were great. Muhammad gets tired walking long distances, so they had a golf cart meet us by the car and took him around the outfield and onto the field. It was neat to see 20,000 fans stand up and cheer for him. [Los Angeles manager] Joe Torre and some of their players came over. It was awe-inspiring to see the universal love and respect that Muhammad received. As we sat at our seats, a little to my left was Wayne Gretzky, and George Brett, who I think is one of the top 10 baseball players of all time, was a few feet in front of us. So "The Great One" was to my left, the Royals great was in front of me, and "The Greatest" was two seats to my right. Afterward, the golf cart took him out, and there was a group of parents from the Royals organization with their kids. Muhammad just lit up. It was a magical evening.

54 Super Fans

Although nearly every team has its famous fans, the list of famous Chiefs fans includes actors Kevin Costner—who has said that he first became a fan of the Chiefs when he watched Len Dawson in Super Bowl IV—David Koechner, Rob Riggle, Paul Rudd, and Eric Stonestreet. Koechner, Riggle, Rudd, and Stonestreet all grew up either in the Kansas City area or not too far away. "The guy who's a huge Kansas City sports fan, especially the Chiefs, is Paul Rudd," Koechner said of his *Anchorman* co-star. "He's nuts about the team. We all know Rob Riggle is a huge Chiefs fan, but Paul Rudd is right there with him."

Rob Riggle grew up on the Kansas side of the state line in Overland Park. He has lived two distinct professional lives—as a Marine and as an actor/comedian. His national break came in 2004, when he joined the cast of Saturday Night Live. *Since then he has been in television shows and movies, including* Modern Family, Step Brothers, The Hangover, 21 Jump Street *(and the sequel,* 22 Jump Street*), and* The Lorax. *Riggle and his "Riggle's Picks" have been a favorite segment on* Fox NFL Sunday. *Riggle, who always picks the Chiefs to win, shared his memories of the Chiefs.*

"Being a die-hard Chiefs fan has cost me a lot with Riggle's Picks. I take them every week, even when they were struggling in recent years. I wasn't going to stop. It doesn't matter who they're playing or how they're playing—I'm picking them to win every week and then the Super Bowl. Unfortunately, their fate is your fate as a fan. That can be bad when you're talking about the teams we had here in the mid-1970s through the early 1980s. My first game at Arrowhead was in 1975. I was too little to appreciate what was going on, but I remember throwing a football around in the upper deck. It was easy to play catch up there because no one was there!

"That changed when Carl Peterson and Marty Schottenheimer arrived. Suddenly, the stadium was full, and there were great players with memorable names: Derrick Thomas, Deron Cherry, and Dan Saleaumua as part of a great defense and then names like Christian Okoye and Steve DeBerg on offense. Then in 1994 I was stationed in Pensacola, dating a good Kansas City girl who was living in Houston, and we went to the Astrodome to see Joe Montana and Marcus Allen lead the Chiefs to a playoff win over the Oilers. (It just hit me that the Chiefs haven't won a playoff game since then.) Great teams are like great casts on *Saturday Night Live*—they stand out. We've had good teams. And after a couple lost chapters with Todd Haley and Scott Pioli, it looks like owner Clark Hunt has made a commitment to winning with John Dorsey, Andy Reid, and Alex Smith.

"Speaking of Montana, what Chiefs fan can forget the *Monday Night Football* game in Denver? John Elway against Joe Montana. Just like that, Elway and Denver did it to us again, taking a decisive lead with less than two minutes. Oh, but wait...we have a guy with just as much—if not more—magic than Elway named Joe Montana. He reached into his pocket and pulled out some gold and drove us down the field for the winning touchdown.

"One of my greatest Chiefs memories will be when the Chiefs asked me to come out to Arrowhead and beat the big war drum with the tomahawk mallet. I was beating that thing so hard that I actually broke the mallet! As far as I know, I was the first and only person to do that. I'm going to keep beating the drum for the Chiefs and keep picking them on *Fox NFL Sunday*. I'm going to keep picking them to win the Super Bowl. I want to see the Chiefs dominate and make it to the Super Bowl before I die. I want to see

Super Fans Part II

Since every team has its rabid fans—the ones who are spotted during game broadcasts every week—Visa and the NFL decided to start honoring them. A select group from each team has been inducted in the Pro Football Hall of Fame. Though we're biased when we say the Chiefs have the best fans in the NFL, there are three in particular who are recognizable and distinguished as super fans.

Arrowman, aka Monte Short: Arrowman was the first of the Chiefs super fan representatives in Canton, Ohio. Short usually wears the jersey and hat of the Chiefs opponent impaled with multiple Chiefs-logo arrows. He started dressing up in costume in 1992. One year while dressed up like Arrowman at a Chiefs-Cowboys game in Texas, someone tapped him on the shoulder unexpectedly. "I turned around, and it was Lamar Hunt," Short said in the book, *For Chiefs Fans Only!* "He'd seen me from his suite in the stadium and came down to talk to me. I couldn't believe it."

Weirdwolf, aka Lynn Schmidt: Weirdwolf, who was selected in 2002 for the Visa Hall of Fans, has been a Chiefs fan since 1971. Weirdwolf, Schmidt says, is "in the spirit of the Wolfpack," which was a raucous group of fans at Municipal Stadium in the 1960s and '70s. Weirdwolf can be spotted with a red-painted face, bandana with wolf ears, sunglasses, and a red and yellow uniform that has various buttons and patches. "This is more than football to this community," he said. "It is a community that happens to love football and a team."

The X-Factor, aka Ty Rowton: X-Factor is best known as the fan who wears a spandex outfit with patches and lettering on it, adorning beads, a bandana, and sunglasses. And it's all topped with an arrowhead. Rowton says his first costume looked more like Ronald McDonald than a superhero. With modifications throughout the years, he's developed several costumes that he wears during the season.

that trophy go to Arrowhead with a huge parade. We deserve it, and you have to believe it can happen."

David Koechner is originally from Tipton, Missouri, which is approximately two hours from Kansas City. He jokes about being "that guy" on TV shows and movies, but since getting his national break on the cast of Saturday Night Live in 1995, Koechner has appeared in more than 120 television and movie roles, including parts on Mad About You, The 40 Year-old Virgin, Talladega Nights, and Semi-Pro. His most notable roles have been as Todd Packer in The Office and sports newscaster Champ Kind in Anchorman and Anchorman 2. Koechner shared his memories of the Chiefs.

"As far as I can remember, the Chiefs were my introduction to pro football when I was a kid. There weren't many games on TV when I was that age, but my cousins were huge Chiefs fans. I even had a Willie Lanier poster in my room when I was growing up. And I remember watching the infamous Christmas Day game in 1971 at my grandmother's house. I've thought so often about kicker Jan Stenerud and how here's this guy who had so many triumphs in the NFL and is in the Hall of Fame, but many people remember him for the missed field goals against Miami that day.

"Fast forward almost 20 years and you have Steve DeBerg in the 1990 playoffs with the mangled finger that was in that huge cast with the pin sticking out. The Chiefs were in the playoffs, thanks largely to DeBerg, but then he has the bad finger. I was waiting tables in Chicago at that time and I kept sneaking a peak at the TV to see how the Chiefs were doing on that cold day in Buffalo. That took an incredible amount of heart for DeBerg to go out there.

"My memories of the Chiefs and Bills aren't all bad, though. On September 14, 1997, the Chiefs were hosting Buffalo. A little more than eight months before that, I was dating a Kansas City girl named Leigh. She had told me about a dream that she was at

Lake Kanakuk, where she was a camper growing up, and that I was dressed as a clown and asked her to marry me.

"I think she regretted telling me that story as soon as she said it. Well, we were in Kansas City for a wedding, and on that Thursday after going skeet shooting with her dad, Dr. Dick Morgan, I asked for his daughter's hand in marriage. He thought for a moment and just said, 'Well, I know she's crazy about you.' It was not necessarily the glowing welcome to the family I had envisioned, but by that statement, I had his blessing. Sunday morning my brother, who had done some clowning in Tipton, let me borrow his costume. I had some balloons, including one with the ring, and I asked her if she'd marry me. (The last balloon she popped was the one with the ring.) Her dad had four tickets on the 50-yard line for the Chiefs-Bills game, so after proposing we headed out to Arrowhead. I don't think she watched three minutes of the game that day, which the Chiefs did win. So Arrowhead and the Chiefs have a special place in my heart."

55 Eat at Chappell's

Jim Chappell is full of stories. One of his many favorites involves the Chiefs and the thousand or so helmets that hang from the ceiling at Chappell's restaurant. "Joe Montana would come in here with Greg Manusky, who went to Colgate," Chappell said. "To give Manusky a hard time, Montana would say, 'Hey, Jim, where's your Colgate helmet?' Of course, we didn't have one. Finally, one day, Greg asked if he could use my phone. He called Colgate and said, 'This is Manuz. I need a Colgate helmet. Send it to...' And he

170

gave my address. About a week-and-a-half later, the helmet showed up."

That's just one of the stories. There are countless others. When taking a tour of Chappell's Restaurant and Sports Museum with Chappell, it's like you're getting a history lesson from that uncle who always spins the greatest yarns at family reunions. You could point to practically any of the gazillion or so pieces of memorabilia in the restaurant and get an anecdote behind it, which leads to another story about another item. If you want to view sports history while getting a good meal and possibly spot a Chiefs legend, Chappell's is a must for any Chiefs fan.

As Chappell walks around the restaurant in North Kansas City, located approximately 20 minutes from Arrowhead Stadium, you'd swear he's running for office. He stops by a table of old friends and chats for a few moments before going to a table with six young business folks. And then he visits with a young family, handing Styrofoam baseballs with his likeness emblazoned in maroon to the two children.

It's no surprise that Jim Chappell comes across as a politician. He's dabbled in politics, and his office walls are jammed with photos of Jim posing with a who's who of local and national politicians. And this restaurant began as a political and sports bar.

Since the establishment at 323 Armour Road opened in 1986—and quickly dropped the political aspect, thankfully—Chappell's (pronounced like the place of worship, not like some fancy joint that could be found on the Champs-Elysees) has become one of the best sports museums in the Midwest. Among the Chiefs-related items inside the restaurant: a rare Len Dawson Super Bowl IV MVP football, Dawson's signed Dallas Texans warm-up jersey, and countless autographs, photographs, and pennants.

Besides the Chiefs memorabilia, though, it's been common throughout the years to see former Chiefs at the restaurant. On any given day, one might see Bobby Bell, Ed Budde, Deron Cherry,

Dawson, Bill Kenney, or Ed Lothamer, to name a few. That's not to mention that on a few occasions Chiefs founder Lamar Hunt could be seen giving his friends tours of the restaurant. "What a unique place! There are restaurants that have sports memorabilia, but I've yet to see one that has this extensive of a collection," said Dawson, who besides eating there, often used Chappell's as a place to interview athletes and coaches for KMBC-TV. "At Chappell's, Jim has put together a collection that includes Kansas City's sports history, but it has memorabilia from colleges and high schools and other pro sports teams, not to mention all of the football helmets hanging from the ceiling."

Chappell's is one of those places where you could eat 81,677 times and be fascinated by a new photograph or trinket each time, even if it's been in the same place for years. It might be Tom Watson's putter, the signed photograph of baseball legends Jackie Robinson and Satchel Paige posing in Monarch uniforms, one of two Olympic torches, the 1973 Oakland A's World Series trophy, Paul Hornung's Heisman Trophy, or baseballs signed by the likes of Babe Ruth, Lou Gehrig, and Ty Cobb. Then there are the football helmets on the ceiling—more than 1,000, Jim says, and somehow he can lead you to the one from your college or favorite NFL team.

Chappell's has gained national attention and popularity. *Sports Illustrated* selected the restaurant a few years ago as one of the top 10 sports bars in America. So did the *Chicago Tribune*.

As recently as January 2014, *USA TODAY* gave it the same distinction. "There's some really awesome stuff," said ESPN's sports business reporter Darren Rovell, who helped compile the list for *USA TODAY*. "Tons of football helmets, autographed baseballs. It's the closest thing to *Cheers*. You feel like you're back in time."

Even non-Chiefs celebrities have stopped by Chappell's during trips to Kansas City, including Franco Harris, Brooks Robinson, artist LeRoy Neiman, and country singer Vince Gill. "Jim has one of the biggest sports collections around, and I like to show people what Kansas City's about," said Hall of Famer Bobby Bell. "It's an opportunity to be with Jim, and I always have fun kidding with him. I can't tell you how many times people have come in here thinking I own the place. I've been known to greet visitors and take them to a seat. That has been going on for years. It's an amazing place!"

56 Grigs

For nearly 50 years (1963–2009), Bill Grigsby's voice and trademark "Beeeeuuuteeful!" were synonymous with Chiefs football. "He loved people," said Len Dawson, who got to know Grigsby first as a player in the mid-1960s and then as a broadcast partner. "He loved to tell stories and he was very good at it."

One story Grigsby loved to tell was from 1964. He and Hank Stram were invited to Fort Leavenworth to speak at the Command Staff School. They figured they'd get some type of payment for speaking, but they didn't know exactly how much. While Stram was speaking, a general handed Grigsby an envelope. Not wanting to be rude, Grigsby takes the envelope to the bathroom, opens it, and finds four $100 bills. We'll let Grigs pick up the story from here:

"I think to myself that's really too much, so I take one of the four bills and stick it in my pocket, put the other three back in the envelope and seal it. Hank asked if I knew anything about the money, and I handed him the envelope as I was getting ready to speak. As we were driving back to Kansas City that night, I asked him how we did. He said, 'Those tight bastards, they gave us only $200!' That was Henry for you."

And that's classic Bill Grigsby, a prankster and a storyteller, for you.

During his 62-year broadcasting career, Grigsby called Kansas City A's baseball, Kansas City Scouts hockey, the NAIA men's basketball tournament, Chiefs football, and even professional wrestling. Along the way he broadcast two Super Bowls (I and IV) and the first national broadcast of the NCAA Final Four.

It was with the Chiefs, though, that most people knew Grigsby. During his time associated with the organization, Grigs became friends with nearly everyone associated with the team from front-office people to players. He especially lit up, though, when talking about Chiefs founder Lamar Hunt. "Oh, Lamar was one of the finest gentlemen I've ever known in sports, not just in Kansas City or with the Chiefs," Grigsby said. "He had many offers from people in places such as Los Angeles to move the team. But he wouldn't do it. He loved Kansas City, which wasn't easy when he first moved the team here. The team didn't have great fan support. But Lamar stuck with it, which is wonderful for the people of this city. With Charles Finley moving the A's to Oakland, leaving the Chiefs as the only major league sport in Kansas City in the late 1960s, Lamar saved this town. If we didn't have pro football and Major League Baseball in Kansas City, this place wouldn't be the same."

Grigsby was so popular in Kansas City that when Carl Peterson joined the Chiefs and was basically cleaning house after years of bad football, Grigs went to meet with Peterson to introduce himself and, Grigsby hoped, to save his job. "Oh, I knew who Bill Grigsby was before he walked into my office," Peterson said. "Based on fan reaction, there was no way we were going to get rid of Bill Grigsby. He was an institution in Kansas City, not just with the Chiefs."

Grigsby, who was one of Kansas City's best storytellers of any kind, passed away on February 26, 2011, at the age of 89.

57 Tragedy Strikes Organization Early

By nature of being a violent sport, pro football has had its share of devastating injuries. And, of course, as happens in life, players have their tragedies on and off the field. It's been rare, though, that a pro sports team has had two such events so early in its existence and occurring so closely together as the Chiefs experienced in the 1960s with Stone Johnson and Mack Lee Hill.

Stone Johnson

Coach Hank Stram called Stone Johnson the team's "Mr. Lightning." Johnson, who had been clocked in the 100 at 9.3, was fast enough that he was a sprinter on the 1960 U.S. Olympic track team. Three years later the franchise selected the 23-year-old Johnson in the 14th round out of Grambling.

With the organization moving that season from Dallas to Kansas City and the combination of both the players and the fans being lukewarm about the other, Stram saw Johnson as a way to inject some excitement. "He was special," Stram said. "He was brand new and enthusiastic—something all of us appreciated under the circumstances."

It seemed to be somewhat of a miracle that Johnson was even walking, let alone a world-class sprinter. As a high school freshman, Johnson suffered a back injury and was bedridden for three months. "The doctor who operated on my back told me I might not walk again," Johnson told *The Dallas Morning News* before the 1960 Olympics. "One day I decided I was going to get up and take a step. I did. After a while I was walking again and then running. And a funny thing about my running: I was a lot faster. Before I was crippled, I couldn't even make the sprint relay team."

The Chiefs' No. 2 flanker, the speedy Johnson was back to return a kick during the team's final exhibition game on August 31, 1963, in Wichita, Kansas, against the Houston Oilers. When the ball sailed to Jim "Preacher" Pilot, Johnson started blocking. He dropped his head as he put it into the stomach of an Oilers player. Johnson went down to the ground paralyzed. Doctors would discover he had fractured his fifth cervical vertebrae.

Johnson died a little more than a week later on September 8 in a Wichita hospital. "What happened to Stone was tremendously tragic," Len Dawson said. "He was just getting started."

Even though he never played a regular-season game for the Chiefs, the team retired Johnson's No. 33.

Mack Lee Hill

Coming out of Southern University in 1964, Mack Lee Hill was passed on by every AFL and NFL team in their drafts. His last two years in college were stalled by injuries and a new coaching staff.

With the death of Johnson and the decline of Abner Haynes, the Chiefs needed help on offense. So they signed Hill for a $300 signing bonus. (Even in the days before the mega-contracts and even for an AFL team, $300 still amounted to mere pennies.)

Hill, whose 5'11" and 235-pound frame helped him garner the nickname "the Truck," showed the Chiefs he was worth the… um…investment. As a rookie in 1964, Hill was an AFL All-Star as he rushed for 576 yards and four touchdowns on 105 carries— second to Haynes' 697 yards and four touchdowns.

Hill followed up his rookie campaign with 627 yards rushing and two touchdowns on 125 carries. He also caught 21 passes for 264 yards.

In Buffalo for the next-to-the-last game of that 1965 season, Hill injured his right knee when he was tackled after making a catch. When the team returned to Kansas City, doctors determined that he ruptured a ligament and needed surgery. He was admitted to the hospital on Monday night and went into surgery early afternoon on Tuesday.

Surgery seemingly went fine, and Hill was placed in a cast. Suddenly, though, Hill's temperature spiked to at least 108. Doctors rushed to perform ice relief to cool Hill. Nothing worked. A little less than two hours later, he died of what doctors called a "sudden and massive embolism." He was 25. "Mack Lee Hill was a fine gentleman and a great football player," coach Hank Stram said. "He was probably one of the most unselfish players I have ever coached."

Unlike Stone Johnson's death, though, Hill's didn't have a negative effect on the team. The team used it as motivation. Perhaps it was the circumstances of each, including how it was a few days before the team's final game of 1965. "He became a legend as he should have," lineman Jerry Mays said of Hill. "And I think he became an inspiration for the kind of effort he had always given... There were no bad sides to the guy. He was all good. I think he became an inspiration to our ballclub."

Since 1966 the Chiefs have given the Mack Lee Hill Award to the rookie or first-year player who "best exemplifies the spirit of the late Mack Lee Hill." The Chiefs retired Hill's No. 36, and he was inducted into the team's Hall of Fame in 1971.

58 Marv Levy

Marv Levy badly wanted to coach the Chiefs in the post-Hank Stram era, and legendary Washington Redskins coach George Allen recommended Levy, one of Allen's former assistants, to Lamar Hunt. Instead, the Chiefs went with Paul Wiggin—and then Tom Bettis.

But because of the disastrous Wiggin and Bettis tenures, Hunt met with Levy about the job when it opened up again in December of 1977. In hindsight, except for the experience gained as an NFL head coach by coaching the Chiefs, Levy might wish he hadn't succeeded Stram or Bettis, especially if he knew how his story would play out.

The Chiefs won only two games in 1977 under Wiggin (1–6) and Bettis (1–6). After the rough five years the Chiefs had gone through dating back to the end of Stram's tenure, they needed a proven winner. By the time Levy came to Kansas City after the '77 season, he had established himself as one of the best coaches in the Canadian Football League. His Montreal squad won the Grey Cup twice in his five years there, including 1977.

For Levy, who was being courted by the Redskins, too, he saw the Chiefs as a young team ready to get drastically better. And he liked what he heard from president Jack Steadman. "The most compelling lure in Kansas City would be the nature of responsibilities I was promised during my negotiations with the Chiefs," Levy wrote in his autobiography, *Where Else Would You Rather Be?* "I would have sole authority over all matters relating to selection of the coaching staff and player personnel. Without interference I was to determine which players we played in the games, which players we would release, and which players we would retain on our roster."

Levy and the Chiefs agreed to terms, and in December 1977, he became the fourth head coach in Chiefs history. During the press conference, Hunt called Levy "one of the brightest people I ever met."

He is certainly an intellect. Levy can quote works of literature as well as great leaders in history. He has a master's degree from Harvard and he entered law school before deciding to become a football coach. Since he retired from coaching, he's written a novel—in addition to his autobiography.

One thing Levy learned early in his time with the Chiefs was that he couldn't completely believe everything he says he understood during negotiations with Steadman. "As our pre-draft meetings intensified, I became increasingly aware of how often Jack Steadman would pop in," Levy said. "His interest I could understand, but then I began to notice how vigorously he would express opinions about so many of the areas which I believed fell into the category—as it had been described to me during my interview—of football operations. Jack knew business and he knew it well. He knew a lot about a lot of things, but he didn't know much about football."

That theme, Levy wrote, became a common one while he was with the Chiefs.

On the field, the team improved. It certainly became better than what it showed throughout the 1970s. Under Levy, who was more of a defensive-minded coach, the Chiefs installed the Wing-T offense and became the No. 2 rushing team in the NFL. During Levy's five seasons, the Chiefs improved at quarterback with Bill Kenney, running back with Joe Delaney, wide receiver with Carlos Carson, and kicker with Nick Lowery replacing future Hall of Famer Jan Stenerud. Defensively, in his first draft alone, he added Sylvester Hicks, Gary Spani, and Art Still. Kansas City went from winning four games in his first season in 1978 to winning nine games in 1981.

The Chiefs were 1–1 in 1982 before a strike wiped out seven games. When play resumed in late November, the Chiefs floundered with only two wins in their seven games. Stinging from the strike and the losses, Chiefs fans displayed their disgust by avoiding the final two home games, as less than 25,000 went to Arrowhead for the San Francisco 49ers game the day after Christmas, and then only 11,902 showed up for the season finale against the New York Jets on January 2. The small crowd who was there saw Levy's finale as Chiefs coach.

A few days after the Jets game, Steadman told Levy they were going to make a coaching change; 31–42 in five years wasn't good enough. Levy, who refused to resign, was fired with one year remaining on his contract. Three years later he became the head coach in Buffalo, where he'd take the Bills to four straight Super Bowls, a feat that earned him induction into the Pro Football Hall of Fame.

Steadman admits that firing Levy was his most major gaffe as Chiefs president. "I kept getting advice that Marv had lost the team and we had to make a change," Steadman said. "Had Marv stayed here, we would not have encountered the problems we had with here in the 1980s. That's the biggest mistake I made, and I've learned from it."

59 Failure to Develop a Quarterback

Make sure you're not standing near a ledge or within reaching distance of any sharp objects when you read the next sentence. Ready? Don't say you weren't warned. Here you go: Before Patrick Mahomes led the Chiefs past the Denver Broncos in the final regular season game of 2017, Todd Blackledge was the last quarterback drafted by the Chiefs to lead the team to a win. That is so wrong on so many levels.

Blackledge is considered one of the biggest draft busts in Chiefs history. And yet before Mahomes, *he's* the last quarterback the Chiefs have drafted who's led them to a win. That happened on September 13, 1987, the season opener at Arrowhead against San Diego. And saying that Blackledge *led* the Chiefs to a win that day might be a slight overstatement. In the 20–13 win, Blackledge was 6-of-15 for 79 yards and one interception. The Chiefs' two touchdowns that day came on a 43-yard run by Christian Okoye and a 95-yard kickoff return by Paul Palmer. The Chiefs proceeded to lose their next nine games. During that time head coach Frank Gansz inserted Bill Kenney as the starter. Essentially, Kenney, whom the Chiefs signed as a free agent before the 1980 season and was originally the second-from-last player selected in the 1978 draft, ousted the Chiefs' first-round pick (seventh overall) in the '83 NFL Draft. And for the Chiefs, that's the last "winner."

Consistent NFL winners like the Patriots, Packers, and 49ers draft and develop quarterbacks. Yes, there are exceptions. And, yes, the Chiefs have reached the AFC Championship Game with the likes of Steve DeBerg and Joe Montana. But for whatever reason, they haven't had much luck in developing homegrown quarterbacks. Here's a look at the quarterbacks not named Patrick Mahomes whom the Chiefs have drafted since Blackledge's win in 1987.

Danny McManus—1988, 11th round: McManus, who was an outstanding player at Florida State, led the Seminoles to a win in the 1988 Fiesta Bowl over Nebraska with 375 passing yards. He was the Chiefs' third-string quarterback in '88, never seeing the field during the regular season before embarking on a 17-year career in the Canadian Football League, where he threw for more than 50,000 yards.

Mike Elkins—1989, second round: When Marty Schottenheimer became head coach before the '89 season, he knew he needed a quarterback. The Chiefs drafted Elkins and tried to develop him. He played in one game that season and none the next year before the Chiefs released him. "The biggest thing had to do with the inconsistency of his accuracy," Schottenheimer said when Elkins was released. "That was the No. 1 concern. Mike worked his tail off. He did everything he could in terms of his preparation."

Matt Blundin—1992, second round: Blundin seemed like a decent second-round pick out of Virginia. Instead, during two seasons with the Chiefs, Blundin played in two games and threw for 15 yards, no touchdowns, and one interception.

Steve Matthews—1994, seventh round: Matthews, who set all sorts of passing records at Memphis State, never saw regular-season action for the Chiefs in three seasons. He played one season for Jacksonville and one for Tennessee.

Steve Stenstrom—1995, fourth round: Stenstrom played in 17 games during his four-year NFL career, but none of those games was with the Chiefs. Stenstrom was an unusual situation in that he signed with the Chiefs for three years and $2.15 million one day and then was placed on waivers the next day. The Chiefs gambled that no other NFL team would pick him up for his base salary of $627,397, but one did: Chicago.

Pat Barnes—1997, fourth round: Barnes was a bit of a loose cannon when the Chiefs selected him in '97 out of Cal and he didn't catch on with the Chiefs or any other NFL team.

James Kilian—2005, seventh round: Kilian, who was a two-year starter at Tulsa, beat out Heisman Trophy winner Jason White for a spot on Kansas City's practice squad. In two seasons that's as far as he got.

Brodie Croyle—2006, third round: Croyle had the football pedigree (University of Alabama legend) but was too frail. He was injured at both Alabama and with the Chiefs, having the misfortune to suffer a torn ACL on three occasions. He also has the dubious distinction of playing more games than any Chiefs-drafted quarterback since Blackledge, but he ended his Kansas City career after five seasons and a 0–10 record. "The surgeries, the injuries—I wouldn't trade any of it," Croyle told *The Birmingham News*. "It was a great ride. All those things build character. All those things are placed in your life to teach you something."

Ricky Stanzi—2011, fifth round: During possibly the roughest stretch in recent Chiefs history, the fans clamored to see Stanzi play. What would the Chiefs have lost by playing Stanzi? Oh yeah, possibly another game in their 7–9 and 2–14 seasons when he was with the team. Instead, Stanzi never saw action in a regular-season game.

Aaron Murray—2014, fifth round: Murray, whom the Chiefs drafted out of the University of Georgia, never saw the field for Kansas City. After the Chiefs cut him in September 2016, Murray didn't see the field for the Arizona Cardinals, Philadelphia Eagles, or the Los Angeles Rams either. Murray caught on with the Tampa Bay Vipers of the revamped XFL in 2020.

Kevin Hogan—2016, fifth round: Unlike Murray, Hogan played in eight NFL games. Just not with the Chiefs. In fact, the Chiefs cut Hogan before the start of the 2016 regular season. The former Stanford star landed with the Cleveland Browns, where he played in eight games during the 2016 and '17 seasons.

60 Gary Spani

The concept of team was important to Gary Spani, the unselfish linebacker who played nine seasons for the Chiefs following a Hall of Fame career at Kansas State. Although he was an outstanding individual player, averaging more than 12 tackles per game during his college career and 8.1 a game with the Chiefs, he would have traded those tackles for a championship season. "When you don't win the war as a team, it's hard to have good memories. I don't know if you can have a good memory of a war you didn't win," said Spani, who was Kansas State's first consensus All-American in his senior season. "Personally, the joy I had of playing football and the friends I met stick out to me the most."

During Spani's time at K-State, the Wildcats won nine total games in four seasons and only one conference game. But the Chiefs drafted Spani, who also went to high school in Manhattan, Kansas, in the third round in 1978.

His teams didn't fare much better in Kansas City. In Spani's nine seasons with the Chiefs from 1978–86, the team finished above .500 only twice and went to the playoffs only once (1986).

But Spani was one of the reasons Chiefs fans had a reason for hope. During his nine-year career, Spani became the Chiefs' all-time leading tackler with 999. He also recorded 9.5 sacks, recovered nine fumbles, and scored two touchdowns. During the '86 season, though, Spani says he started to sense the end of his career was close. That ended up being his most memorable year. "The trend was turning toward the big running backs and smaller linebackers," Spani said. "That was the first year in my life that I didn't start. I was the captain of the team...but I had to make some hard decisions on how to react. I learned to be a captain and make some sacrifices to help the team win. We came down to the last three games of the year needing to win. Before those games I had worked myself back into the starting lineup. We beat Denver, the Raiders, and the Steelers, and went to the playoffs for the first time since 1971. To be honest, I felt God told me that we were going to win the last three games. I told the guys that, and we stepped up and won. We didn't have enough talent to go very far in the playoffs, but we made it."

As a non-starter most of the season, Spani spent more time on the field during practice, going up against the first-teamers. In one practice Spani ruptured a disc in his back and was never again up to full speed. He had surgery right after the season. In 1987 Spani was on the physically unable to perform list and didn't play another game. His last game was the 35–15 playoff loss against the New York Jets.

He ended his career one tackle shy of the 1,000 mark. How frustrating is that? "The hardest thing for an athlete to do is to retire. At least for me it was. I did something I loved doing. I played football," Spani said. "The worst thing is probably retiring and then having second thoughts. We had a press conference announcing my retirement. A friend of mine at church was an older gentleman who didn't watch football and didn't know much about the sport, but saw [the press conference] on TV. He called me when I got home that day and said, 'In the book of Corinthians, there are nine gifts. I don't know why God had only nine. In the book of Galatians, there are nine fruits. I don't know why God chose only nine. And your wife is pregnant, and if I'm not mistaken, it still takes nine months to complete a birth. I think you completed what you were supposed to do. You can move on.'

"I have never looked back since he told me that. It freed me up. I completed a period in my life and I could move on. It's funny to be only one tackle away from 1,000, but 999 is perfect for me."

Inducted into the Chiefs Hall of Fame in 2003, Spani is the only Kansas-born player in the team's HOF and has been in the front office for the Chiefs since 1989, most recently as the director of special events.

61 The Nigerian Nightmare

The Chiefs owe a huge thanks to the Nigerian Olympic Committee. In 1984 the committee decided not to take the African record holder in the discus, who had qualified with several tosses of more than 200 feet, to the Olympics. Little did anyone know that decision would lead Christian Okoye to football and a few years later to becoming the most punishing and one of the best running backs in Chiefs history.

Okoye, who grew up as a soccer goalie in Nigeria until he was 17, was a sprinter and thrower in track and field throughout high school. He was so good that he got a track scholarship to Azusa Pacific, then an NAIA school. He became dominant in NAIA track and field. Throughout his career he won eight individual national championships in shot put, discus, and the hammer and was a 17-time NAIA All-American in field events.

After being passed up for the Nigerian Olympic Team in 1984, the disheartened Okoye decided to drop track. He talked to Azusa Pacific football coach Jim Milhon about playing football. After two weeks Okoye was ready to give that up, too. "I didn't like it," Okoye told the (Miami) *Sun-Sentinel* in 1987. "I didn't understand it. It was stupid to me: people hitting each other all the time, the game stopping a lot, not like soccer."

Christian Okoye, the "Nigerian Nightmare," barrels through Los Angeles Raiders tacklers during 1989.

Sticking with it for two years, though, Okoye got the hang of it, and used his 6'1" and 253-pound frame to his advantage. "I like running the ball," he said. "What I like about it is running and getting away from people. When somebody tries to hit you, you hit him first. It's kind of fun."

Although other NFL teams were banking on Okoye being around for the second and third rounds, the Chiefs snagged him early in the second round (35th overall) in the 1987 NFL Draft. During the next six seasons, Okoye became Kansas City's intimidating hammer—a linebacker-sized runner with speed whose mammoth shoulder pads made No. 35 look even more imposing.

After two modest seasons in the Chiefs backfield, Okoye led the NFL in rushing during his third year in the league. That year of 1989, which happened to be Marty Schottenheimer's first as Chiefs head coach, he ran for 1,480 yards on 370 attempts. Okoye, who earned the nickname the "Nigerian Nightmare," had a career-best 12 touchdowns. "When Marty came, he said, 'Christian, I want you to be prepared; we're going to run the ball and we're going to run it a lot,'" Okoye said. "All I wanted is: hand me the ball, and I'll run it as many times as you want it, and they did. I loved it."

Okoye retired before the 1993 season because of a knee injury. Years later, on an NFL Films program, Okoye expressed some regret about the way his career ended. "Not playing football growing up," he said, "it was too easy for me to walk away. When I started getting injuries here and there, I felt it was time for me to go."

Regardless of whether the time was right for that, it's a good thing for Chiefs fans that the Nigerian Olympic Committee decided not to take him to the '84 Games. When he retired, Okoye, a two-time Pro Bowl player, was the team's career rushing leader with 4,897 yards (he's now fourth) and single-season rushing leader with 1,480 yards (now sixth). At that time he also had the most 100-yard rushing games in a season and a career and most rushing touchdowns in a career (40).

62 Ed Podolak

In 1971 Ed Podolak became a Christmas legend and a nationally recognized name. Sure, Chiefs fans already knew about Podolak, the running back out of Iowa who wore No. 14. But on that fateful December 25, Podolak compiled a Chiefs record 350 total all-purpose yards against the Miami Dolphins. Fateful? Unfortunately, Podolak's efforts came during "the longest game," the Chiefs' double-overtime playoff loss to Miami at old Municipal Stadium. Podolak's Chiefs record stands today.

Podolak, whom the Chiefs drafted in 1969, has often joked about how people wouldn't have known about him without that Christmas game. People stop him in airports. Members of the media often call him in December. "I really enjoy a nice notoriety because of that," Podolak said. "That was early in my career, so because of that, people tuned in to some of the things I did later. That was a springboard into recognition as I travel around the country."

One of those times he was recognized, it developed quickly into a friendship with musician Jimmy Buffett. "After I retired I was at a bar in Aspen," Podolak said, "and Jimmy's manager came up to me and said, 'Ed, if I'm offending you in any way let me know, but Jimmy Buffett is a big fan of yours because of the Miami game and following your career after that. We're playing softball this afternoon, and if you'd like, he'd love to have you join us.'

"Little did he know that Jimmy's song, 'Changes in Latitudes, Changes in Attitudes' was my anthem when I was quitting football.

I used to drive around in my car with the top down, singing, 'If it suddenly ended tomorrow, I could somehow adjust to the fall.' I knew all the words to Jimmy's songs. We hit it off right away. We became like brothers and have been ever since."

Buffett even wrote a song for Podolak in the early 1980s called "We Are the People Our Parents Warned Us About." After working with People's Bank in Kansas City during his playing days, Podolak bought part of a real estate company in Aspen in 1971. Since retiring from the Chiefs and pro football in 1977, he has been a successful real estate developer in the Aspen area. He helped develop and open Club Del Mar, a boutique resort in Costa Rica, golf resorts near Basalt, Colorado, and in California's Santa Rosa Mountains. Podolak calls himself "very fortunate."

A second-round draft pick in 1969, Podolak did it all for the Chiefs—rushed, caught passes, and returned kicks. He led the team in rushing four times, receiving three times, and punt returns three times. He finished his career with 8,178 career combined yards. He also scored the first touchdown at Arrowhead Stadium, albeit in preseason, and was one of the first running backs whose face mask had the vertical bar down the middle. The Chiefs inducted Podolak into the team's Hall of Fame in 1988.

But despite those accomplishments and distinctions and the recognition garnered from his record-setting game against the Dolphins on Christmas Day in 1971, Podolak doesn't live in the past. He's adjusted well to life after football. He's in a pretty good place, literally—his own Margaritaville, if you will. "I live in Basalt [just outside Aspen], which is a small town very similar to where I grew up in Iowa," he said. "I don't see any reason to change any of this."

63 L.J. and the Bad Boys

Larry Johnson had the talent to be one of the best running backs in NFL history. Larry Johnson had the attitude to be one of the biggest pains in the ass in NFL history. Each sentence is equally true.

Johnson, whom the Chiefs selected out of Penn State in the first round (27th overall) of the 2003 NFL Draft, grew up studying the great running backs in NFL history the same way a writer would study Hemingway or a musician would study Mozart. With the encouragement of his dad, Larry Sr., who was a coach at Penn State, Larry Jr. watched old highlights of Jim Brown, Franco Harris, and Tony Dorsett. He studied their moves, the way they navigated the line of scrimmage, how they held the ball. He wanted to be just like them. "I go out there every Sunday to see if I can live up to those guys," Johnson told NFL Films early in his career. "Every time I touch the ball, I'm trying to make them proud."

And on the field, he could make them proud. Johnson was a powerful and fast running back. In 2005 and '06, his third and fourth years in the league, he ran for more than 1,700 yards each season—1,750 in '05 and 1,789 in '06—and was selected for the Pro Bowl both seasons.

He ran with a chip on his shoulder the size of Pikes Peak. That's not always a good thing. "L.J. was incredibly talented, but for me he was frustrating at times," said quarterback Trent Green. "L.J. had unbelievable ability to run the football. His tenacity was incredible. Some of that was being hard-headed, which has affected him in other areas. I think Larry could've been one of the best in NFL history, but he let too many external factors get in. There were times when I'd have a one-on-one meeting with him, tell him what

Troublemakers!

Much like every NFL team, the Chiefs have had players—besides Larry Johnson—who weren't exactly pillars in the Kansas City community. Here's a look at some of them:

Dale Carter: An outstanding defensive back of whom coach Marty Schottenheimer once said, "I've never coached a better athlete than Dale Carter—at any position." Off the field, though, Carter had a couple issues. During his NFL career, which included brief stops in Denver (1999), Minnesota (2001), New Orleans (2002–03), and Baltimore (2005), Carter was suspended for drugs and arrested for assault, gun possession, and driving under the influence. In 1993 he was involved in a shootout outside a Kansas City nightclub. While on probation for weapons and alcohol charges in 1994, Carter was charged with beating a Chiefs season-ticket holder in a bar restroom.

Bam Morris and Tamarick Vanover: In 1998 the Chiefs signed Bam Morris, who'd been a solid running back for Pittsburgh and Baltimore, *after* he'd been busted for having six pounds of pot in his car. With the Ravens he failed an alcohol test (which was on his banned substance list after the plea deal from the marijuana) and spent 89 days in jail.

While with the Chiefs, Morris became close with Tamarick Vanover, who was in his fourth year with the team as an electrifying kick returner. The two of them ended up going into business together, selling drugs and stolen cars. Evidently, stolen vehicles were Vanover's specialty. He was busted in a theft ring that stole cars in North Carolina, took them to Missouri, re-titled them, and sold them elsewhere around the country.

Victor Riley: The offensive tackle/gem of a human who the Chiefs selected in the first round of the 1998 draft, Victor Riley was charged in 2001 with aggravated assault and criminal damage to property, misdemeanor counts of child endangerment, and leaving the scene of an accident when he rammed his wife's car with his SUV—while his wife and their infant child were in the car.

we needed, and it'd seem like everything was fine—until we got into the huddle during the game. Then there'd be times when he'd have a vacant look on his face when I was talking to him, but then I'd hand him the ball, and he'd end up with 200 yards rushing. That was a struggle for me because I felt I was good about figuring out the guys and finding ways to lead them. For whatever reason, though, I had difficulty finding Larry's button."

Green wasn't the only one who had difficulty with Johnson. In 2004, after Johnson had been complaining about his playing time and was likely going to be filling in for an injured Priest Holmes, coach Dick Vermeil made the well-publicized (and somewhat facetious) statement during his press conference: "It's time, young man; it's time to take your diapers off and go to work." Johnson reacted negatively through the media and ended up not seeing action for the next four games.

Johnson had issues away from the field, too. In 2003, the same year he was drafted, he was charged with aggravated assault and misdemeanor battery after allegedly arguing with his girlfriend. Five years later he was involved with two incidents with women in Kansas City nightclubs. In the first one, he was accused of shoving a woman. In the second he was accused of spitting on a woman. Since 2008 he's been charged with disturbing the peace and misdemeanor domestic battery and assault in different cases.

Never a fan favorite, Johnson was the topic of an online petition commanding the Chiefs not to let him break the team rushing record. His use of a gay slur in 2009 resulted in his second suspension of the year, and he was released shortly thereafter—seven games into the season. He finished the year with Cincinnati and then played two games in 2010 for Washington and one game for Miami in 2011. Perhaps more fitting for Johnson, he was reportedly seen working as a DJ at a Miami strip club in 2013.

64 From Heisman Winner to Super Bowl Champ

Mike Garrett was a spark when the Chiefs needed one. Still recovering from the deaths of Stone Johnson and Mack Lee Hill and the trade of Abner Haynes, the team was getting depleted in the backfield. In the 20th round of the 1966 AFL Draft, the Chiefs selected Garrett, who'd won the Heisman Trophy at the University of Southern California in 1965.

Garrett became a mainstay for the Chiefs, starting during his entire career in Kansas City from 1966–70. He ran for 3,246 yards and 24 touchdowns. He also played on both the Super Bowl I and IV teams for Kansas City.

Each Super Bowl experience was special for Garrett. In the first one at the end of his rookie season, the Chiefs faced the storied Green Bay Packers in Garrett's hometown of Los Angeles. Against Minnesota in Super Bowl IV, he ran for a 5-yard touchdown in the Chiefs' win. "What I remember most about scoring is thinking about how the people of Kansas City were going to be beside themselves if we won," he said. "They loved us, and it was great to be a part of a team that represented Kansas City the way it should be."

After his NFL career ended with the San Diego Chargers in 1973, Garrett, among other things, received his law degree, ran for Congress, bought and managed properties, ran a program for delinquent kids, and worked for former Lakers owner Dr. Jerry Buss.

He says that he turned down a job as assistant athletics director with USC at least three or four times. But he finally acquiesced and took over the department two years later in 1993 when AD Mike McGee left to take the same job at South Carolina. "I always dreamt of being the athletics director [at Southern Cal] and turning the program around, but I never thought it'd actually happen," Garrett said. "It was serendipitous. When I finally got there, there wasn't much the job presented that I hadn't done before. The job has anything and everything. It's very demanding...Problems never cease to exist. When you're losing, you have losing problems. When you're winning, you have winning problems. But I like winning. So you can always give me the pleasant problems."

Garrett ran into some unpleasant problems, namely those involving football's Reggie Bush and basketball's O.J. Mayo, and was pushed out in 2010. (He, though, did lead a USC football resurgence after firing Paul Hackett, a former Chiefs offensive coordinator, as head coach and hiring Pete Carroll.) Then in 2012 he took over as athletics director at Langston University, a traditionally black NAIA school in Langston, Oklahoma.

Even though Garrett doesn't make it to the Kansas City area much anymore and he's lost touch with most of his teammates, Kansas City remains a favorite city, and he cherishes his time playing for the Chiefs. "I really remember the locations around town as much as anything else," he said. "I found that Kansas City was a very unique place after living in Los Angeles. The topography of Kansas City captured me. And Municipal was a great, quaint stadium. It was one of the greatest places to play. Those Chiefs teams were probably the best I played for in my career. It was wonderful to play with guys that were so talented. We didn't realize at the time how good we were. As time went on, we appreciated it more and more."

65 Visit Municipal Stadium and Eat at Bryant's

It's hard to believe that this is actually the place. It looks so different now—just a smattering of newer homes. It's quiet on this summer afternoon. There's no construction on this swath of open space, but the aroma of Arthur Bryant's has made its way up here. If you didn't stop to look, it would be easy to miss the indiscreet black and white photos of former baseball and football players. Ah, indeed, this is the site—22nd and Brooklyn—of the old Municipal Stadium, the Chiefs' original home.

This is where it all began for Major League Baseball in 1955 and then in 1963 for the Chiefs. Professional baseball had been played here since the stadium first opened in 1923, and it housed two NFL teams in the 1920s—the Blues in 1924 and the Cowboys during 1925–26. (The team had two different names.)

But the combination of the Philadelphia Athletics moving to Kansas City in '55 and the forethought of Charlie Bryant to move Arthur Bryant's just down the road in '58 helped put the restaurant—and Kansas City barbecue—on a national map. So grab a beef sandwich and some fries from Bryant's and head to this spot to imagine (or remember) what it was like to pull for the early Chiefs on a cold December day.

As with other multi-sport stadiums at that time, which was before the cookie-cutter stadiums began popping up in cities such as St. Louis, Pittsburgh, Atlanta, and Cincinnati, fitting a football field inside a baseball stadium posed interesting challenges, especially during cold weather. The upper deck, which had been installed when the A's moved from Philadelphia, cast a shadow on the football field. "So the field would be frozen on one side, and the other half of the field would be slush," former wide receiver Chris Burford said. "And you had both the teams on the same sideline."

For the time being, it had to do, which was fine for Lamar Hunt. The team was moving from the spacious—and often empty—Cotton Bowl, which held more than 75,000, to Municipal, which held about 49,000. After a scouting trip to Kansas City when Hunt saw Municipal, he remarked that he was "impressed with the stadium facilities. I had seen so many bad ones in Boston, Buffalo, and other places."

AFL stadiums couldn't compare to their NFL counterparts—even by 1960s standards. "We had an exhibition game in Oakland in Frank Youell Stadium," Ed Budde said. "There are a lot of high schools that have nicer facilities than that one in Oakland. That was the worst stadium I ever played in. We had to take turns taking a shower because they had only two showers."

"Buffalo was the same way," Bobby Bell said. "People watching didn't understand what was happening in Buffalo because right after the game we were all running off the field. We did that because all of the hot water would run out after three showers, and it was freezing after that."

Municipal Stadium was luxurious compared to some others. In New York the Jets (known in the early years as the Titans) called the Polo Grounds home for their first three seasons. Players say they had to leave lights on in the locker room the night before a game to keep the rats away from their equipment. In Denver most of the floor of the visitors' locker room in the original Mile High Stadium was dirt, including where the players got dressed.

The main thing those other places didn't have that Municipal could boast: Arthur Bryant's, which has become one of the most iconic barbecue restaurants in America, at 17th and Brooklyn. Known for its vinegar and paprika-tasting sauces, Bryant's has hosted such luminaries as Steven Spielberg, Jack Nicholson, Bryant Gumbel, and presidents Harry Truman and Jimmy Carter, along with, of course, nearly every member of the Chiefs, A's, and Royals for a decade. "There was an old German shepherd that sat next to Arthur by the register," Burford said. "'The Platter' was my favorite with brisket, ribs, pickles, a half-loaf of white bread and Arthur's red original sauce—washed down with a mug of beer! I visited again [in 2013]. A little had changed, but not all that much."

When the A's moved to Kansas City, a second deck was added to Municipal Stadium, and A's owner Arnold Johnson purchased the old Braves Field scoreboard in Boston for $100,000 and put it in right-center field. (With the football configuration, that scoreboard was near the corner of an end zone.) During that 1955 season, the Kansas City Athletics drew a whopping 1,393,054 fans, a far cry from the 304,666 in their final season in Philadelphia. The attendance in '55 was the largest ever in the history of Municipal, including the Royals' four seasons there.

Excitement for the Chiefs wasn't that high. Even though mayor Roe Bartle promised 3,000 permanent seats and 11,000 temporary seats as part of the incentive to move to Kansas City, that was way more than needed. The team drew 5,721 for their first exhibition game on August 9, 1963, against Buffalo. (By comparison they drew 11,000 for a preseason game three weeks later in Wichita, Kansas, against Houston.) "I remember turning to whoever was next to me and saying, 'Is this what we left Dallas for?'" defensive tackle Jerry Mays said in the book, *Winning It All.* Although more than 30,000 showed up for the San Diego game on October 20, attendance faded for the 5–7–2 Chiefs after that. They didn't even hit 25,000 for their final two games—combined.

Things didn't improve drastically for the Chiefs at Municipal Stadium until the 1966 season, aka the season of Super Bowl I. For the first time in the organization's history, it eclipsed 275,000 fans in total home attendance (preseason and regular season combined for 284,341). Excitement continued to mount, especially in the quaint quarters of Municipal. "I loved playing at Municipal,"

Fred Williamson said. "It was great, very friendly, very charismatic. People could reach out and talk to you."

In 1967 after Charlie Finley—who bought the A's from Johnson and failed in talking Lamar Hunt into moving both the A's and the Chiefs to Atlanta—left Kansas City for greener pastures in Oakland. The Chiefs played four years alone at Municipal.

The team's final game at Municipal Stadium was on Christmas Day 1971, the double-overtime loss to Miami in the NFL's longest game. Burford probably needed something stronger that day than a mug of beer with The Platter from Arthur Bryant's.

Blackledge and Other Draft Busts

Every NFL team has its draft busts—players who never perform to expectations because of either injuries or other issues (such as lack of relative talent). Of course, the Chiefs have had some doozies. Here are some of the biggest first and second-round draft busts in Chiefs history. They're in chronological order...though in many fans' eyes, the first one happens to be the worst.

1983 Draft

Todd Blackledge
Taken in the first round of a famed quarterback class that included John Elway, Jim Kelly, and Dan Marino, Todd Blackledge had the Penn State credentials to be selected ahead of Kelly and Marino—or so it seemed. In actuality, who could forget the October 20, 1985, game, when Blackledge threw a team-record six interceptions against the Los Angeles Rams? Blackledge never turned into the franchise quarterback the Chiefs needed and thought they were

The Short Career of Leon Sandcastle

For those paying close attention to some of Alex Smith's postgame interviews inside the Chiefs locker room during the 2013 season, they might've noticed something peculiar in the background: a Leon Sandcastle bobblehead. Sandcastle had a short rendezvous with the Chiefs in 2013, but he wasn't necessarily a bust.

The Sandcastle legend started with a commercial that the NFL launched two months earlier during the Super Bowl. Former NFL star Deion Sanders is shown in it in his disguise as he goes through the NFL Combine. It ends with commissioner Roger Goodell announcing: "With the first pick in the 2013 NFL Draft, the Kansas City Chiefs select Leon Sandcastle."

The NFL Network and NFL.com even reported on April 1 that the Chiefs were going to select Leon Sandcastle, who "already has been stamped with legendary status," with the overall No. 1 pick in the 2013 NFL Draft.

The subsequent interview with NFL Network's *Total Access* was pure gold. Sandcastle was decked out in dark sunglasses and a red pullover, and one couldn't help but notice his hair. NFL.com reported that the Chiefs "couldn't turn down the opportunity to bring aboard that afro and terrible facial hair."

Among the highlights from the groovy-talking Sandcastle:

What about the money? Because I assume it must be about the money.
Leon Sandcastle: It must be the money and I go to sleep to that jingle every night...But the last time a team wrote Leon a check, the bank bounced.

There's a new quarterback there, Alex Smith. Do you believe in Alex?
LS: I don't know that I believe in Alex as of yet, because Alex has not been on the field with Leon. Alex's responsibility is to get the ball to Leon just as much as the center gets the ball to Alex.

Is there anything you can't do, Leon?
LS: No, there's nothing that Leon can't do. There's nothing that Leon has not attempted to do.

Sandcastle, who was at the Chiefs practice facility earlier in the day, ended the interview by blowing a kiss to the camera.

The Sandcastle gag brought about Sandcastle bobbleheads and Sandcastle Chiefs jerseys. And it gave the Chiefs some fun national attention. As humorous as it all may have been, Sanders—um... Sandcastle—might've performed better in 2013 than many of the busts the Chiefs have had throughout the years.

choosing. He played in 40 games for the Chiefs and threw for 4,510 yards. He finished his NFL career with more interceptions (38) than touchdowns (27).

Chiefs could have drafted: Kelly (14th overall by the Bills) or Marino (27th overall by the Dolphins).

1986 Draft

Brian Jozwiak

The seventh overall pick in 1986, it might seem unfair to put Brian Jozwiak on this list. Can a player who's injured be a bust? Yes, especially when he started only three games in his three seasons with the Chiefs. He was an All-American at West Virginia before a hip injury ended his NFL career.

Chiefs could have drafted: defensive end Leslie O'Neal (eighth overall by the Chargers).

1990 Draft

Percy Snow

The Chiefs' first-round selection (13th overall) in the 1990 NFL Draft out of Michigan State, Percy Snow was seen as a great addition to the defensive line that featured the top picks of '88 and '89, Neil Smith and Derrick Thomas. And sure Snow started at inside linebacker during his rookie year as the Chiefs reached the playoffs. However, during training camp the next season, Snow fractured his ankle while driving a motor scooter. He missed all of the '91 season and never returned to form.

Chiefs could have drafted: running back Emmitt Smith (17th overall by the Cowboys).

1995 Draft

Trezelle Jenkins

The Chiefs drafted 6'7", 317-pound tackle Trezelle Jenkins (31st overall) in the first round of the 1995 NFL Draft. In spite of his size, Jenkins never adjusted to the NFL. He played in just nine games for the Chiefs from 1995–97. He signed with the New Orleans Saints and Minnesota Vikings but never appeared in a game for either team.

Chiefs could have drafted: cornerback Craig Newsome (32nd overall by the Packers).

2002 Draft

Ryan Sims

Want to see a Chiefs fan cry or sock you in the nose? Mention Ryan Sims, the sixth overall pick in the '02 draft. His name elicits about the same response from recent Chiefs fans as Blackledge's name from two decades earlier. In five seasons with the Chiefs, Sims, a defensive tackle out of North Carolina, registered five sacks, one interception, and 65 tackles. In the following four seasons with the Tampa Bay Bucs, Sims had only 3.5 sacks and 48 tackles.

Chiefs could have drafted: defensive end Dwight Freeney (11th overall by the Colts).

2004 Draft

Junior Siavii

After trading their first-round pick (30th overall) to the Detroit Lions, the Chiefs selected defensive tackle Junior Siavii (36th), a projected fourth or fifth-round player. Siavii proved the "experts" correct. In two seasons with the Chiefs, Siavii had one sack and 13 tackles—in 26 games (no starts).

Chiefs could have drafted: safety Bob Sanders (44th overall by the Colts).

Dishonorable Mention:
Glenn Dorsey, 2008 Draft, fifth overall pick
Tyson Jackson, 2009 Draft, third overall pick

67 The Brawl

"Anytime we played [the Raiders], we knew there'd be a fight at some point," said former Chiefs great E.J. Holub. The former line-backer/center would know.

At Candlestick Park in 1961 during one of the first games between the two organizations, Oakland quarterback Tom Flores ran out of bounds in front of the Raiders bench. From out of nowhere, Holub clobbered Flores with a forearm—about four yards out of bounds. "That started a huge fight in front of our bench," Flores said. "Guys were pushing, throwing punches, falling over benches, the works."

Flores, the longtime Raider, though, spent part of the 1969 season as a backup quarterback with the Chiefs. "The Chiefs had a reel that they kept of all their famous fights," Flores said. "When I joined the Chiefs, they showed me the reel of that infamous fight. E.J. Holub, by that time, was the center. He was a wild and crazy guy. He told me, '[Heck], Tom, you ran right into my elbow.' I just shook my head. We talked about how that was one of the best fights between the Chiefs and the Raiders."

But there is one fight in the rivalry between the Chiefs and Raiders that stands out above the rest in terms of timing and importance. It was on November 1, 1970, at Municipal Stadium. At the time the Chiefs, the Oakland Raiders, and the Denver Broncos were duking it out for the top spot in the new AFC West. The Chiefs, leading 17–14 with the ball near midfield, were 68 seconds away from tying for first in the division. On third down and 11, quarterback Len Dawson called for a sweep play to the left. "I told [tackle] Dave Hill to go down the field because I was going to keep the ball instead of handing it off to Mike Garrett," Dawson said. "They were out of timeouts with less than two minutes to go. So if we get the first down, I'd go to a knee, and we'd leave with a win."

And the play worked beautifully. Dawson ran for 19 yards on the bootleg, all but sealing the game. While Dawson was on the ground facedown, Oakland's Ben Davidson speared him in the back with a vicious and extremely late hit. When Davidson stood up, Chiefs wide receiver Otis Taylor, who had run in from about 25 yards away, grabbed Davidson by the neck and threw him to the ground. The benches cleared, and it took several minutes to restore order. Taylor was ejected, and the Chiefs were penalized, negating the first down. "I have to admit that I wasn't surprised when Otis did that because he was that type of player. He was protecting me," Dawson said. "It also didn't surprise me that—once Otis jumped on Davidson, the rest of our teammates jumped in there, too."

Following the imbroglio the Raiders got the ball back on a punt, marched beyond midfield, and kicker George Blanda booted a 48-yard field goal for the game-ending tie. The outcome of the game, combined with a Denver loss earlier in the day, put the Raiders in first, Denver in second, and the Chiefs in third. Kansas City ended its season a few weeks later at 7–5–2.

"Otis was a big-play performer," Dawson added. "He was a complete player—not just a guy that could catch a football. He was a true football player. Even though [going after Davidson] may

Hey, You're Otis Taylor...Sorry About the Headlock

Otis Taylor, in spite of being one of the all-time best Chiefs, was involved in another of the all-time worst incidents in Chiefs history.

In September of 1987, NFL players hit the picket lines in search of free agency and a percentage of the league's revenue. The league cancelled that weekend's games, and then each team brought in replacement players.

Taylor, who was a 45-year-old scout for the Chiefs at the time, was helping a replacement player, who claimed the picketing players slashed his car's tires. That wouldn't be hard to believe. After all, a couple striking players—one was reportedly Dino Hackett—were pacing the picket line in front of Arrowhead Stadium with unloaded shotguns.

While Taylor was walking the replacement player to his car, linebacker Jack Del Rio, who was 24 at the time and in his first year with the Chiefs, started yelling at Taylor, calling him a "dirty scab" and a "lowlife."

There are various accounts of how all of this went down, especially what happened next. In 300 Pounds of Attitude, Jonathan Rand, a former sports columnist for The Kansas City Star, wrote: "Taylor yelled back, and Del Rio rushed him, grabbed Taylor in a headlock, and threw him to the ground."

In The Kansas City Star article, Del Rio said he and Taylor began shouting at each other before Taylor attacked him, knocking a plastic mug out of his hand. He told police that Taylor threw him down and "landed on top" of him.

In Taylor's book, *The Need to Win*, he wrote of walking through the picket line when Del Rio started yelling: "I may have been as much of an instigator as he was because I was taking a firm line, too. I wasn't going to let anybody push me or run over me, and that's what Del Rio was trying to do. We yelled at each other, and he rushed me...He grabbed me in a headlock and flipped me. I lost my balance as he tried to body-slam me and I fell onto the gravel."

There's little debating, however, how the rest of the story played out. The two men scuffled for about three minutes before Hackett broke it up. But not before Taylor had a bloodied face. "I couldn't believe it was happening," Hackett said. "Here's Jack and Otis Taylor, a Chiefs linebacker and a Chiefs legend, wrestling around there on the ground. It was unbelievable."

As Hackett separated the men, he told Del Rio, "Jack, no. No, this is Otis."

According to Taylor, Del Rio then said, "Hey, Otis, I used to love watching you. You were a great player."

Charges were not filed, but a week later, Taylor filed a police complaint and a $1 million lawsuit against Del Rio and the NFLPA. The next day Del Rio filed an assault complaint against Taylor. The case was settled out of court two years later.

have hurt our playoff chances, Otis was being Otis...he was watching out for his teammates."

That play, incidentally, helped change the NFL rules so that a personal foul after the play wouldn't negate the play.

68 The NFL's Best Defensive Backfield

It might be difficult to quantify, but you could make a very strong argument that the Chiefs defensive backfield of the 1980s was the best in the NFL during that decade. It's certainly one of the great ones in NFL history. "It was one of the best without question," Deron Cherry said. "You can look for teams and players that were better, but that collection of players for us was quite an incredible group. You'd have a hard time finding many teams with that talent that stayed together for so long."

The foursome of Cherry, Albert Lewis, Kevin Ross, and Lloyd Burruss patrolled the secondary together from 1984–88. That last year Kevin Porter was added to the mix. He took Burruss' spot in 1989, and that foursome stayed together through the 1991 season.

Each member of the original foursome—Lewis, Ross, Burruss, Cherry—was selected to at least one Pro Bowl. Here are some of their other key statistics with Kansas City:

Lloyd Burruss, Safety (1981–91): Burruss averaged 63 tackles per season, picked off 20 passes, and scored five touchdowns during the '80s. Four of those five touchdowns came on a Pick-6. In 145 career games, Burruss recorded 628 tackles, 22 interceptions, seven fumble recoveries, and 3.5 sacks.
Pro Bowl: 1986. *Chiefs Hall of Fame*: 1998.

Deron Cherry, Safety (1981–91): Cherry recorded six 100-tackle seasons. He led the AFC in picks in 1986 with nine. In 148 career games, Cherry recorded 927 tackles, 50 interceptions, 15 fumble recoveries, and three touchdowns.
Pro Bowl: 1983–88. *Chiefs Hall of Fame*: 1999.

Albert Lewis, Cornerback (1983–93): Lewis picked off 20 of his 38 Chiefs career interceptions during his first four seasons. In 150 career games with the Chiefs, he recorded 555 tackles, 38 interceptions, 11 fumble recoveries, 10 blocked punts, and 4.5 sacks.
Pro Bowl: 1987–90. *Chiefs Hall of Fame*: 2007.

Kevin Ross, Cornerback (1984–93, '97): In 156 games with the Chiefs, Kevin Ross had 826 tackles, 30 interceptions, 12 fumble recoveries, 12 forced fumbles, and four sacks.
Pro Bowl: 1989–90. *Chiefs Hall of Fame*: 2011.

"We all were students of the game and played it at a high level," Burruss said. "We took a lot of pride in how we played. We were four guys, but more than that, we were all one. There were no egos. We all wanted to succeed as a team. If one guy was having a problem, we'd all help out. And if a guy needed help, he'd ask for it."

The Chiefs have had a history of solid secondaries. During the Super Bowl years, the defensive backfield featured the likes of Emmitt Thomas, Jim Kearney, Jim Marsalis, and Johnny Robinson.

Then after struggling as a franchise during much of the '70s, the transition to the best defensive backfield in the NFL of the 1980s began at the end of the 1970s, when the team added Gary Barbaro and Gary Green to a unit that still included Thomas. In 1981 Burruss was added. Then in 1983 Cherry took Barbaro's spot after Barbaro, who started all 101 games in his Chiefs career, left the NFL for the New Jersey Generals of the USFL. In the following year in 1984, Lewis took Green's spot at left cornerback, and Ross became the team's regular right cornerback.

During the 1980s, a few of the Chiefs defensive back coaches were pretty talented, too: Walt Corey (1981–82), Bud Carson (1983), and Tony Dungy (1989–91). But it all came down to the players. "I don't think there was an emphasis placed on the secondary, but there was a philosophy of tradition, and the guys who were there upheld the tradition from the older guys," Cherry said. "Green and Barbaro picked that up from Thomas. Then Green, Barbaro, and Eric Harris held us accountable as rookies. We tried to make the young guys such as Jayice Pearson accountable. After I retired in '91, Lewis and Ross held the young guys, Dale Carter and Martin Bayless, accountable. You knew there was a certain standard and you had to uphold that."

69 Chiefs Player at Center of KU-MU Dispute

Missouri vs. Kansas according to the MU media guide: 57–54–9
Kansas vs. Missouri according to the KU media guide: 55–56–9
Oddly, that figures.

You wouldn't really expect anything other than at least a mild discrepancy in the all-time football series record between the bitter rivals, would you? Getting Jayhawks and Tigers to agree on it would be like the Chiefs and Raiders agreeing on anything. But in the game, played more than a half-century ago, that provides the difference in record, the implications were enormous.

The player at the center of the controversy, former Chiefs running back Bert Coan, jokes that he "didn't have much of a career" at Kansas. Coan certainly had all the makings for a good career at running back with his size (6'4", 210 pounds) and 9.4 speed, but things didn't pan out. After playing his freshman season at Texas Christian, Coan enrolled at Kansas. He redshirted one season, played a season, and then suffered a season-ending injury the next year after he broke his leg in spring practices.

At that time in college football, the national champion was crowned before the bowl games with the team ranked No. 1 at the end of the regular season selected as the national champ. Heading into the season finale, the Tigers found themselves undefeated at 9–0 and ranked No. 1 in the country. The only obstacle between the Tigers and the national championship was a home game against the Jayhawks, which was easier said than done.

And the Jayhawks dominated the Tigers. Missouri didn't get a first down until the clock showed 9:06...left in the third quarter. They didn't get another until the fourth quarter. Coan led all rushers in the game with 67 yards. He also scored two touchdowns as the Jayhawks went on to win 23–7.

As Ernie Mehl wrote in *The Kansas City Times*: "Not even the most partisan Missouri fan could deny that the better team on the field in this classic came away with the heavy end of the score. It was so completely convincing there was nothing to look back upon as a turning point."

Missouri's victory would come off the field as the Big 8 Conference looked closer at the season for KU, which already had been placed on one-year probation for the recruitment of Coan. About a month after the contest, the Big 8 ruled that Coan was ineligible and the Jayhawks needed to forfeit wins against Colorado and Missouri. (Coan was limited to those two games because of a shoulder injury.)

Coan, a Texan by birth, ended up at Kansas in part because Houston Oilers/Tennessee Titans founder Bud Adams, a former KU football player and member of the AFL's "Foolish Club," hosted him on a flight to Chicago. "I guess it's safe to say it now, but I was illegally recruited off the TCU campus," Coan said. "I was working, driving a concrete truck, and [Adams] called me and asked if I wanted to go up [to Chicago]. He was about to create a new [American Football League] team, and all of the owners were meeting in Chicago at the Hilton, which was part of the reason for him being there. I thought he might want me to play with the Oilers, so I went with him. I had no idea he was going to talk about Kansas the entire time. When I first visited the KU campus, [head coach Jack] Mitchell was leery and I don't think he had any idea what was going on."

Coan went on to spend seven years in the AFL—1962 with the San Diego Chargers and then 1963–68 with the Chiefs. He rushed for 1,259 career yards and 15 touchdowns and was part of the Super Bowl I Chiefs team. "I liked playing in Kansas City. They treated me better than I deserved because I was injured quite a bit," Coan said.

As far as the infamous 1960 game, Missouri quickly changed its overall record after the forfeit was announced. Kansas hasn't been so quick to do so. "If you look at the record, it shows they forfeited, but we didn't win that game," said Andy Russell, who was a sophomore linebacker and fullback for the Tigers before becoming a member of the famed Pittsburgh Steelers teams of the '70s. "They beat us. That's all there is to it."

70 Will to Succeed

Will Shields has always seemed to have perfect timing. When the Chiefs drafted him in the third round, they needed a right guard to help protect future Hall of Fame quarterback Joe Montana and block for future Hall of Fame running back Marcus Allen—a tall task for many rookies. Shields, who didn't start his first pro game against Tampa Bay, was up for the task and more. And the road grader/pass protector performed beautifully well for 14 seasons.

He was so good that in 2015 he was enshrined in the Pro Football Hall of Fame. Here are the main numbers that stand out: 224 (the number of games he played in 14 seasons), 223 (the number of games he started, which is third on the all-time list since 1970), and 12 (Shields' number of consecutive Pro Bowl appearances).

Shields will go down as one of the best and most durable offensive linemen in pro football history—and one of the best Chiefs ever. But he's meant much more to the Kansas City community than 224, 223, and 12. Helping the community isn't a vehicle for Shields; it's who he is. It's his life. "I always put my best foot forward and did everything I possibly could, on the field and off it," Shields said. "My goal was to be the best teammate, the best player, and the best person I could be. I hope that's how I'm remembered by my teammates and the Kansas City community."

More than 100,000 people have been helped by Shields' foundation, Will to Succeed. Not to mention the countless people he's encouraged, trained with, or otherwise worked with at his training facility, 68's Inside Sports.

68's Inside Sports, which is located in Overland Park, Kansas, is technically two buildings within a few blocks of each other. One location is more of a traditional fitness facility, which is where you can find Shields most days, while the other is an indoor sports training facility. It includes a large turf field, where Shields has conducted various football camps, plus batting cages and pitching tunnels.

In an era when many pro athletes use their charitable work as a public relations vehicle or let it go by the wayside after their playing careers, Will Shields isn't that way. In fact he was active with Boys & Girls Clubs while he attended the University of Nebraska. In 2003 the NFL recognized Shields' work away from the game as the Walter Payton NFL Man of the Year award winner.

Since arriving in Kansas City as a third-round pick out of Nebraska in 1993, Shields has been making a difference in the community. Will to Succeed, which Shields began during his rookie season, has raised more than $1 million for various charities and causes, mostly helping women and children.

71 The Cheetah

"That's what speed do" was a popular phrase for the Kansas City Royals during their incredible postseason runs in 2014 and '15. They showed the world what it meant to have speed on the bases and in the outfield. The Chiefs showed the world what could happen when a quarterback with a bazooka for an arm could throw to perhaps the fastest player in the NFL. It created an intimidating target: a 5'10", 185-pound cheetah known as Tyreek Hill, whom the Chiefs selected in the fifth round of the 2016 NFL Draft out of West Alabama.

Hill's biggest problem, though, has not been on the field. In fact, the Chiefs drafted Hill, knowing he was bringing ugly baggage. Hill's college career started at Garden City Community College before he transferred as a junior to Oklahoma State. It was there in 2014 that he was arrested and eventually pleaded guilty to domestic assault and battery after choking his then-pregnant girl-friend Crystal Espinal. He was dismissed from the OSU football and track teams shortly after the incident. He played one season at West Alabama before entering the draft and being selected by the Chiefs. "There has to be a certain trust here, but there's just things that we can't go into and go through," Reid told reporters at the time, "We uncovered every possible stone that we possibly could and we feel very comfortable with that part of it."

Shortly after being drafted, Hill acknowledged the fans questioning the Chiefs' decision. "The fans have every right to be mad at me," he said. "I did something wrong. I let my emotions get the best of me and I shouldn't have did it. They have every right to be mad…I'm fixing to come back, be a better man, be a better citizen, and everything takes care of itself, and let God do the rest."

While Hill earned the community's trust and became an electric player on the field, *The Kansas City Star* broke a story in March 2019 that Hill and Espinal, who became his fiancée, were being investigated for battery after their son suffered a broken arm. Things became uglier and more convoluted over the next several months as the Johnson County, Kansas, district attorney's office investigated, and a Kansas City TV station released audio of a recorded private conversation between Hill and Espinal, during which Hill allegedly made threatening comments toward Espinal. The Chiefs suspended Hill. He was reinstated in July when the NFL announced that after its investigation—and taking the lead from the Johnson County DA office—that there wasn't enough evidence to suspend Hill. (It was discovered later that the TV station released an edited version of the conversation. In the unedited audio, Hill denies the 2014 domestic charge as well as hurting their son.)

Hill returned to team activities just in time for training camp. But during the first regular-season game in 2019, Hill left the game and was hospitalized after suffering a shoulder injury (technically, a sternoclavicular joint injury). He missed four games with that. Later in the year, during the Chiefs' game against the Los Angeles Chargers in Mexico City, Hill suffered a hamstring injury but did not miss any time. In spite of those injuries, Hill ended up with 860 receiving yards. Without Hill, which included games without Mahomes, Kansas City's offense had to work harder for points. As fans saw in the fourth quarter of Super Bowl LIV with the play known as *Wasp*, Hill is one of the toughest weapons in the NFL to defend.

The biggest question isn't injuries or what Hill brings on the field. It's whether he can avoid issues off of it. "My journey has been rough, man. I've been through a lot in my life," Hill said after Super Bowl LIV. "I'm really thankful for those things that I went through in my life that made me better, who I am today, which is a loving father, a loving person…I'm very thankful for my journey."

72 1969 AFL Playoffs

There's something to be said for determination and motivation. The Chiefs had both heading into the 1969 season. In spite of having one of the best teams in the AFL, they didn't have much to show for it in the two seasons after Super Bowl I. In 1967 they finished second in the AFL West. And then in '68, they won a franchise-best 12 games but got smoked by Oakland 41–6 in their first AFL Divisional Playoff game.

As the Chiefs learned from Super Bowl I, they had a good offense, but their defense was lacking. Coach Hank Stram made sure defense wasn't his team's shortcoming again. So, during the previous two seasons, the Chiefs added players such as Emmitt Thomas, Jim Kearney, and Jim Marsalis to the defensive backfield, along with linebackers Jim Lynch and Willie Lanier.

There was a little extra motivation, though, that season. It was the last season for two leagues. Whichever team won the AFL championship and went to the Super Bowl would be the last American Football League franchise to win the AFL title. Since Lamar Hunt had the foresight to start the AFL, it was only fitting that the Chiefs reach this particular game.

Getting there wouldn't be easy. Len Dawson missed four games because of a knee injury. In the quarterback's first game out, his replacement, Jacky Lee, injured his ankle and would be out for three weeks. That left the Chiefs with one quarterback, Mike Livingston, before they signed former Raiders quarterback Tom Flores, whom the Bills had just cut.

So that his injury-plagued team could reach the Super Bowl, Stram had previously instituted stricter rules and a system of fines, which make his players laugh today. "Hank had a really big fine system," Ed Lothamer said, "but the biggest one was if you were caught with a girl in your room. That was $2,500."

Stram made his stance perfectly clear when former Raiders quarterback Tom Flores joined the team during the season. "Under Hank's regime, everybody had to be clean-shaven—no mustaches, beards, or sideburns," Flores said. "The first day that I arrived, the team was getting ready to practice. I had long sideburns. I had signed a contract with the Chiefs after being released by Buffalo, where the rules weren't quite as stringent. Before I left Hank's office, he said, 'Oh, Tom, we don't have long sideburns here.' I told him that I'd shave them that night. He said, 'There is shaving gear in the bathroom.' I realized he wanted me to do it right then. Of course, I had about two minutes to get out on the field for practice. I asked him how short he wanted my sideburns. He said, 'About where mine are.' Well, he didn't even have any.

"So, I rushed into the bathroom, already dressed for practice, slapped some shaving cream on my face, and did the best I could to cut down about an inch on each sideburn and get them even. I know they were not even. Plus, I was bleeding because I did it so fast. When I finished, I grabbed my headgear and ran out the

Behind the Photo

It's one of the most famous photographs in Chiefs history. Otis Taylor drawing up the play in the dirt as Len Dawson watches—like a couple of kids would do in the backyard. In this case the backyard was Shea Stadium during that 1969 playoff game against the Jets.

While the Chiefs defense was halting the Jets on first and goal at the 1 late in the game, Taylor was tossing an idea out to Dawson. "I'd go to all of the guys on offense from the linemen to the receivers if we had an idea for a formation or a blocking scheme or anything like that, but I'd ask the receivers what they wanted to do. After all, they know better than anybody out there what they're able to do against that day's defense," Dawson said. "In that photo [Taylor] was diagramming and telling me, 'Before we switch to go out to the slot, the cornerback is not there. It's the safety. So if we go on a quick count and he has to guard me, if you can contain the safety on the other side, I can beat this guy.'"

Kansas City's defense stopped New York, making the Jets settle for a field goal that tied the game at 6. "Otis was right! It broke wide open, and a slower safety couldn't handle it," Dawson said. "Otis got out. If you remember that day, the wind was swirling like crazy, and if you didn't get a good release on the throw, the ball wouldn't take off. I ended up getting a hell of a release, and it took off. In fact, when it left my hand, I thought, *Oh, no, I've overthrown him.* But Otis Taylor had different gears. He took off, came up with the ball, and took it inside the 20."

One play after that 61-yard bomb, Dawson hooked up with Gloster Richardson for a 19-yard touchdown that ultimately gave the Chiefs the 13–6 win. And it started with a play drawn in the dirt.

door. When I got outside, it was as if everybody was expecting me to come out looking like I did—bleeding and shaving cream on my face. All my new teammates were laughing and applauding. They knew exactly what I was doing. They knew that I needed short sideburns, but not one guy said anything about it. I was sitting right next to Lenny Dawson, and he didn't tell me. Mike Livingston didn't tell me. Buck Buchanan didn't say anything. Not one guy told me. They just waited for it to happen because they knew it would."

The 11–3 Chiefs lost their regular-season finale at Flores' former team, Oakland, 10–6. That meant the Raiders finished 12–1–1 and won the division. And in the four-team playoffs, the Chiefs opened on the road at Shea Stadium against the defending world champion New York Jets.

After a couple field goals, the Chiefs led 6–3, heading into the fourth quarter. With the Jets driving, the Chiefs were flagged for pass interference, giving New York first and goal at the 1-yard line. The Jets failed to score on their first two running plays, setting up a crucial third down. With tears running down his face, Lanier pleaded with the defense to make a stop. The group rallied and held the Jets to a field goal. "When a grown man comes in the huddle and is crying, that's bonding," Kearney said. "We had that bond and we had an incredible desire. We played for the love of the game."

With the game tied at 6, the Chiefs went on to score the lone touchdown of the contest, when Gloster Richardson caught his only pass of the game from Dawson and took it in for a 19-yard touchdown play. "The wind was gusting that day," Richardson said. "The wind was always blowing in Shea Stadium. I was watching the flight of the ball, and the wind was making it do all sorts of things. That ball took all day to get to me. I thought it'd be up there until the game was over. That was tough concentration, but I'm glad I made the play."

The Chiefs' 13–6 win over New York meant a return trip to Oakland-Alameda County Coliseum, where the Chiefs had lost two weeks earlier. Incidentally, remember how the Chiefs lost only three games that season? Two of them came against the Raiders. In fact, since the first Super Bowl season of 1966, the Raiders held a 7–2 advantage in games between the two teams. (Not to mention, the Raiders embarrassed the Chiefs in the '68 playoffs.)

This AFL Championship Game, the final one in the league's 10-year history, however, became the grudge match expected between the two hated rivals. Although Kansas City's new vaunted defense didn't help much in the previous nine games against Oakland, it paid off this time.

The Chiefs held Oakland quarterbacks Daryle Lamonica and George Blanda to 154 yards on 17-of-45 passing. The quarterback tandem also threw four interceptions. Amazingly, the Chiefs lost the ball four times on fumbles, including three times on their end of the field in the fourth quarter, yet the defense stepped up and stopped Oakland each time.

In the end the Chiefs won 17–7 for their third AFL championship—the final one in the league's history—and second trip to the Super Bowl.

73 The KC Wolf and Other Mascots

For the young of all ages, seeing KC Wolf either at Arrowhead Stadium or some other function around the Kansas City area is sure to provide entertainment—if not some inspiration.

When Carl Peterson became president and general manager of the Chiefs in December 1988, he promised sweeping changes with

Other Symbols of Chiefs Nation

KC Wolf has become the most visible Chiefs mascot during the past 25 years or so, but there have been three other symbols or "mascots," if you will, that are unique to the Chiefs.

Warpaint

Bob Johnson and Warpaint sounds like a pair of sidekicks for Bozo the Clown or Captain Kangaroo (apologies to those who are too young to remember Bozo and Captain Kangaroo). Instead, Warpaint and Bob Johnson were the horse and rodeo cowboy, respectively, who ran around the Municipal Stadium and then Arrowhead Stadium fields after the Chiefs scored. (Truth be told, Warpaint was more than one horse over the years.) With the introduction of KC Wolf, Warpaint and Johnson were sent to pasture in 1989. However, in 2009, as part of the team's 50th anniversary celebration, the Chiefs resurrected Warpaint with a new rider, Susie, a Chiefs cheerleader and world champion rider. Warpaint can now be seen in and around Arrowhead before games, during halftime, and, of course, during games. If you're looking for the ultimate experience and you can't book KC Wolf, you can book Warpaint and Susie for corporate and personal events. Call the Chiefs at 816-920-4525 for more information.

Tony DiPardo and the TD Pack Band

For more than 40 years, at the personal request of Lamar Hunt, Tony "Mr. Music" DiPardo and the TD Pack Band entertained Chiefs fans at Municipal and Arrowhead stadiums. DiPardo's enthusiasm, thumbs-up signal, and red trumpet became legendary in Chiefs Nation. He was seen as such a big part of the Chiefs that coach Hank Stram made sure DiPardo received a Super Bowl IV ring. On December 16, 2010, DiPardo died at the age of 98. His daughter, Patti, led the TD Pack Band for the last 20 years of Tony's life.

The Wolfpack

If you ever wonder why the Chiefs mascot is a wolf, it comes from the Wolfpack, which started simply as a small section of ardent fans at Municipal Stadium. The name originated from a postgame interview, when the group of fans behind the bench were described as wild as a "pack of wolves." The group gained so much recognition, including notable attention in a 1966 *Sports Illustrated* article, that it became an official "club" for Chiefs fans.

plans to change the culture. He wanted to improve the team on the field, of course, but he wanted to bring back the fan base, too. One of the changes for that 1989 season was the addition of a 7'2", overweight instigator—the mascot, KC Wolf.

The man behind the costume is Dan Meers, who was the University of Missouri's Truman the Tiger and the St. Louis Cardinals' Fredbird before becoming KC Wolf. That animal refers to the Wolfpack from Municipal Stadium. (See sidebar.) He entertains fans in and around Arrowhead Stadium with his antics, including a grand entrance on a zip line, motorcycle, or four-wheeler, and belly flopping on a stuffed dummy dressed like that game's opponent.

One stunt, however, went horribly—and nearly tragically—wrong late in the 2013 season. Meers was going to enter the stadium on a bungee cord. During the Saturday rehearsal, there was a malfunction that sent Meers crashing into the upper-deck seats at Arrowhead. He was in the hospital for nearly two weeks.

After a long recovery, Meers is back at it. Either as KC Wolf or himself, Meers makes more than 150 speaking appearances each year on behalf of the Chiefs. He has been to Germany, Japan, Mexico, and numerous Pro Bowls. He speaks to audiences at churches, schools, businesses, and countless other types of groups. As of 2014, according to the Chiefs official website, appearances, which can last anywhere from 10 minutes to six hours, range in price from $150–$325. He can be booked through kcchiefs.com or by calling 816-920-4212. "Chiefs fans truly are the best around," Meers said, "which helps make my job so much fun."

74 *MNF* Returns to Arrowhead

Chiefs fans had waited a long time to see a *Monday Night Football* game at Arrowhead Stadium—eight years to be exact—and it would be only the fourth time since the stadium opened nearly 20 years earlier. So the anticipation of the Buffalo Bills visiting Arrowhead on October 7, 1991, started building as soon as the NFL and ABC announced the schedule.

With the ageless Steve DeBerg at quarterback, the Chiefs were coming off an 11–5 season and a trip to the playoffs in 1990 (a 17–16 loss at Miami). The Bills were coming off what would be the first of four straight trips to the Super Bowl. They came to Kansas City with a lot of confidence and momentum as the AFC's only undefeated team (5–0) remaining.

Some say that Arrowhead was as loud as it had been before or since, as 76,120 euphoric fans filled the stadium. It was the largest home crowd for the Chiefs in two seasons. And they weren't disappointed.

The Chiefs took an early 3–0 lead when Nick Lowery hit a 41-yard field goal two minutes into the game. Lowery added kicks from 40, 24, and 22 yards on a perfect 4-for-4 night. The Chiefs extended their lead in the second quarter with the game's first touchdown on a 1-yard pass from DeBerg to Pete Holohan. Scott Norwood hit two field goals for the Bills during the second quarter, cutting the Kansas City lead to four at 10–6. That's the closest Buffalo would come.

With a 13–6 lead coming out of halftime, the Chiefs kept the ball on the ground and poured it on during the third quarter. The "Nigerian Nightmare," Christian Okoye, added touchdown runs of five and two yards as the Chiefs cruised to an unlikely 33–6 win. Okoye rushed for 122 yards on 29 carries, setting a Chiefs record with his 13th career 100-yard game. Harvey Williams also ran 20 times for 103 yards. All told, the Chiefs racked up 389 yards and held the Bills' high-scoring offense to 211 yards and two field goals. "If a team can succeed in running the ball as well as they did, you're in for a long night," said Bills head coach Marv Levy, who coached the Chiefs from 1978–82. "They just overpowered us. I hope we're not as bad as we looked. I think most routs—and this was a rout—are not indicative of the difference between the two teams."

Besides holding the Bills to less than half of the 450 yards they'd been averaging in 1991, the Kansas City defense sacked quarterback Jim Kelly six times—four by Derrick Thomas and two by Bill Maas. Buffalo suffered its worst defeat since the Indianapolis Colts beat the Bills 47–6 with replacement players during the 1987 strike, as the Chiefs caused five fumbles and held the Bills without a touchdown for the first time since December 1988. "We gave them so many gifts, they should be happy until next Christmas," said Kelly, who threw for 189 yards on 17-of-23 passing.

Maas helped lead that defensive charge. "There was a lot of energy, a lot of adrenaline flowing," he said. "Our defense shut down the No. 1 offense. Our offense held the ball and ran and ran and ran. It was a night to remember. By the time the fourth quarter rolled around, it was glorious."

"We've all been around long enough to know that wasn't the Buffalo Bills football team," said Chiefs coach Marty Schottenheimer. "It was one of those nights where everything fell our way."

The game helped put Arrowhead—along with the pregame tailgating and deafening crowd—on the national map again. With the win over the Bills on the field, the Chiefs began a six-game *Monday Night Football* winning streak, which lasted into the 1994 season. The first five of those games were at Arrowhead.

Often forgotten is that three weeks after beating the Bills, the Chiefs beat the Los Angeles Raiders 24–21 at home on October 28…on *Monday Night Football.*

75 Arrowhead Stadium, the Home of the…

There's an artist's rendering hanging in a back room of Chappell's Restaurant in North Kansas City that shows a baseball stadium and a football stadium with a funny-looking half-moon thingama-jig between the two structures.

The caption reveals architect Charles Deaton's idea for a rolling roof between what would become the Truman Sports Complex—Royals Stadium and Arrowhead.

Even aside from the rolling roof, the whole idea of two stadiums seemed preposterous. Throughout the 1960s in cities with Major League Baseball and the NFL, the rage was multi-purpose or cookie-cutter stadiums that could hold both baseball and football. And they were sprouting all over the country: Atlanta, Pittsburgh, Philadelphia, Cincinnati, and St. Louis to name a few.

In the late 1960s, the Chiefs and A's were looking for funding for new stadiums. A's owner Charlie Finley had threatened for years to leave if he didn't get one. After going to the first Super Bowl, the Chiefs needed one, too. Chiefs owner Lamar Hunt and team president Jack Steadman didn't want a cookie-cutter stadium, fearing that Finley might move the A's and they'd be stuck with a stadium that didn't fit their needs. After much politicking Jackson County voters approved $102 million in general bonds, $43 million of which would be used for the Jackson County Sports

Complex, including a rolling roof. They broke ground in July 1968 and finished four years and one month later.

With the new Sports Complex being built, many of Kansas City's signature buildings started sprouting. Kansas City International Airport was dedicated in 1972. Crown Center opened in 1973 as did Worlds of Fun. Construction of Kemper Arena began in 1973 for the NBA's Kings, and Bartle Hall opened in 1976. "All of that boom in Kansas City came from the sports complex," Steadman said. "From the point the funding was approved, everything started going crazy around here...all of a sudden, everything started moving in Kansas City in a big way."

Arrowhead wasn't completely finished when it opened in 1972 with a preseason game between the Chiefs and the St. Louis

Arrowhead Stadium provides not only one of the best home-field advantages, but also one of the NFL's best tailgating atmospheres. (AP Images)

Cardinals, but it was still quite an improvement from Municipal Stadium. Ticket prices then ranged from $6 in the end zone to $10 in the club section. "As a player, although I enjoyed playing at Municipal, Arrowhead's facilities were incredible," said Hall of Fame quarterback Len Dawson. "I think we had one commode in the locker room at Municipal. Can you imagine? At that time there weren't many good stadiums in the American Football League, but we enjoyed the switch from Municipal to Arrowhead."

The total cost of the Truman Sports Complex was $70 million, which was $37 million more than the bonds. For more than 20 years, though, the stadium in its original form worked perfectly. In the mid-1990s, the stadium went through some upgrades, including going from artificial turf to grass, expanding the concession areas, and adding video boards to the scoreboards at both ends of the stadium.

The biggest renovation to date began when Jackson County voters approved a sales tax that would bring nearly $250 million in Arrowhead upgrades. Those upgrades included a new press box, the Founder's Plaza, a new Chiefs Hall of Honor, an upgraded sound and video board, and concourses that were double the size of the 1972 version. The renovations were completed at the start of the 2010 season to a total cost of $375 million. (The Hunt family kicked in $125 million.) "We wanted to give our fans all the amenities of a first-class stadium while preserving the iconic elements of Arrowhead," Clark Hunt told *The Kansas City Star* when the "new" Arrowhead opened. "I'm delighted to say we've exceeded my loftiest expectations, and we're extremely proud to be able to show our fans the results."

The one renovation that still didn't happen is the rolling roof. Ardent football fans in Kansas City lament the fact that the Chiefs won't host a Super Bowl with an open-air stadium. In the same way that costs and construction delays forced Deaton's original idea to be scrapped, a roof idea hasn't made it very far on at least

Home of the...

You love it or you hate it. There doesn't seem to be much middle ground in the great controversy over the way Chiefs fans end the National Anthem at Arrowhead Stadium.

Since the resurgence of the Chiefs and Arrowhead Stadium under Carl Peterson in the late 1980s, Chiefs fans began substituting "Chiefs" for "brave" at the end of the Star-Spangled Banner. And most fans don't just sing "Chiefs." They shout it. During a chat with fans on ESPN.com, Hall of Fame quarterback Joe Montana wrote: "What they do with the National Anthem, wow…It's crazy."

Former Raiders kicker Joe Nedney, who was returning to Kansas City with the San Francisco 49ers in 2006, described Arrowhead to the *San Francisco Chronicle*: "It's a neat environment…Not much else goes on in that area, so Chiefs fans are very enthusiastic. One thing I remember is on the last phrase of the National Anthem instead of 'Home of the Brave,' they say 'Home of the Chiefs!'"

Although the song revision has lasted for nearly a generation, it's not popular with everyone. Kansas Jayhawks fans in Allen Fieldhouse adopted the "Home of the Chiefs" chant, but in November 2013, Kansas basketball coach Bill Self urged fans to stop altering the ending. (Fans do the same at K-State and Missouri games, too.) *The Kansas City Star* sports columnist Vahe Gregorian wrote about it three months earlier, calling the insertion of the Chiefs "tacky and disrespectful."

If you're more in line with Self and Gregorian, you could follow the lead of actor/comedian Rob Riggle, who served 23 years in the Marines (nine years active duty and 14 years in the reserves before retiring on January 1, 2013, as Lieutenant Colonel). "I usually sing 'Home of the Brave' and then scream Chiefs right after that," said Riggle, who grew up in Overland Park, Kansas, and graduated from Shawnee Mission South. "Think of it as an echo of what everyone in the stadium just screamed. It usually gets a chuckle or two…But that's a tricky one because I love the U.S.A. and I love the Chiefs."

two other occasions. In 1984 the Jackson County Sports Authority looked into various ways to add a fabric roof before deciding it was too expensive. Then in 2005 the NFL announced the Chiefs would host a Super Bowl—presumably in 2015 or '17—*if* voters approved a rolling roof as part of the renovations. Evidently, $200 million was too hefty of a price for a Super Bowl.

76 Art Still

The kids call him the dictator—or at least that's what he says. He jokes a lot, so you aren't completely sure if that is indeed a nickname. Assuming a tyrannical role might be understandable.

After all, it isn't easy raising two or three children. Or even one for that matter. But try 11. That's the life for former Chiefs defensive end Art Still. "Before we got married, we were talking about the future and kids," Still said, remembering the conversation with his then-future wife Liz. "She said she wanted a big family and to live in the country. I told her I could make that happen. I wanted 15 [children], and she wanted 10."

So they settled for 11—six boys and five girls—with 19 years separating the oldest and the youngest. "They say you know you're too old when you're in diapers the same time as your child," Still said. "The most challenging part is the kids think they're smarter than you, so you have to prove them wrong."

A dedicated father, Art Still used to be devastating to opposing offenses. Chiefs fans remember Still as an aggressive player who racked up 72.5 sacks, 992 tackles, and 11 fumble recoveries from 1978–87. During Still's Chiefs Hall of Fame career, which began as the second overall pick of the 1978 draft out of the University of

Kentucky, he led Kansas City in sacks six times and was a two-time team MVP.

One highlight came early in his career when Still sacked Oakland Raiders quarterback Ken Stabler four times in one contest. The rival Raiders were actually Still's favorite team growing up. "To always admire somebody like Stabler and then to be laying on top of him after a sack, whispering sweet nothings to him," Still said. "That game brings back some unique memories."

But the games and accolades really aren't what pop into Still's mind when he thinks back to those days. "As an athlete you think that if you played football, you'll think of the games first," Still said, "but I think of the relationships and the people that I met, not only on the field but away from it. I think of people like Lamar Hunt and Walt Corey, who coached me on defense throughout my career. I think of players that I played with like Walter White. And then I think of guys who played before me like Bobby Bell and Buck Buchanan. You develop great relationships with guys that almost become a part of your family."

In 1988 Chiefs traded Still to Buffalo, where he played for two seasons before retiring. He remained near Buffalo until the late 1990s, when he moved his family back to the Kansas City area. "I wanted to start a business and I figured that if I was going to start one, I wanted to be where I had some contacts and a place that had good people," Still said.

77 Watch *Chiefs Kingdom*

Most professional sports teams these days have video production crews that handle video board entertainment as well as various features on the team's website. The Chiefs' version of this is appropriately named 65 Toss Power Trap Productions (after Hank Stram's famed play call), and it's taken in-house video production one step further with the development of a television show called *Chiefs Kingdom*. "The Hunt family and the entire *Chiefs Kingdom* have created a culture rich in tradition and ripe for storytelling," said Jodain Massad, 65 TPT's director of production, to kcchiefs.com. "*Chiefs Kingdom* is dedicated to telling those stories."

In 2011, 65 Toss Power Trap Productions became the first NFL in-house production crew to win a medal at the New York Festivals. In 2014, 65 TPT won its fifth consecutive New York Festivals world medal. Before rolling your eyes about a film award that may be unfamiliar, entries for the New York Festivals come from around the world and include networks ESPN and TNT, among others. Additionally, 65 TPT has won 21 Emmy awards in three years. "We sincerely believe we have the best fans in the league," Massad said. "We are inspired to celebrate their stories and the stories of their favorite team in a manner they can't find anywhere else."

Haven't watched any of the *Chiefs Kingdom* episodes yet? No problem. You can catch up through the Chiefs website. The show features incredible Chiefs fans throughout the country, but some of the more notable episodes have been:

- "Joplin," which focused on fans who were impacted by the devastating tornadoes in Joplin, Missouri in May 2011.

- "Paul Rudd and Rob Riggle," which, as you may have guessed, features actors Paul Rudd and Rob Riggle, who are both Kansas City area natives and die-hard Chiefs fans.
- "Chappell's," which featured Chappell's Restaurant and Sports Museum, a favorite hangout for Chiefs players and fans in North Kansas City.
- "Lt. Col Birdwell," who was a 9/11 survivor at the Pentagon. The moving show relives his memories of 9/11 and all of the incredible things that have happened because of his love for the Chiefs.
- "David Koechner," an actor who has starred in movies, including *Anchorman*, and who happens to be a huge Chiefs fan.
- "Jim Birdsall," who is a Kansas City native and a longtime Chiefs fan. Oh, he happens to be one of the most recognizable voices for NFL Films, too.

Chiefs Kingdom, along with other programs from 65 Toss Power Trap Productions, is must-see TV for all Chiefs fans. If you don't want to wait for the shows to hit the team's website, the shows are seen weekly in more than 10 markets throughout Kansas, Missouri, Iowa, Arkansas, and Oklahoma.

78 Steve Bono

If there's one game Steve Bono could redo out of the 88 in which he played, it'd be the playoff game on January 7, 1996—Kansas City and Indianapolis. "It's the worst loss I've ever had; I definitely struggled with it," Bono said by phone from the San Francisco area, where he's lived since he first started playing for the 49ers in

1989. "I threw three interceptions, we missed three field goals, and the weather was bad. We still should've won. We were running the ball well, but then all of a sudden, we started throwing it more for some reason. We put in different protections because of things Indianapolis was doing defensively. We didn't stick with what got us there."

So, instead of a trip to the AFC Championship Game, Bono ended his best NFL season—and one of the best regular seasons for a Chiefs franchise—with a 10–7 loss. "That Indy playoff game is something I think about more often than I would like," Bono said. "It is the one regret I have about my career—that I never got another chance to prove myself in a playoff game."

With Bono starting at quarterback for an entire season for the first time in his career after sitting behind Hall of Famer Joe Montana in both San Francisco and Kansas City, the Chiefs weren't expected to do much in 1995. But after winning its first three games and losing one at Cleveland, Kansas City rattled off seven straight victories. Overall, the Chiefs won the AFC West with a 13–3 record and secured home-field advantage for the playoffs.

One of the most memorable plays that season came the week after the loss to the Browns. Playing in a scoreless game at Arizona, Bono went to the sideline to talk with head coach Marty Schottenheimer during a timeout in the second quarter. Schottenheimer started to get a "funny grin" on his face. Then he called for a bootleg. "I must've had that same funny grin because when I got back to the huddle, I didn't call the play," Bono said. "I just looked at everybody and shook my head. They knew. We had worked on it three or four times in practice that week. Usually things like that don't necessarily work because you can't set up the defense to do exactly what the opponent will do. It's amazing it happened like that."

It could not have transpired more perfectly, as Bono, who was not exactly fleet of foot, ran for a 76-yard touchdown. It was the longest touchdown run by a quarterback in NFL history. (Bono is now tied for third. Pittsburgh's Kordell Stewart broke the record in '96 with an 80-yard run; Washington's Robert Griffin III tied Bono's feat—or feet—in 2012; Oakland's Terrelle Pryor set a new record in '13 with a 93-yarder against the Steelers.)

Bono had not seen the broadcast TV version of that play until he came across an unmarked VHS tape in his home office a few years ago. He popped in the tape, and it happened to be that play. "I just started laughing," he said. "It was so ridiculous. It was hysterical. [Tackle] Joe Valerio was out in front, pulling me along, yelling at me to hurry up. But there was no one else even close."

K.C.-S.F. Quarterback Connection

The Chiefs seem to like those San Francisco 49ers quarterbacks. Steve Bono was the third in the long list of former-49ers-quarterbacks-turned-Chiefs that began in 1993.

1998: Chiefs signed Steve DeBerg, who played for the 49ers from 1978–80. Apparently, San Francisco decided it would rather start some guy named Joe Montana.

1993: Montana, safety David Whitmore, and a third-round draft pick in 1994 came to the Chiefs in exchange for Kansas City's first-round pick in '93. The Chiefs used that third-round pick (92nd overall) on wide receiver Lake Dawson. (The 49ers used the '93 first-round pick to trade down and select former Kansas defensive lineman Dana Stubblefield.)

1994: Chiefs traded their 1995 fourth-round pick to the 49ers for Bono.

1997: Elvis Grbac left San Francisco as a free agent to sign with Kansas City.

2013: New Chiefs coach Andy Reid and general manager John Dorsey acquired Alex Smith from the 49ers in exchange for that year's second-round pick and a conditional pick (which turned out to be the second round) in 2014.

The 1995 season was by far Bono's best. That year Bono, who played for seven teams during his 14-year pro career, threw for 3,121 yards and 21 touchdowns. He received his only Pro Bowl selection that season.

In November 1995, though, *Sports Illustrated* ran a feature on Bono. In it were these two sentences: "Bono puts down his micro-brewed beer and changes the subject to his favorite topic: food. Last year he joked that 'the worst restaurant in San Francisco is better than the best restaurant in Kansas City.'"

Needless to say, proud midwesterners weren't happy with the quote. When asked via email if he regretted that statement or if it was taken out of context, Bono replied: "The restaurant quote was all [*SI* writer] Michael Silver. Unfortunately he quoted me as saying it. He has admitted to me and apologizes for it to this day. People that know me know I love to eat, and we enjoyed plenty of good restaurants in K.C."

As Bono thinks about his time in Kansas City, one person who comes to mind is the late Lamar Hunt. "He was just a very kind, gentle, down-to-earth person," said Bono, who has spent the majority of his time since retiring from football in 1999 in the financial field. "He'd come to the locker room and talk to each player, genuinely wanting to know how we were doing. I had an opportunity to be around him since playing there, and it was incredible to see how he was a great man and a great family."

In spite of the one game he wishes he could have back, as fans remember Bono's three years in Kansas City—and his whole career for that matter—he hopes they think of him as a winner. "Statistically, I was never great; I was always okay," he said, "but I'd like to think that not only in my NFL career, but also in high school and college, that I could get it done."

79 Curtis McClinton

Curtis McClinton spent eight seasons for the Chiefs from 1962–69, following a solid collegiate career at the University of Kansas. During that time he played on all three AFL championship teams, including the two Super Bowl squads.

His resume, however, reads more like that of a lifelong business leader instead of an eight-year pro athlete. Since his playing career ended with the Chiefs following Super Bowl IV in 1970, McClinton has received his master's and doctorate degrees; been Amtrak's national director of real estate management and marketing; worked for the Department of Commerce, overseeing economic development for cities and counties throughout the U.S.; served as the deputy mayor for economic development in Washington, D.C.; and was the founding president of the Black Economic Union of Greater Kansas City, which ushered in the 18th and Vine district. There have been many other endeavors—all geared toward helping others. "My mother was a teacher, and my father was a businessman and Kansas state senator," said McClinton of two of his main influences. "I was very blessed to know at a young age that education was very important. I've converted the education into knowledge and the knowledge into the ability to interact with all sorts of people."

After working in Spain and Jamaica in international development, McClinton, a Wichita, Kansas, native, moved back to Kansas City in 1992 and found a niche in the investment banking and development market.

Of course, McClinton is best known for what he accomplished during his stint as a fullback/tight end for the Chiefs, which included being selected as the American Football League Rookie of the Year in 1962 and receiving three invitations to the AFL All-Star Game. That came on the heels of his time at KU during which he was an All-Big 8 football selection and three-time high hurdle champion in track.

After the Chiefs moved from Dallas in 1963, McClinton scored the franchise's first touchdown in Kansas City, a 73-yard run during a preseason game against Buffalo. A few years later, he scored the AFL's first touchdown in a Super Bowl, on a 7-yard pass play from Len Dawson. The touchdowns, though, aren't what McClinton wants fans to remember. "My great love in football was hitting and defense," McClinton said. "The greatest honor I had was protecting and defending Lenny. I loved to block; I loved to hit. I tried to be the best blocker and hitter in the league."

As a result of what he accomplished on the field, the Chiefs inducted McClinton into the team's Hall of Fame in 1995. He's also a member of both the Kansas Sports Hall of Fame (2003) and Missouri Sports Hall of Fame (2007).

When looking back on his Chiefs career, though, McClinton diverts attention from himself and credits his coach, the late Hank Stram. "He was a teacher and he had the capacity to build his teaching and convey his philosophy with wit," McClinton said. "He had humor, but it had some bite to it. You didn't know if you should be perturbed or if it was a challenge. I always admired that about him. I'm just thankful for God's gifts and opportunities to play for Coach Stram and a great owner, Lamar Hunt, with good players and a wonderful franchise."

McClinton, who also is an accomplished singer, has performed in France, Spain, China, and Africa and sung the national anthem before Chiefs games. Undoubtedly, in life and in football, Curtis McClinton struck all the right notes.

80 Anatomy of a Great Fourth-Quarter Comeback

Quarterback Trent Green told me that the 2003 Chiefs had a feeling that they would win every game, that someone on defense and special teams could make a game-changing play that would give the ball to the high-scoring offense. And they nearly did win every game that year, finishing the regular season at 13–3 before losing to Indianapolis in the AFC playoffs. That confidence began building in Weeks 4 and 5 with fourth-quarter wins against the Baltimore Ravens and Denver Broncos. It reached a crescendo in Week 6 at Green Bay's historic Lambeau Field. The Chiefs trailed the Packers by 17 points, 31–14, in the fourth quarter.

With a short field early in the fourth, Kansas City went 42 yards and scored on a 1-yard run by Priest Holmes to make it 31–21. On Green Bay's next drive, on third and 6, Jerome Woods picked off a Brett Favre pass and returned it 79 yards for a Pick-6. Now it was 31–28. Three minutes later and with 5:41 left in regulation, Morten Andersen kicked a 34-yard field goal that tied the game at 31. By this point every Cheesehead was stunned, but the Chiefs weren't surprised because they expected to win the game. The comeback was sparked by Green, who completed 9-of-16 passes for 159 yards in the fourth quarter. He ended the day with 400 yards on 27-of-45 passing. Since it was one of the biggest passing days in Chiefs history and is tied for the biggest fourth-quarter comeback in team history, it seems only appropriate to let Green take you through overtime.

"We passed so much in the fourth quarter that as we started overtime with the ball, our first nine plays were to Priest for a run, and he was doing the job. Nine plays and 41 yards later, we were at the Green Bay 31. At that point we faced third and 3. The Packers

Diagramming a 99-yard Touchdown

At Arrowhead Stadium on December 22, 2002, quarterback Trent Green found receiver Marc Boerigter for a 99-yard touchdown play against the San Diego Chargers. The play tied an NFL record and set a Chiefs record for the longest play from scrimmage. (The second longest for the Chiefs was 93 yards from Mike Livingston to Otis Taylor, who then lateralled to Robert Holmes, against the Miami Dolphins on October 19, 1969. The longest run from scrimmage is 91 yards by Jamaal Charles in 2012 against New Orleans.) The Green to Boerigter play, though, was a fortuitous situation for the Chiefs. We'll let Green describe:

"That was a crazy play because we went to our big personnel group—Priest Holmes and Tony Richardson in the backfield, Jason Dunn and Tony Gonzalez at tight end, and then Boerigter—as part of our short-yardage package. When you see that personnel group as a defense, you're sure we're going to run. Plus since we were backed up at our own 1, it normally would be a run. Our plan was to go to Gonzalez for 12 to 15 yards up the middle to give us some space. Boerigter was going deep as a decoy to keep the safeties and corners back. It was a play-action pass, so the two tight ends were lined up on my right side. The order of my read was Dunn, Gonzalez, and then Priest. I was going to look at Dunn to draw the underneath coverage, which would leave Gonzalez open.

"On the snap of the ball, though, San Diego safety, Rodney Harrison, who was very aggressive, started chasing Tony. I realized that by chasing Tony, Rodney left the whole center of the field open. I knew there was another safety, so it depended on Marc's angle. As the play was designed, Marc's landmark was the middle of the field and straight toward the goal post, which would've put the free safety too close for me to throw. Instead, Marc flattened the angle of his post route from the uprights to the far numbers. After the play fake, when I saw all of that happening, I looked at Tony to keep Rodney committed and then threw it out to a wide-open Boerigter at the numbers. He caught it around the 50 and then took off. (continued on next page)

"Believe me, that was not supposed to be a big yardage gain. In two years we probably ran that 30 to 40 times in practice. Never once did we throw that ball. It was either option one, two, or three. But I used to tell our guys, never make the read for me. You run as hard as you can, as fast as you can, and get to your spot. The defense will dictate where I'm going with the ball. Fortunately, Marc bought into that. We got that touchdown against the Chargers because Marc was hustling, and the line did a great job of holding their blocks."

came with an all-out blitz when we were going to pass, and all I could do was throw it away. Then Morten's field-goal attempt was blocked.

"On Green Bay's second play after taking possession, starting on their own 39, Ahman Green ran the ball, but Jerome Woods knocked it loose, and Mike Maslowski recovered it at our 49. Since Priest had just run the ball nine straight times, minus the last incomplete pass, we called for 989 Pump, which was double-pumps on the outside with a play-action to Priest. On that play, the receivers would go about 10 or 12 yards, make a stutter move to slow down the defenders, and then go. As with much of our offense, that play was about match-ups.

"Earlier in the game Green Bay's starting cornerback had gotten hurt, so he was in and out of the game the rest of the time. As I walked to the line for this play, they had a young player, Bhawoh Jue, covering Eddie [Kennison]. I couldn't believe it! I knew at that moment I wanted to go that way with the ball. While I went through my cadence, their strong safety, who was to my left, started creeping into the box. In our pass protection on that play, if he comes, we don't have anyone to block him, giving him a clean shot to me. When Casey Wiegmann snapped the ball and I dropped back, I did a quick check to the left side to see if the safety was coming. If he was, I'd have to get rid of the ball quickly.

As the play unfolded, I realized he was in the box to protect against the run. With the strong safety in the box, I knew we had man-to-man coverage and, sure enough, Eddie stuttered and blew by Jue and I hit him for a 51-yard touchdown."

That gave the Chiefs the 40–34 win and improved Kansas City's record to 6–0. The Chiefs wouldn't lose until Week 11, on November 16 at Cincinnati, 24–19.

81 Psycho

Sherrill Headrick's nickname of "Psycho" was coined after he suffered two severed vertebrae from a pregame collision in 1960. "I played a game right after they say I broke my neck," Headrick said. "It sounds worse than it was, but I still had no business playing. When Lenny Dawson first came to the team [in 1962], he said, 'You played with a broken neck? You're psycho!' From that moment on, that was my nickname."

Headrick, the Texans/Chiefs middle linebacker from 1960–67 not only left it all on the field, but also in the locker room, considering he would get so worked up before every game that the team wouldn't take the field until Headrick vomited.

Headrick would also get guys loosened up, doing anything to get a laugh from his teammates. One of the best stories to demonstrate both Headrick's pain tolerance and appreciation for a laugh came after one of his two hemorrhoid operations. Both times he had the operation on Thursday and then played three days later. "I'll never forget after one of those games he came out of the locker room, and he had the ring that he was supposed to be sitting on," said Bert Coan, who played with Headrick at Texas Christian and then later with the Chiefs, "on top of his head like a hat. It was hilarious."

Then there was the game against Denver in 1962. The Texans needed to beat the Broncos to have a shot at the playoffs. Headrick hadn't played because of back spasms that were giving him so much pain that he barely could trot. The Broncos were moving down the field with a trap play up the middle, a play they ran rarely with Headrick on the field. "Hank [Stram] came over and asked if I could go in," Headrick said. "I told him I didn't think I could play, but Denver didn't know that, so I went out there, hoping nobody would run over me. They stopped running the play, and we ended up winning the game. A lot of what I did in my career was stupidity, but some of it wasn't so bad after all."

Playing with myriad significant injuries is why his Psycho nickname is so appropriate. "He could endure pain more than any player I played with," Coan said. "I saw him get a compound fracture of his thumb during a game. He was making a face like it hurt a little, but he just came to the sideline, the trainer taped it, and he went back in. Besides being tough, though, I would say in 1962 he was the best linebacker in professional football, AFL or NFL."

Headrick, a four-time AFL All-Star who intercepted 14 passes for the franchise, three of which he returned for touchdowns, was a small linebacker, even by 1960s standards. Although he was listed around 220 pounds, Headrick says he never got above 208. He was too small to blitz because "the offense would use a big guy to knock me down." But he studied an opponent's offense so much, he could tell within one or two plays what they were going to do. "People who know me think I was a cutup and didn't pay attention," Headrick said, "but I prided myself in watching the team that we were going to play and figuring out anything that would help me play bigger. Hank was a good coach, and we loved him, but he didn't know much about defense. So he'd ask what I thought about different plays and situations…Our coaches were very knowledgeable, but they'd listen to our ideas."

Eventually, Headrick's toughness caught up to him. He played his final season with Cincinnati in 1968 before a slipped disc ended his career at the age of 31.

Life was less than ideal for Headrick after he retired. Much of his post-playing life was spent in hospitals, including being confined to a hospital bed for his first year away from the game. Headrick had three discs removed plus replacement surgeries for his shoulders, knees, and hips. The physical ailments, which left him crippled, made it nearly impossible for Headrick to find employment. He did work at various jobs, thanks to friends, including a contract administrator for the construction of 22 fast food joints.

In October 2007 Headrick returned to Kansas City for the annual Chiefs alumni weekend. Eleven months later on September 10, 2008, Headrick lost a battle with cancer. He was 71. Perhaps sensing that uphill bout, alumni weekend was a chance to see old friends one more time. It certainly served as a reminder to him of why he endured so much pain. "It's amazing how close we've been all these years," he said in November 2007, a few weeks after alumni weekend. "Everyone says we didn't make any money back then. Shoot, I was afraid they'd realize that I would pay them to let me play. I loved football. Who in the world can say they had as much fun as me playing this game?"

82 The Father of the Touchdown Dance

Before Jamaal Charles and his touchdown celebration of dusting off the "haters," you had Johnnie Morton and the worm and Tony Gonzalez and his slam dunk of the football over the goal post. Before Tony G there was Neil Smith, who'd celebrate a sack with a home run swing. Before all of them, though, was Elmo Wright.

During the first game of the 1969 college football season, University of Houston's outstanding receiver caught a pass against University of Florida defensive back Steve Tannen. As Wright took a couple steps, Tannen dove and grabbed Wright's feet. Instinctively, Wright started high-stepping to break from Tannen's grasp. It worked, as Wright broke free and continued high-stepping all the way to the end zone. "It felt so good that I did an accelerated version of the high step," Wright told *The New York Times* in 2005. When he returned to the sideline, his teammates were telling him how he just "danced" into the end zone. Before that Wright spiked the ball when he reached the end zone, which the NCAA—being the NCAA—outlawed.

The Chiefs picked Wright in the first round of the 1971 NFL Draft. That year he enjoyed the best season of his pro career, when he caught 26 passes for 528 yards and three touchdowns. As he reached the end zone upon scoring one of those touchdowns, Wright began the high-stepping move he used against Florida two years earlier, but he wasn't breaking away from a defender nipping at his heels. He was dancing in the end zone.

From that point on, Wright and the NFL wouldn't be the same. Wright's high-stepping move became his signature touchdown celebration. Unfortunately, he didn't have many opportunities to display it. Wright played in 51 NFL games during five seasons (four with the Chiefs) and scored seven touchdowns. He spent the last season of his career with Houston and New England.

Over time, touchdown celebrations became more elaborate and outrageous. And although some players have gone to extremes to make sure the attention is on them after a touchdown—see former Chiefs receiver Joe Horn, who hid a cell phone in the goal post to use as a celebration prop while playing for New Orleans—Wright tried to offer an explanation to the *Houston Chronicle* in 2007. "People would say, 'Why do you dance?'" Wright said. "The bottom line is: when you put out that kind of effort, to me it was natural to emote. I would simply ask someone: what is it in your life that you feel so passionate about that once you accomplish it, it made you feel like dancing?…And then when it's over, 60,000 people are cheering. That's an unusual situation to be in. And just imagine: before you do it, you just went running down the field [with] people trying to knock your head off."

Wright may not be one of the best Chiefs of all time, but whenever the history of the touchdown celebration is mentioned, you'll find Elmo Wright and the Chiefs.

83 The Tomahawk Chop

Whether you love it, hate it, or are ambivalent toward it, the tomahawk chop has been a tradition at Arrowhead Stadium since the early 1990s. In case you've missed it, the chop is basically an arm swing in the same motion as using a tomahawk. Keep your palm in, extend your elbow, bring your arm up to your shoulder…and make a downward chopping motion. Of course, it's accompanied by a war chant.

Florida State introduced the sports world to the tomahawk chop in 1984. It remained there, peacefully, until "Prime Time" Deion Sanders started playing for the Atlanta Braves. In Atlanta during the spring of 1991, a few Braves fans began a chant and chop when Sanders went to the plate. The whole stadium soon caught on. Former Royals general manager John Schuerholz, who was with the Braves in a similar role at the time, perpetuated the chant by encouraging the use of the song and the chant more often. (After all, it helped give the Braves a tremendous home-field advantage at Fulton County Stadium and not only when Sanders was hitting.) That season the Braves went from worst to first and eventually lost in the World Series to Minnesota.

As the Braves were making their run toward the postseason that fall, the chop became prevalent at Arrowhead Stadium. It became a prominent national symbol of the Chiefs and Arrowhead during the *Monday Night Football* blowout victory in October against the Buffalo Bills.

So why Arrowhead and the Chiefs? Was it a mockery of Native Americans? Was it the Chiefs ripping off Schuerholz's Braves? The answer to the last two is no. The answer to the first is somewhat simple.

The Northwest Missouri State marching band was performing at Arrowhead during a Chiefs game in November 1990. The band, which was directed by Florida State alum Al Sergel, started the chant. Coach Marty Schottenheimer and the Chiefs players loved it. And it stuck.

Since then there's been a love-it or hate-it type relationship with the chop and chant. The people who love it generally think it makes Arrowhead more ominous for visiting teams. On the flip side, some people find the chop annoying and as degrading to Native Americans.

Amid complaints and protests by Native Americans at Arrowhead in 1992, the Chiefs and their sponsors stopped encouraging the

Arrowhead's Guinness Attempt

For years Chiefs fans have been saying that Arrowhead Stadium is the loudest in the NFL. In 2013 the Chiefs wanted to officially prove that to the world. After Seattle broke the record at CenturyLink Field in September against San Francisco with 136.6 decibels, Kansas City fans set out to break the record in October against Oakland. And they succeeded. The Chiefs flew in the same *Guinness World Records* official from the Seahawks-49ers game for the Raiders contest. The Arrowhead scoreboard showed the decibel level of Chiefs fans, which reached a level of 137.5. (That's close to the equivalent of a jet engine at 100 feet.) "They destroyed any Premier League hopes of attaining this record, I can tell you that, and I'm a Brit that loves the Premier League," Philip Robertson, the Guinness official, said after the game. "It was extraordinary."

It also happened to be short-lived. On an early December Monday night against New Orleans, Seattle reclaimed the title as Seahawk fans hit 137.6. (Chiefs fans like to argue that—besides not being a completely wide-open stadium like Arrowhead—CenturyLink Field also pumps in some-artificial noise.)

That wasn't the first time that the Seahawks and Chiefs have been embroiled in a record noise attempt. In October 2000 the Chiefs attempted to set the "on-site" NFL attendance record during a Monday night game against Seattle. The plan was to fill Arrowhead and use Kauffman Stadium as a second site, showing the game on the video board. Only 4,391, however, went to Kauffman to watch the game. The total between Arrowhead and Kauffman ended up at 82,893, about 8,000 short of the record. At least the Chiefs won the game 24–17 and set the team attendance record, which still stands.

chop. But that's not to say they completely disallowed it. "We are just more or less discontinuing the promotion of it," Bob Moore, Chiefs longtime director of public relations, said at the time. "We will not censor the public."

The Chiefs stopped playing the Tomahawk Chop background music during games at Arrowhead, but the fans kept doing the motion anyway and singing the chant. The stadium ended up reinstituting the music, which still plays today, and it likely will remain a controversial tradition for the foreseeable future at Arrowhead Stadium.

84 Chris Burford

Chris Burford wasn't the speediest receiver, but he had good hands and was particularly adept at hauling in receptions along the sideline. "There's nothing I ever did that would make me jump up and down," he said. "I had a good career and I know where I fit in the scheme of things. I'm just proud of the fact that I was one of the original guys in the AFL, and the league made it. A number of us contributed, in whatever minor ways, to the league's success. To see what it is today, and knowing that if we hadn't done a decent job early on that it wouldn't be as strong as it is today, is satisfying."

When he retired in 1967, Burford had played in 103 games, caught 391 passes for 5,505 yards, and scored 55 touchdowns. He was inducted into the Chiefs Hall of Fame in 1975. For seven seasons Burford was a sure-handed—oftentimes outstanding—receiver. His best season was 1962, when he caught a team-record 12 touchdown passes. Due to an injury, however, he missed the team's final three games of the season.

Today, Burford lives in Reno, Nevada, with Cathi, his wife of more than 30 years. Burford spent 40 years (1970–2010) as an attorney and actually earned his law degree at UMKC while he was with the Chiefs. At the end of his playing career, he also dabbled in television as a color commentator for NBC and as the sports director/sports anchor at WDAF-TV. "Lenny [Dawson] had started at Channel 9 about six months before I did," said Burford, who was at WDAF from 1967–69. "I went down to the station and said, 'Lenny's doing a great job over at 9, and I think I could do something for you at 4.' They gave me a shot. Television definitely wasn't as competitive back then."

After setting an NCAA record at Stanford with 61 receptions in 1959, Burford was a first-round draft choice of the Chiefs (then the Dallas Texans) in 1960. Despite the normal high expectations for a first-round pick, Burford didn't feel as if he was under the spotlight, simply because he was joining a brand new league—the American Football League. "The big pressure wasn't on me as much as it was on the league," Burford said. "We didn't know if the league would make it or not. But our team had success with great players. Lamar [Hunt] and his people did a super job. I don't think anybody ever outmanned us."

Even though Burford has moved west, he says he wouldn't trade his time in Kansas City or with the Chiefs for anything. "I loved Kansas City," he said. "Once the team moved there, I stayed year-round. Kansas City is one of the great, undiscovered big cities in the U.S. Plus, we had some great players back in the 1960s. That's what made it fun. We never felt there was a game that we couldn't win. That's a good feeling."

85 Fantastic Fullbacks

The Chiefs have had great running back-fullback combos, but for a stretch of 15 seasons, they featured two of the NFL's best fullbacks of that era, Kimble Anders and Tony Richardson.

The Chiefs signed Anders as a free agent out of the University of Houston in 1991. After appearing in only two games that year and then rushing for only one yard during two starts in '92, Anders established himself as a top fullback during the next six seasons. Part of the turnaround for Anders was the break he received in '93, blocking for Hall of Fame running back Marcus Allen and playing with Hall of Fame quarterback Joe Montana, both of whom joined the Chiefs that year. "I watched Joe Montana when he came to Kansas City," Anders said. "Here's one of the best ever, a veteran, and he was in the back of the room taking notes and asking questions. He never stopped studying. When you see a guy like Joe doing that, what are you going to do?"

An effective blocker who was best known as a sure-handed receiver in the West Coast Offense, Anders became a three-time starting fullback in the Pro Bowl for the AFC. Though he never rushed for more than 400 yards in a single season, he finished his 10-year Chiefs career with 2,261 yards. When the Chiefs released him after the 2000 season, he had 369 receptions, which was the most ever by a Chiefs running back. He saved his best game for one of his last in a year the Chiefs were actually planning on using him as their primary runner. In the 1999 home opener against Denver, Anders—who served as the starting halfback while Richardson played fullback—ran for a career-high 142 yards. Late in the game, he suffered a season-ending Achilles injury.

He tried to make a comeback in 2000, but he couldn't get back to form. "Kimble Anders was a valuable performer on the field for the Kansas City Chiefs the past 10 seasons," president and general manager Carl Peterson said at the time. "Just as important Kimble was an active member of our community and was a fine representative of our team as a citizen off the field."

Midway through Anders' career, the Chiefs signed Richardson, another free agent, in 1995. "T-Rich" started 16 games in 1999, the year Anders injured his Achilles, and rushed for a then-career best 387 yards. The only other season in his career that eclipsed that was 2000, when he ran for 697 yards to go along with his 468 receiving yards.

When Trent Green became the Chiefs quarterback the next year, he learned quickly that he could lean on Richardson. "T-Rich is a natural leader," Green said. "He was the glue of the backfield. As much credit as Priest Holmes and Larry Johnson get, Tony was the leader in the classroom and the leader on the field in that group. He was the constant communicator with those guys. If we really needed to make sure a play happened a certain way, I'd talk to T-Rich. He carried enough respect in that huddle that he could get in guys' faces or encourage them to get them going. I could lean on him to help with that process."

Richardson signed as a free agent with Minnesota in 2006 and then played the final three years of his career with the New York Jets. All told, Richardson's longevity was amazing, as he played in 234 NFL games in 16 seasons, rushed for 1,727 yards, and had 1,543 receiving yards.

He's also been one of the most likeable and community-oriented players in Chiefs history. "I just wanted to adopt him," said former Chiefs coach Dick Vermeil, who coached Richardson for five seasons from 2001–05. "In my coaching career, he's one of the most special human beings I ever met."

86 Stram's Race Relations

Ask anyone who played for him or even knew him and you'll learn quickly that Hank Stram was as popular as they come. Out of all he did for the game, though, one of his decisions helped make him a trailblazer—at least by 1960s standards. At a time when black

Carried off the field on his players' shoulders after winning Super Bowl IV, Hank Stram also broke boundaries by signing several African Americans from Historically Black Colleges. (AP Images)

players were dotting NFL and AFL rosters, Stram selected the best players regardless of color when he became the organization's first coach in 1960. "During that period of time, there were a lot of racial issues in our country, including in football," Stram said. "We never had any trouble with that at all. To our guys race didn't make a difference. I told them whether they were black, white, or polka dotted, we just wanted winners."

America was in the midst of the civil rights movement then. So, even though some major universities had begun (albeit slowly) to integrate their football teams, most African American players went to Historically Black Colleges such as Grambling, Prairie View, Southern, and Morgan State.

That didn't matter to Stram and his staff. He wanted to win. So, they drafted and signed the best players possible. They even employed an African American, Lloyd Wells, a former sportswriter in Houston—and later a Muhammad Ali confidant—as a scout. As pro football's first full-time African American scout, Wells helped sign eight players who had All-Pro careers with the Chiefs, including Otis Taylor, Emmitt Thomas, Buck Buchanan, and Curley Culp.

In the 1965 AFL Draft, the Chiefs chose Taylor from Prairie View, Gloster Richardson from Jackson State, and Frank Pitts, who played for the Chiefs during 1965–70, from Southern. "Mack Lee

Stram's Ingenuity...or Lack Thereof

In addition to his racial tolerance, Hank Stram was known for his innovative ideas. When he went to restaurants, he would constantly be doodling plays on the napkins. "He was always thinking, always trying something," Len Dawson said.

But not all of Stram's brainstorms worked. He had timed the snap from the center to the punter, who stood 15 yards back in punting formation. From his calculations Stram had figured that Dawson would have plenty of time to get rid of the football before the rush got to him. So During a 1967 preseason game in the Los Angeles Coliseum against the Rams, Stram tried putting Dawson back there for a fake punt on fourth down.

But unlike in a normal third-down situation, the Chiefs didn't have a tight end in to block because it was a punting formation, and the Rams featured Deacon Jones on their "Fearsome Foursome" defensive line. The Hall of Fame pass rusher nearly creamed Dawson. "When I got back there, I looked to my right, and Deacon Jones was on the end for the Rams," Dawson said. "He split out in a three-point sprinter's stance and nearly beat the ball to me. I got it away quickly, but I decided that was the last time that play was going to be called. Hank always wanted to find ways to get an advantage of the opposition. That was just his personality."

Hill, who was a few years ahead of me at Southern, was the main reason I signed with Kansas City," said Pitts, a fourth-round selection. "He told me they'd sign for what I wanted. It was all new to me. I didn't know what they were paying or what I was worth, but as long as you had talent, Hank was going to get you out there. When you think about it, he was one of the first coaches who had almost a dominating team of black players."

By 1966 eight of the Chiefs' 22 starters were black. Three seasons later as the Chiefs headed for their world championship win in Super Bowl IV, the team had 23 African American players on its roster—13 of whom were starters. "Imagine if there had been no AFL and no Kansas City Chiefs," said Willie Lanier, who went to Morgan State and was one of the 13 starters in 1969. "Maybe I have to wait five years for my chance [to play in the NFL], for the chance to play middle linebacker. And five years in football is an eternity."

And that started at training camp in 1960 with one man—Hank Stram—who helped eliminate racial barriers through football. "At first [players] wouldn't even drink out of the same water buckets on the field," he said. "But after a week of banging on one another in 103-degree heat, they were drinking from the same buckets and the same dippers. It was a small sign of something much bigger about them as individuals and as a group. They were changing, learning respect for each other, and becoming a team."

87 Jovan Belcher Tragedy

His career looked bright. In 2012, his fourth professional season with the Chiefs, Jovan Belcher had started 10 of the team's 11 games at inside linebacker. A year earlier he had a career-high 120 tackles while starting all 16 games. For an undrafted free agent out of Maine, his football career was certainly off to an auspicious beginning. Off the field, Belcher was usually positive, upbeat. He made annual trips to his high school, West Babylon (New York), to deliver motivational talks. He and Kasandra Perkins, his girlfriend, had a beautiful infant daughter, Zoey.

However, in a stunning tragedy on the morning of December 1, 2012, Belcher shot Perkins 10 times, drove to the Chiefs practice facility, and killed himself in front of coach Romeo Crennell and general manager Scott Pioli. It's an incident that will haunt Crennell, Pioli, and countless others forever. "It doesn't sink in," former teammate Eric Winston said a year later. "You don't grasp immediately what happened. I went from grieving for him and mourning to anger and to frustration and just simple disbelief. When you have something like that happen, you really run the gauntlet of human emotion."

Police found Belcher sleeping in his idling Bentley in front of Perkins' apartment in the wee hours of December 1. They didn't smell alcohol, and he wasn't violent when they woke him and asked him to turn off the car and go inside. (Belcher's autopsy revealed that his blood-alcohol level at the time of his death, about five hours after police saw him, was 0.17, which is more than twice the legal limit of 0.08 in Missouri.)

At 6:45 Saturday morning, Belcher and Perkins began arguing. About an hour later at 7:50, Belcher's mom, Cheryl Shepherd, who moved in with the couple a few weeks earlier, heard gunshots. When she reached the bedroom, she saw Belcher kneeling over Perkins' body. He then kissed Perkins, Shepherd, and Zoey; apologized; and sped off toward Arrowhead, where the Chiefs scheduled a team meeting that morning.

Crennell, Pioli, and linebackers coach Gary Gibbs pleaded with Belcher to drop his gun. According to the police report, Belcher told them, "You know that I've been having some major problems at home and with my girlfriend. I need help! I wasn't able to get enough help. I appreciate everything you all have done for me with trying to help…but it wasn't enough. I have hurt my girl already and I can't go back now."

As police arrived at Arrowhead, Belcher walked toward the back of the parking lot and took his own life. A year later on December 31, 2013, Shepherd filed a wrongful-death lawsuit against the Chiefs. The lawsuit states that Belcher was subjected to "repetitive head trauma" as a player, and the Chiefs didn't take proper precautions. She asked for $15,000 in damages. Chronic traumatic encephalopathy (CTE) is a degenerative neurological condition that has been linked to concussions and various problems for various athletes but particularly current and former NFL players.

Meanwhile, Zoey's custody was awarded to Sophie Perkins, a cousin of Kasandra Perkins, after a short custody battle between the two families. Sophie Perkins is the sister of Whitey Charles, Jamaal Charles' wife. "[Belcher's] daughter and my daughter were born on the same day," said former Chiefs defensive back Javier Arenas, "so I always want to be there for my daughter. Be a better parent. Not that he wasn't, it's just the situation."

88 Revolving Coaching Door

Before Andy Reid became the head coach before the 2013 season, the Chiefs had only four head coaches who lasted at least five seasons: Hank Stram (1960–74), Marv Levy (1978–82), Marty Schottenheimer (1989–98), and Dick Vermeil (2001–05). Those five coaches have chapters throughout this book. With the exception of those five, plus Paul Wiggin and Andy Reid, whose first season was 2013, here are the others who have coached the franchise.

Paul Wiggin (1975–77): It's always tough to be the first coach after a legend. Paul Wiggin might've been better off had he not been Hank Stram's successor, but the Chiefs did what many pro teams do when one coach is fired: hire the opposite. Wiggin— low key, unassuming, and humble—definitely was the antithesis of Stram. Compounded by years of questionable draft picks, the Chiefs were a bad mix of too old and too young during Stram's final three years. Only five players from the previous six drafts— which included a convicted felon—were on the roster when the Chiefs hired Wiggin. Even home attendance during Stram's final three seasons, which happened to be the first three seasons in the new Arrowhead Stadium, had dropped from more than 800,000 to less than 600,000. That's what Wiggin inherited in 1975. Kansas City lost its first three games in 1975 before winning three straight, including wins over Oakland and Denver. But late in the year, quarterback Mike Livingston suffered a season-ending knee injury, and the Chiefs lost their last four games of another 5–9 season. After another 5–9 season in '76, the Chiefs got off to a horrible start in '77, losing their first five games. They then won at San Diego before losing to Cleveland. Two days after the Browns game, owner Lamar Hunt announced that the Chiefs fired Wiggin.

The Chiefs players didn't like the decision with many crying when they heard the news. The players went so far as releasing a statement that read that they were "shocked and saddened with what has happened here today. Every man on this football team feels a deep sense of guilt for the actions that were taken. It is our fault that we lost a fine man and a great individual—Paul Wiggin. One of the great crimes in life is to have someone else suffer the consequences of your own actions. We feel this is the case today."

Tom Bettis (1977): Perhaps in hopes of not alienating all of their players with the firing of Paul Wiggin after a 1–6 start in 1977, the Chiefs hired Tom Bettis, a longtime Stram and Wiggin assistant, as the interim coach. Bettis, who had been with the Chiefs for more than 11 years under Stram and Wiggin, originally wasn't going to take the job because of his friendship with Wiggin until the former coach suggested otherwise. "You're 43 years old, and I think you've got to take this chance," Wiggin told Bettis. After 11½ years with the Chiefs as an assistant, Wiggin's tenure was about finished. The Chiefs won their first game, 20–10 over Green Bay, under Bettis but then lost the last six games of the '77 season. Kansas City finished with a then-franchise-worst 2–12 record. Bettis and the entire coaching staff were fired. "The circumstances were not very good," Bettis said. "If I had to do it over, I probably wouldn't do it."

John Mackovic (1983–86): After 11 consecutive seasons without a playoff berth and three straight defensive-minded head coaches, the Chiefs hired Dallas Cowboys quarterbacks coach John Mackovic as Marv Levy's replacement in February 1983. "We feel John is the most outstanding young coach in professional football," team president Jack Steadman said during Mackovic's introductory press conference. If that's the case, pickings for young coaches were slim in 1983.

With Mackovic as head coach, the Chiefs selected quarterback Todd Blackledge with their first pick in the 1983 NFL Draft, but Blackledge never produced on the NFL level. Perhaps the same could be said of Mackovic. After finishing near the bottom of the division for his first three years, Mackovic led the Chiefs to a 10–6 record and playoff berth, where they lost to the New York Jets. Mackovic, who went 30–34 as Chiefs head coach, was fired after the season, partially because of a player revolt, which leads to…

Frank Gansz (1987–88): An odd chain of events led to the hiring of Frank Gansz as head coach in 1987. Defensive coordinator Walt Corey, who helped the Chiefs become one of the NFL's top defenses in '86, was offered a job with Buffalo. Gansz, who had been assistant head coach and special teams coach under Mackovic, announced shortly thereafter, on January 7, 1987, that he was going to resign and pursue other opportunities, presumably a head coaching job. So the two guys in charge of the defense and special teams—the two best parts of the Chiefs at the time—were leaving. After hearing the shocking news that Gansz was leaving, eight players met with Lamar Hunt and Jack Steadman at the home of players' rep Nick Lowery to question the direction of the team. A few hours later, Mackovic was fired. Two days later Gansz was not only rehired but was announced as the new head coach. "I never wanted to harm John Mackovic," Gansz said. "When I resigned at that time, I was under the impression everything was stable and set."

Hunt said later that the meeting with the players was not the sole reason for firing Mackovic and hiring Gansz. "If I could characterize that meeting, it would be that it was extremely positive for the Kansas City Chiefs. Nobody in that room took an anti-John Mackovic stance," Hunt said. "The meeting was not a decisive factor in my decision, up or down." (Incidentally, Mackovic faced a similar situation in 2003, when the University of Arizona complained about Mackovic to the administration. Five games into the next season, he was fired.) As much as the players liked Gansz (and probably didn't like Mackovic), they weren't able to carry the momentum from '86 into '87. During two seasons under Gansz, the Chiefs went 8–22–1. At the end of the 1988 season, Steadman resigned as president, general manager Jim Schaaf was fired, and the Chiefs hired Carl Peterson as president and general manager. Peterson fired Gansz and hired former Cleveland Browns coach Marty Schottenheimer.

Gunther Cunningham (1999–2000): Perhaps more than any other coach in Chiefs history, Gunther Cunningham paid his dues before becoming a head coach in the NFL. After spending 30 years in various coaching jobs at the college and pro levels—the last 18 as an assistant in the NFL—Cunningham, who'd been Kansas City's defensive coordinator for four seasons under Schottenheimer, became the Chiefs head coach on January 22, 1999, just 11 days after Schottenheimer resigned. "I think this last season the Chiefs lost their way a little," Cunningham said of Kansas City's 7–9 record in 1998. "It's like walking in a forest, and the Chiefs took the wrong path." As popular as Cunningham was with players and other coaches, the Chiefs still struggled to find the right path. After a respectable 9–7 rookie season, good for second in the AFC West, the Chiefs went 7–9 in 2000. To make matters worse, they lost six of their last eight games. Peterson made the difficult decision to fire Cunningham. By the time the news of Cunningham's departure had gotten out, it was rumored that Dick Vermeil was set to become the team's next head coach.

Herm Edwards (2006–08): Herman Edwards and his famous "you play to win the game" mantra came to Kansas City in 2006 to replace Dick Vermeil. Edwards was familiar with the Chiefs, having served as the defensive backs coach in 1993–94 under Schottenheimer. Evidently, Edwards couldn't convince his Chiefs that they played "to win the game" because, with the exception of a 9–7 campaign in 2006, Kansas City didn't win much. During his next two seasons, the Chiefs went 6–26. Their 2–14 mark in '08 represented the least amount of wins by a Chiefs team since going 2–12 in 1977. Edwards had trouble finding the right quarterback. His main option that year was Tyler Thigpen after Damon Huard and Brodie Croyle went down with injuries.

On January 23, 2009, new president and general manager Scott Pioli fired Edwards. "This is going to be a very good football team," Edwards said in his statement. "The support of Chiefs fans across the country has been tremendous. They are truly passionate about their football team. Chiefs fans will be proud to cheer for this team for many years to come." With the departure of Edwards, the rumor mill began spinning immediately toward former Denver coach Mike Shanahan. The Chiefs went a different direction for 2009.

Todd Haley (2009–11): When he was introduced on February 6, 2009, as Edwards' replacement, Todd Haley seemed like a good fit. Although he hadn't been a head coach before, he had good bloodlines. His father, Dick, was Pittsburgh's director of player personnel for 20 years, including the Steelers' dynasty of the 1970s. And most recently Todd was the offensive coordinator for an Arizona team that lost in Super Bowl XLIII. It became apparent over time, however, that Haley and general manager Scott Pioli weren't on the same page. They got along as well as a fox and a chicken. Haley helped lead the Chiefs to a surprising AFC West title in 2010. Less than a year later with three games remaining in the 2011 season, Pioli fired Haley. At the time the Chiefs were 5–8, having lost five of their last six games under Haley, who went 19–27 overall with Kansas City. "I don't perceive Todd Haley as a mistake," Pioli said during his press conference. "Todd Haley is a good football coach. I'll say that. What we need to do is figure out what direction we're headed in and how we're going to continue to make progress, how we can get some consistency back."

Romeo Crennel (2011–12): Pioli hoped that "consistency" would come in the form of Romeo Crennel, Haley's defensive coordinator and former NFL head coach. Crennel's personality was the opposite of Haley's. Whereas Haley could be volatile at times and dress down his players, Crennel was the favorite uncle who's more like a father figure. Unfortunately the old adage of nice guys finishing last happened to Crennel. After leading the Chiefs to a 2–1 record in their final three games of 2011 as interim coach—including a win over the undefeated Green Bay Packers—Crennel was hired as the full-time coach for 2012.

That season, amid injuries and Matt Cassel and Brady Quinn as the team's quarterbacks, the Chiefs finished with a wretched 2–14 record for the second time in five seasons. Pioli, unsure about his own future, fired Crennel. "Obviously I'm very disappointed in the way our season went. At the end of the day, the NFL is a performance-based league, and we weren't able to win," Crennel said in a statement. "I want to thank the Hunt family for the opportunity as well as our players, coaches, and fans for their support during my time in Kansas City." A few weeks later, the John Dorsey-Andy Reid era began in Kansas City.

89 Frank Pitts

The 1965 American Football League Draft was all about speed for the Chiefs. They selected Frank Pitts in the fourth round out of Southern in Baton Rouge, Louisiana. During that same draft, Kansas City chose two other burners, receivers Otis Taylor and Gloster Richardson. (Coincidentally, the Chiefs' first pick in the draft was former Kansas star Gale Sayers, who decided to play for the NFL's Chicago Bears.)

The threesome came along at a time when the 40-yard dash was first being recorded on a regular basis. Pitts, the speediest of the three, clocked a 4.4. That speed led to one of the Chiefs' most effective plays during their Super Bowl seasons. "[Coach Hank Stram] got excited when he saw how quick I was in a short distance and came up with a reverse," Pitts said. "We mastered it during the 1966 season, when we went to the first Super Bowl. Then we perfected it two years later."

In 1968 the Chiefs "perfected" the reverse. That helped lead to the best season for Pitts, who played for Kansas City from 1965–70, statistically. He ended with 107 rushing yards on 11 carries and 655 receiving yards and six touchdowns on 30 catches. The next season the Chiefs reached Super Bowl IV in New Orleans. Pitts was fired up again except for a slightly different reason. It was close to where he attended college in Baton Rouge, and Southern's marching band played at halftime. "I was plum excited," Pitts said, "and I tried to show off."

Did he ever. Two reverses to Pitts and another long pass play set up two Jan Stenerud field goals and a Taylor touchdown. Pitts finished with 37 yards rushing and 33 yards receiving as the Chiefs manhandled the Minnesota Vikings 23–7.

Pitts also made his presence known in the first Super Bowl, called the AFL-NFL World Championship Game at the time, as the Chiefs faced the Green Bay Packers in the famed Los Angeles Coliseum. The Packers and the NFL both were seen as superior to the Chiefs and the AFL. The Chiefs were out to prove that wrong. But that doesn't mean that the players weren't excited—especially Pitts. "Before the game I'll never forget running by Green Bay coach Vince Lombardi, and I stopped, started shaking his hand, and said, 'I've seen you on TV so much and I'm out here in Los Angeles, and it's so great to meet you,'" Pitts said. "[Lombardi] said, 'It's great to have you out here. Now get back to the other side!'

"When we got ready to kick off, Elijah Pitts was playing for Green Bay. I made the tackle on him during the kickoff. When I got him, I was hugging him and falling to the ground and I said, 'This is your namesake making a tackle.' He just said, 'Fine, now get up.' That was a big highlight for me. That was my second year as a pro."

Sadly, though, in 2005 burglars took two of Pitts' prized mementos from his Super Bowl appearances: his two Super Bowl rings. "They trashed our room," said Pitts, who lives in Baton Rouge. "They went into our computer room and didn't take anything. They also didn't take anything from our front room, which is where I have pictures and paraphernalia from my days [in the NFL]."

Pitts, who's a sergeant-at-arms in the Louisiana Senate, had been wearing the rings because the senators with whom he works were traveling to areas affected by Hurricane Katrina. Some of the senators felt that it would be enjoyable for their constituents to see the rings. It would be something to briefly take their minds off the overwhelming tasks at hand.

But this story does have a happy ending. A year after Pitts' Super Bowl rings were stolen, several Louisiana senators and the New Orleans Saints helped make sure that he received replacements. Senator Ken Hollis began the fund-raising drive, which was aided by a $5,000 check from the Saints. In early December 2006, Pitts was presented with the replacements before a Saints game at the Superdome. Don't look for Pitts to take off those rings ever again.

90 Arrowhead's First Win

The game already featured drama. It was a match-up between the Chiefs and Raiders, one of the biggest rivalries in football—and all of sports—and the Chiefs were looking for their first win in their brand new stadium. Oakland running back Marv Hubbard only stoked the flames with some pregame trash talking before the Raiders visited Arrowhead Stadium for the first time ever on November 5, 1972.

Heading into the contest, the Chiefs had won each of their four road games but had yet to win in three attempts in their new digs. Hubbard thought the Chiefs would be easy pickings when he told reporters during the week: "When we go to Kansas City, we're going to kick some rear. It's going to be some kind of fight."

It sure was some kind of fight—for Hubbard. Every time he touched the ball, all 10 times, the Kansas City defense, led up front by Willie Lanier, Buck Buchanan, Curley Culp, and company, was there to make sure "some rear" got kicked. Hubbard ended the game with 18 yards rushing on eight carries and eight yards receiving on two catches. He also fumbled the ball.

"We won," Lanier said afterward, "because we attacked Oakland throughout the ballgame on offense and defense. We played football."

To Lanier's point, as good as Kansas City's defense was that day, the offense was equally impressive. En route to a 27–14 victory, the Chiefs jumped out to a 17–0 lead in the first half. Quarterback Len Dawson completed 10-of-18 passes for 181 yards, three touchdowns, and no interceptions, and running back Ed Podolak had 115 yards rushing and 42 receiving with one touchdown.

During the final few minutes of the fourth quarter, Oakland coach John Madden took Hubbard out of the game. The raucous Arrowhead crowd started chanting, "We want Hubbard. We want Hubbard." After the game Hubbard backtracked on his incendiary comments. "I don't know where that got started," he told reporters. "I don't want to say anything about you press boys, but us players know what's goin' on…well, well, I guess you got to make a living."

Besides being the Chiefs' first win at Arrowhead Stadium, the game marked the largest crowd in the stadium's history—then, now, and probably forever—as a standing-room only audience of 82,094 witnessed the game.

Chiefs owner Lamar Hunt, who probably enjoyed beating the Raiders as much as anyone in the organization, said after the game that it was "a proper beginning for our old AFL friends!"

91 Visit Big Charlie's Saloon

About 1,122 miles east of the actual Arrowhead Stadium is a place that has been called Arrowhead East. Once you step into the back room of Big Charlie's Saloon, a small sports bar in South Philadelphia, you'd swear you were in Kansas City instead of the "City of Brotherly Love," a frenzied sports town infamous for booing and throwing snowballs at Santa Claus at the end of an abysmal Eagles season. "We take that same passion for the Chiefs," said Anthony Mazzone, a lifelong friend of bar owner Paul Staico and a converted Chiefs fan.

As it did from Staico to Mazzone, that passion spreads to their friends. On any given Sunday, there can be as many as 60 or more people crammed into the back room to watch the Chiefs. "There's 40 or 50 people that come together as family," Staico said. "We have a common interest in the Chiefs...We make people feel at home. It's not like it's just our thing. Everybody's invited."

The back room at Big Charlie's is more than the viewing room for Chiefs games—it's a shrine to the Chiefs. The walls are decked out with various photographs of players and Arrowhead Stadium, Chiefs barstools and tables, bobbleheads, footballs, helmets, and countless other Chiefs bric-a-brac.

Unlike some "Chiefs bars" around the country that were opened because the owner was a Kansas City transplant, Staico and his buddies are Philadelphia natives. Most are South Philly natives, to be exact. Staico's love of the Chiefs began innocently enough in the early 1970s. Staico's father, Charlie, enjoyed dropping a few bucks on NFL games every now and then. During the '70 season, Charlie told Paul, who had been wanting a new bicycle, that if the Chiefs won that weekend, he'd buy his son a bike. The Chiefs won. Paul Staico got his new bike, and his love for the Chiefs began.

When Paul took over Big Charlie's in 1983, he converted it to a Chiefs bar. Since then, as word has spread that a group of passionate Chiefs fans are in the heart of Philadelphia, many Chiefs players, coaches, and others, including Derrick Thomas, Joe Valerio, Marty Schottenheimer, Rich Gannon's family, Mitch Holthus, and Scott Pioli, have stopped by to meet Staico, Mazzone, and the rest of the crew.

In May of 2003, NFL Films arranged for Chiefs coach—and iconic Eagles coach—Dick Vermeil and his staff to make a surprise visit to Big Charlie's. The group of fans was gathered—they thought—to watch the 2002 Chiefs highlight film, thanks to NFL Films, and told they'd be getting a call from Kansas City. Vermeil called from his cell, but instead of doing so from his office at Arrowhead Stadium, he was about to walk inside Big Charlie's with his coaches. "When I walked in there, it was beyond my expectations," Vermeil said in the NFL Films Emmy-award-winning program. "It only took a few seconds to get into the feeling of warmth and respect and how much these people care about the Chiefs...It was fun to share a beer with them and laugh and have them tell some stories about games."

So the next time you're in Philadelphia on a Chiefs Sunday, know that you have a friendly home at Big Charlie's. You can't miss the little bar on the corner of 11th and McKean—it's the one with the red and white exterior sign with the Arrowheads on it.

92 Scott Pioli

He was the right-hand guy in a championship organization. He was a hot commodity for years with options to land in sexier spots. He was looking forward to the challenge in Kansas City. He had family from this area.

Through much fanfare and hype, general manager Scott Pioli came to the Chiefs in January of 2009 after helping guide the New England Patriots to 14 playoff wins since 2000, including three Super Bowl championships as Bill Belichick's right-hand man. He started working with Belichick in Cleveland in 1992 as a Browns pro personnel assistant.

During the press conference announcing Pioli's hiring, he delivered a quote about humility, though that would hardly seem the case during his tenure. "This isn't about me; it isn't about my ego," he said. "This is not daunting at all…This is opportunity."

The opportunity was similar to when the Royals hired Dayton Moore as their general manager in 2006. Moore was 39 when the Royals hired him; Pioli was 43. Moore was born in Wichita; Pioli's wife, Dallas, was born in Wichita. Moore came to the Royals after being a part of 14 consecutive National League East division winners with the Atlanta Braves as John Schuerholz's go-to guy. Pioli had a major role, alongside Belichick, in the Patriots' great success.

But Pioli was no Moore. Unlike Moore, who worked to build relationships with other members of the Royals front office, the media, and fans, Pioli seemed to do the opposite. A major control freak, he fired longtime Chiefs staffers, acted as if the media was a nuisance, and alienated fans.

According to *The Kansas City Star*, Pioli sent emails telling employees to keep their office blinds closed when the team was practicing. During his first year, Pioli noticed a candy wrapper in a stairwell at the Chiefs facility. After monitoring it for a week and seeing that no one cleaned it up, he placed the wrapper in an envelope, which was used as a focal point for a lecture to employees on lack of attention to detail.

Pioli's first order of business was firing the likeable, though ineffective, head coach Herm Edwards and hiring Arizona offensive coordinator Todd Haley, who helped guide the Cardinals a few days earlier to Super Bowl XLIII. The hiring of Haley seemed like a high-ego version of *The Odd Couple*, and Haley was immediately saddled with quarterback Matt Cassel. Trading with New England for Cassel wasn't bad for Pioli, but as soon as he acquired Cassel, Pioli signed his new quarterback to a six-year contract for $63 million—a bit much for an unproven quarterback.

Though helped by an easy schedule, the Chiefs impressively won the AFC West during Haley's second year with a 10–6 record but then lost nine straight games (including the 2010 regular-season finale, wild-card loss to Baltimore, four 2011 preseason games, and first three contests in the 2011 regular season). When things didn't improve in spite of four straight wins, Pioli fired Haley with three games remaining in the 2011 season. He then hired Romeo Crennel, whose team won as many games in his three interim games of 2011 (two) as it did in all of 2012. As popular as he was with his players, he wasn't given a chance beyond 2012.

Perhaps the biggest knock on Pioli was his ability—or perceived lack thereof—to draft needed players. Here are the first two picks in each of his four drafts as general manager. (You can judge whether you think the picks were good.)

- 2009: Tyson Jackson (first round, No. 3 overall); second-round pick traded to Patriots for Cassel.
- 2010: Eric Berry (first round, No. 5 overall); Dexter McCluster (second round, No. 36 overall).
- 2011: Jon Baldwin (first round, No. 26 overall); Rodney Hudson (second round, No. 55 overall).
- 2012: Dontari Poe (first round, No. 11 overall); Jeff Allen (second round, No. 44 overall).

Following an abysmal 2–14 season in 2012 and struggling to find a quarterback and a coach to lead a group of players that included five Pro Bowlers (plus with Kansas City nearing a contract with coach Andy Reid, whom many say wanted a general manager he knew), Pioli and the Chiefs parted ways in January 2013. "The bottom line is that I did not accomplish all of what I set out to do," Pioli said through a statement sent by the Chiefs. "To the Hunt family, to the great fans of the Kansas City Chiefs, to the players, all employees, and alumni, I truly apologize for not getting the job done."

93 Kennison Silences Broncos

Eddie Kennison needed a change of scenery. He was a gifted, speedy receiver who happened to be well-traveled in the NFL by the age of 28 when he signed with the Chiefs, his fifth team in less than six seasons, on December 3, 2001.

His most recent stop, Denver, ended abruptly and with hard feelings in the 2001 season. In early November, the night before the Broncos were to play the San Diego Chargers, Kennison told Denver coach Mike Shanahan that he had lost his love for football. Kennison had overwhelming personal concerns. His wife, Shimika, was having complications from her pregnancy, and his father was recovering from a heart attack. Although Kennison tried to recant his retirement request, Shanahan was done—as was Kennison's career in Denver. The Broncos players believed Kennison was a quitter, that he was finished playing in the NFL.

Thanks to Dick Vermeil, who coached Kennison for two years when the St. Louis Rams selected him in the first round of the 1996 draft out of Louisiana State, Kennison got another chance. It wasn't easy.

Shanahan was asked about facing Kennison, which, coincidentally, the Broncos would be doing 13 days later. His response carried a dash of salt. "If he's still there," Shanahan quipped.

Denver linebacker John Mobley also didn't mince his words. "Knowing the way our defense felt about that situation, I think there could be a lot of cheap shots if he gets out on that field," he said. "I don't think he'll suit up against us. He won't want to play against our defense."

For the most part, the talk was one-sided. Kennison, in particular, didn't respond. Vermeil did. "I know Eddie better than anybody on that [Denver] roster knows him," he said during his weekly press conference. "I'm not saying Eddie hasn't had some problems, but they've had some other guys on that roster who have had some problems, who have been suspended from the league. What does that make them?...I'd think they'd show more class in evaluating their own people."

Kennison had to adjust to his new teammates, most of whom had formed an opinion on what happened in Denver. And there was learning the Chiefs offense, which was similar to what the Rams ran when he was there. Quarterback Trent Green helped Kennison pick up the offense and certainly a valuable lesson early that would serve both of them well for the next several years.

"We were running a pass route in practice, and he was on the back side—more of a decoy on a clear out," Green said. "Based on the rotation of the defense, I threw the ball to Eddie, but it went by him because he wasn't going all out. When he got back, I told him that he needed to run hard every time because I could throw it to him on any route, depending on the defense. He looked at me and said, 'I will never let that happen again.' And he never did. We played together through 2006, and he went hard every time. If we went through all the film of him, there are probably 20 throws where he was not part of the read at all, but I threw the ball to him, and he made the play. That might not sound like a big number, but if he wasn't ready, that could be 20 incompletions or interceptions. After that one time in practice, he never again took for granted whether he was the main guy on a route. He just wanted to make a statement here in Kansas City."

And he did, starting with the Denver game at Arrowhead. From the opening kick, it was apparent that the Chiefs wanted to utilize Kennison as much as possible against the Broncos. That game plan paid off. During the Chiefs' first drive of the day, Kennison had two receptions. The first resulted in a first down, which Kennison emphatically helped signal. The second catch resulted in a 51-yard field goal by Todd Peterson, giving the Chiefs an early lead. Later in the quarter, Kennison drew a pass interference penalty on the 12-yard line, which resulted in a 12-yard touchdown run by Priest Holmes that put the Chiefs up 10–0.

Kansas City went on to win the game 26–23 in overtime, thanks to a Peterson 32-yard field goal. The loss to the Chiefs happened to kick the Broncos out of the playoff picture that season. Kennison finished the game with 62 receiving yards on three catches. He also added 14 yards rushing. As big of a contribution, though, may have been the way he supported the team, encouraging everyone from special teams to Vermeil. "That shows his character and what type of person he really is. Everybody on the team sees that and relishes it," said tight end Jason Dunn. "Regardless of what happened in Denver or anywhere else with him, he came here and he let us understand what was going on with him. We knew this game meant a lot to him, and everybody embraced that. He did his job, a great job, and he was very determined to go out there and prove something against Denver. He did it. He put his arms around us, and we did the same to him. This is a family atmosphere, and I think he found that out."

"I don't think words can really express the way I feel with everything that went on and the way this organization embraced me," Kennison said. "For all the people out there that thought I wanted to quit or that I did quit, that's their answer. The comments that the Broncos made during the week said enough. I didn't need to speak. My actions spoke louder than anything I could've said. And winning this game is speaking louder than anything I could have said during the course of this last week or any other time."

Kennison's actions continued to speak for the next five-plus seasons for the Chiefs. By the time the Chiefs released him in 2007, the 34-year-old Kennison had the fourth-most 100-yard receiving games (17) and ranked seventh in Chiefs history with 5,230 career receiving yards and eighth in receptions with 321.

In 2008 Kennison appeared in three games for St. Louis. Then after not playing in 2009, Kennison technically ended his career in 2010 where he was most comfortable and played the majority of his games. In July he signed a one-day contract with Kansas City so he could retire as a member of the Chiefs. "I am honored and humbled to officially conclude my NFL playing career as a member of the Kansas City Chiefs," Kennison said in a statement. "My family is extremely grateful to the Hunt family, Scott Pioli, and the Chiefs organization for making this moment possible. Kansas City has a special place in our hearts and has truly become our home. I feel very blessed to have been extended the opportunity to retire as a member the Chiefs."

94 The Holler Guy

It was appropriate that the Dallas Texans selected E.J. Holub in the first round of the 1961 AFL Draft. Seemingly always wearing a cowboy hat and speaking in his Texas drawl, he was a true Texan, a true cowboy. He started working with horses after his retirement from the Chiefs in 1970. He handled breeding programs for horse farms in the Dallas area, St. Louis, and Oklahoma, where he spent 25 years, before landing back in his home state of Texas in the early 1990s. "It's fun to sell [the colts] and see them go on the circuit somewhere," Holub said. "It's a challenge to find the right niche, the right trainer, and then there's a lot of luck involved."

The real-life cowboy was known for his intensity and versatility on the football field. Because of the former, Hank Stram even nicknamed him "Holler Guy," as he was always yelling on the sidelines, firing up his teammates.

Known for his toughness and versatility, center/linebacker E.J. Holub stands on the sideline during Super Bowl IV.

His versatility was on display while starring on both sides of the ball. Holub quickly established himself as a great linebacker. He was picked for five AFL All-Star teams and had nine career interceptions as a linebacker during 1961–67. Bad knees, however, forced Holub to offense, where he spent three seasons (1968–70) as the team's starting center. Because of that move, Holub is the rare guy to play defense in one Super Bowl and then offense in another. "I was thankful to Coach Stram for moving me [to center] and extending my career," Holub said, "We had such a great offensive line. I just hiked the ball to Lenny [Dawson] and then backed up in case someone got by one of our other guys. The biggest thing I had to do was center the ball."

His toughness and versatility were also on display during an incident at training camp in stifling Liberty, Missouri, and led to the Chiefs' use of Gatorade. "I was practicing both ways—linebacker and center," Holub said. "I'd sweat a whole bunch. One time I got dehydrated and when I went back to the huddle, I just wilted, passed out. They packed me in ice. Coach Stram had heard about the Gatorade in Florida, so he called them, and we got started on it. From then on we drank Gatorade, and I guess it was because of me."

The Chiefs inducted Holub into the team's Hall of Fame in 1976.

Amidst all of the ups and downs: the pain, the knee operations, the early uncertainties with the AFL, the move from Dallas to Kansas City, and obviously the championships, Holub quickly points out that he had a great career. "I'd do it all again in a heartbeat," he said. "Sure, there's the football but also the camaraderie with the players and the people in Kansas City. I'll always be appreciative to the people there because of how they accepted us.

"All in all, I couldn't ask for anything better."

95 Bill Kenney

The Chiefs have had their fair share of quarterback controversies... umm...competitions. Perhaps no single Chiefs quarterback went through as much competition, though, as Bill Kenney did during his nine-year playing career with Kansas City.

Beginning in 1980 when Kenney, who'd been selected out of Northern Colorado by the Miami Dolphins with the second-to-last pick in the 1978 NFL Draft, made the Chiefs' squad as Steve Fuller's backup, he was in constant competition for the job. He quickly knew that it might be that way. "I was a free agent nobody with the Chiefs," said Kenney, whose name was even misspelled on the back of his jersey—KENNY—when he made his debut late in the '80 season. "[Quarterbacks] coach Kay Dalton believed in me from Day One, but he told me when he saw me work out, 'You understand the game for a quarterback better than anyone I've ever been around...but you can't throw worth crap.'"

During his first three years, Kenney battled with Fuller, a first-round draft pick in 1979. Kenney eventually emerged as the starter but missed some games because of injuries. The Chiefs made a coaching change, firing Marv Levy and hiring John Mackovic.

Then Kansas City took Todd Blackledge with their first-round draft pick in 1983 and traded Fuller. The battle continued for Kenney. "When Blackledge showed up, he looked so good that I told my friends my days were numbered," Kenney said. "He was the quarterback of the future, but he just never progressed."

Kenney responded in that 1983 campaign with a season that remains one of the best for a quarterback in Chiefs history. He piled up 4,348 passing yards—600 yards more than he'd thrown for in his first three seasons combined—which is second behind

Trent Green's 4,591 in 2004. His seven 300-yard games that season are also second to Green's eight in '04. That season he also threw for 411 yards in a December game at San Diego, which is good for fourth all time for the Chiefs. Kenney received the only Pro Bowl invitation of his career in 1983. "It was a combination of a completely different philosophy with Mackovic and my own maturity as a quarterback," Kenney said of his monstrous year.

Kenney battled the younger Blackledge for the starting job through 1987. Blackledge never turned into the quarterback worthy of a first-round pick and he couldn't unseat Kenney. That doesn't mean the Chiefs were successful with Kenney as the signal-caller. In '87 the Chiefs lost a then-team-record nine games in a row. Of course, that wasn't all on Kenney's shoulders. It was mostly the fault of a defense, which gave up an astounding and then-franchise-worst 388 points. (And they played only 15 games that season because of a one-game strike.) Then in 1988 the 33-year-old Kenney lost the quarterback battle...to a 34-year-old

300 Yards Doesn't Guarantee a Win

During his 10 seasons with the Chiefs, Bill Kenney became the organization's all-time leader in 300-yard passing games with 15. (Trent Green later recorded more 300-yard games, and Patrick Mahomes is well on his way to becoming the team's all-time leader.) Of Kenney's 15 games, the Chiefs won less than half (six). In fact, heading into the 2014 season, out of the 17 Chiefs quarterbacks who have thrown for at least 300 yards in a game, only Mahomes (14–4), Joe Montana (3–1) and Mike Livingston (2–0) have winning records. Below are the top five quarterbacks in 300-yard games.

Player	300-Yard Games	Record
1. Trent Green (2001–06)	24	11–13
2. Patrick Mahomes (2017–19)	18	14–4
3. Bill Kenney (1979–88)	15	6–9
4. Len Dawson (1962–75)	9	4–4–1
5. Elvis Grbac (1997–2000)	7	3–4

Steve DeBerg. "They finally brought in an older guy to take my place," Kenney said, laughing. "[Playing for the Chiefs] was such a fun opportunity for me. I was in the right place at the right time."

The competition continued for Kenney after he retired from football in 1989 with the Washington Redskins. He decided in 1994 that he wanted to run for the Missouri state senate. When he informed the local Republicans of his intentions, they couldn't believe it. "They tried talking me out of it because they didn't think I could win," Kenney said.

The former quarterback not only won but also spent eight years in office and became a majority floor leader. "I really enjoyed serving," he said. "The greatest thing about that job was being able to help people."

Kenney, who also owns Bill Kenney Homes, a development and real estate company, remains active in the Kansas City community. And, of course, he remains a big Chiefs fan, even through their repeated quarterback controversies. "You really have to grow with young quarterbacks," he said. "The Chiefs haven't had a lot of success developing quarterbacks. They tried developing two when I was here, and it didn't work."

Grbac vs. Gannon and Chiefs vs. Broncos

A year after not making the playoffs in 1996 for what would be only the third time during Marty Schottenheimer's decade as Kansas City's head coach, two quarterbacks guided the Chiefs to a 13–3 record and home-field advantage for the postseason in 1997. The starter, Elvis Grbac, led the Chiefs to a 7–2 record before injuring his collarbone. The backup, Rich Gannon, filled in admirably with a 5–1 record. In spite of Gannon's hot streak, Schottenheimer stuck with Grbac when he was healthy for the regular-season finale and subsequent playoffs.

That decision didn't sit well with many fans. Gannon got the fans' attention during the 1995 playoff loss to Indianapolis, when he replaced starter Steve Bono and drove the Chiefs to within tying field-goal distance. (To preserve the feelings of Chiefs fans, we'll leave it at that.) After the Chiefs failed to make the playoffs in '96, Bono was out, Gannon stayed put, and the team signed Grbac from San Francisco.

With the AFC West title and home field secured, the Chiefs played host to the Denver Broncos in a 1997 AFC Divisional Playoff Game—the first time the two rivals met in the postseason. Denver came to Arrowhead with a 12–4 record, having split the regular-season series with the Chiefs.

The game was relatively sloppy by both teams with six fumbles through the early part of the third quarter. This might go against popular belief and most memories, but Grbac actually had a fairly solid game. He threw for 260 yards and a touchdown, bettering John Elway, who had 170 yards and no touchdowns.

The Chiefs' final possession, however, did nothing to sway the Gannon fans to Grbac's side. Trailing 14–10 Grbac connected with Andre Rison on a 23-yard pass play that put the Chiefs on the Denver 28 with a little less than two minutes remaining. Schottenheimer called the team's final timeout. For some illogical reason, Grbac dinked and dunked the ball for a whopping eight yards on the next three plays—none of which were near a sideline. With fourth and 2 on the 20 with the clock ticking, Grbac launched an ill-advised throw toward a covered Lake Dawson in the end zone. The ball was knocked away by Darrien Gordon, and the Broncos were advancing, while the Chiefs' season ended in heartbreaking fashion once again. "I didn't have any sense that the time was a problem," Schottenheimer told reporters after the

Elvis, the Sexiest Man, Throws for 500…and Loses

The Gannon-Grbac quarterback controversy also played out in one amusing way. For *People* magazine's Sexiest Men issue in 1998, the publication chose Chiefs quarterback Rich Gannon, then 33, as its sexiest athlete. But *People* simply informed the photographer assigned to the piece that the sexiest athlete was the Chiefs quarterback.

Hence, the photographer took pictures of the Chiefs quarterback…or one of the Chiefs quarterbacks: Elvis Grbac. "The pictures made their way back to the New York offices, and editors were dumbfounded," said Jeff Pearlman, who was working for *Sports Illustrated*, another publication owned by Time, Inc. "Yet upon learning the truth, no one with the magazine had the heart to tell Grbac that an unfathomable mistake had been made." As a result, *People*'s 1998 sexiest athlete remained Grbac.

Gannon left the Chiefs the next year in 1999 and signed with the Oakland Raiders, where he eventually led the team to the Super Bowl and became league MVP. During the 2000 season, the Raiders swept the Chiefs for the first time since 1988. The second game between the teams that season was on November 5 in Oakland. The Raiders won that game 49–31, but Grbac put on a performance for the ages.

Grbac, whose arm wasn't his downfall, threw for an incredible 504 yards while also throwing for two touchdowns and two interceptions on 39-of-53 passing. Nearly half of those yards, 226, came during the fourth quarter. "Man, they never threw the ball like that," said wide receiver Andre Rison, who'd been cut by the Chiefs before signing with the Raiders. "They threw 50 or 60 times and still lost? I'd rather take Rich Gannon's stats—a W."

Solid and reliable, as he'd been during most of his time with both the Chiefs and Raiders, Gannon had 242 yards with four touchdowns and no interceptions.

With his day's performance, Grbac became only the eighth quarterback in NFL history to throw for at least 500 yards. Through the 2013 season, there are 15, including former Chiefs quarterback Warren Moon, who threw for 527 yards as a Houston Oiler against the Chiefs in 1990.

The 2000 season marked Grbac's last with the Chiefs. I guess you can say, a few weeks after practically throwing it out of the stadium, Elvis had left the building.

game. "We started that sequence with about 34 seconds to go, and I thought we could get the ball off. We were going to get it off at 18 [seconds]. Had we been able to convert the first down we would still have had in the neighborhood of 12 seconds to take a shot at the end zone."

That game also marked the end of Marcus Allen's Hall of Fame career. He ran for 37 yards on 12 carries.

97 Monday Night Meltdown

Ugly. That's the only word to describe the Chiefs' 30–7 loss at Arrowhead against Denver on *Monday Night Football* on November 16, 1998. Well, maybe not the only word. There's *embarrassing, disgraceful, shameful, appalling,* and *dreadful.* Although no loss to the Denver Broncos is acceptable to any self-respecting Chiefs fan, this one was magnified by actions on the field.

The Chiefs were flagged for five personal fouls, including three straight by Derrick Thomas, who evidently let the smack-talking Shannon Sharpe get under his skin—all during an 80-yard Denver touchdown drive in the fourth quarter—before Marty Schottenheimer pulled Thomas from the game. Allegedly, Sharpe had gotten a hold of Thomas' girlfriend's phone number and kept repeating it at the line of scrimmage. "My actions were uncharacteristic and in some sense uncalled for," Thomas, whom the Chiefs suspended for one game, said during an apology on the following Tuesday. "Being one of the individuals everybody looks up to on this football team, I have to conduct myself in a manner that is positive at all times."

Defensive tackle Chester McGlockton and linebacker Wayne Simmons also committed personal fouls. The latter's play was so egregious that he was waived the next day. Owner Lamar Hunt said the actions of his team "disgraced this organization as well as the community."

The "Monday Night Meltdown" marked the Chiefs' fifth loss in a row, the first time that had happened since 1988. They'd go on to lose the next week. After his team's disappointing 7–9 finish, Coach Schottenheimer resigned, following the season.

98 Watch *M*A*S*H* with Super Gnat and the Hammer

The classic 1970 film *M*A*S*H* should be required viewing anyway but especially for any Chiefs fan. Written by Ring Lardner Jr., the son of sports columnist Ring Lardner, and directed by Kansas City native Robert Altman, the movie is a comedy about a U.S. medical unit (Mobile Army Surgical Hospital) behind the front lines in the Korean War. It stars Donald Sutherland, Elliott Gould, Tom Skerritt, Sally Kellerman, and Robert Duvall as the main doctors as they deal with patients, war, and everyone around them in a humorous way. Lardner even won an Academy Award for his satiric screenplay.

One of the greatest scenes from the movie is a football game between the surgeons and the generals. The surgeons have recruited a ringer, Dr. Oliver "Spearchucker" Jones, who was played by former Chiefs defensive back Fred "the Hammer" Williamson. The Hammer hauled in 11 interceptions during his three years with the Chiefs. But the cornerback is most famous for having his pregame Super Bowl I smack talk blow up in his face. He bragged that he would blanket Green Bay Packers receivers Boyd Dowler and Carroll Dale. "Two hammers to Dowler, one to Dale should be enough," he said.

Though Dowler injured his shoulder while blocking early in the game, his replacement, the hungover Max McGee, burned the Hammer and his Chiefs teammates for seven catches, 138 yards, and two touchdowns, while Dale caught four passes for 59 yards. Making matters more embarrassing, after Williamson brought down Packers rookie Donny Anderson in the fourth quarter he was knocked out and carried off on a stretcher. "I don't remember a thing," Williamson said, according to ESPN.com. "Did I make the tackle?"

He, though, went on to a successful acting career. *M*A*S*H* was his first movie, but he rose to prominence as one of the first African American male action stars of the "blaxploitation" era of the early 1970s with films, including *That Man Bolt* (1973), *Black Caesar* (1973), and *Mean Johnny Barrows* (1976). He more recently acted in *From Dusk Till Dawn* (1996) and *Starsky & Hutch* (2004).

Former Chiefs player Noland Smith also had a major role in *M*A*S*H*'s football scene, which featured Buck Buchanan in a cameo. Other NFL players in *M*A*S*H* include Ben Davidson, Joe Kapp, Fran Tarkenton, and Johnny Unitas. Howard Schnellenberger, best known as the former coach at the University of Miami, played the referee in the film.

In *M*A*S*H* Smith's character is called "Superbug," an appropriate and funny twist, as he was known during his playing days as "Super Gnat." The team's first true return threat—decades before Dante Hall and Dexter McCluster—Smith played for the Chiefs during 1967–69. He was much more than that, though. Despite playing less than three seasons with the Chiefs, Smith was one of the most electrifying—and smallest—players in Kansas City until Hall came onto the scene.

In fact, even though his teammates called him "Jet," his size of 5'7" and 154 pounds garnered him the Super Gnat moniker from an unlikely source. "[Owner] Lamar Hunt made the statement that I was so small, I looked like a 'super gnat' out there," Smith said.

But Smith had blazing speed. He could break free and return a kick for a touchdown at any time. And even with his slight frame, Super Gnat was fearless. "I can't think of many more plays in a game that are more dangerous than returning kicks," Smith said. "Back when I was playing, they called it the suicide squad. But a long kick return is one of the most exciting plays in football. I don't know of another play that can turn a team on or let a team down so quickly."

Smith, who was the Chiefs' sixth-round draft pick in 1967 out of Tennessee State, proved that. He was the first player in the NFL-AFL's history to be drafted as a punt/kick return specialist. Before then returners mainly were running backs or receivers. "A lot of credit for me being drafted despite my size goes to Hank Stram," Smith said. "There were one or two guys who were small, but Hank making me the first player ever as a kick-return specialist made a lot of people take notice."

Smith made people take notice during his first game in a Chiefs uniform, a contest featuring Chiefs rookies against the Broncos rookies at Municipal Stadium. The first time Super Gnat touched the ball on a punt, he ran it back 80 yards for a touchdown. And he kept improving. During his rookie season, Smith led the league in kickoff return yards with 1,148 on 41 returns (28 yards per return average) and one touchdown.

His highlight that season was a 106-yard return against the Broncos in Denver on December 17, 1967. The return remained tied for the longest in NFL history for 40 years. "The whole game, Denver had been kicking the ball into the end zone. Before half-time, Hank pulled me aside and said how he noticed that their men were pulling up short, knowing I wasn't going to bring it out,"

Smith said. "So, on the first kick in the second half, Hank wanted me to bring it out. I hit a lot of traffic around the 20-yard line, but when I hit the 25, I was home free. They were surprised. Plays like that, as a returner, you don't have time to think; it was a natural reaction to bring the ball out and go as hard as I could."

Having a return specialist was a luxury, however, particularly with a team's 40-man roster. So, despite impressive numbers Smith was released six games into the 1969 season. He ended the year with the San Francisco 49ers, which didn't re-sign him after the season, but he always will remember his time with the Chiefs in a special way. "Since I was very small, NFL teams wouldn't give me a look," he said. "I owe a lot to Hank Stram and the Chiefs for giving me the chance. I often think of Hank and how close we were as a team. It was a brotherhood. We played together and we got along. That helped us succeed."

99 Buy a Bottle of Vermeil Wine

For a unique experience—at least unique to NFL teams—Chiefs fans can buy a bottle of Dick Vermeil's wine. After dabbling with winemaking around the time he retired from coaching the St. Louis Rams, Vermeil and his wife, Carol, went into business with a longtime family friend, Jeanne Frediani, and three members of her family to start the Vermeil Wines label as a business in 2007. "We went from making 150 cases of wine for fun to making 5,000 cases a year for work," Vermeil said.

Winemaking has been in Vermeil's French-Italian roots for generations. His great-grandfather, Garibaldi Iaccheri, who emigrated from Italy to Calistoga in 1906, started the Calistoga Wine

Company. Dick's grandfather, Al Vermeil, made wine in his basement from grapes he picked at the Frediani Vineyards, where Vermeil wine is made today. Many times, Dick helped his grandfather make the wine that ultimately would be served with nearly every family dinner.

Vermeil Wines is dedicated to Iaccheri and Vermeil's other great grandfather, Jean Louis Vermeil. In fact, the first bottle of wine produced by Vermeil Wines is named the Jean Louis Vermeil Cabernet-Sauvignon. "I always thought that some day I'd like to put my dad's name and my great-grandfather's name—both Jean Louis—on a bottle of wine," Vermeil said.

Appropriately, another bottle is called the XXXIV Proprietary Red, named after Super Bowl XXXIV, when Vermeil's St. Louis Rams defeated the Tennessee Titans. "That's the only [Super Bowl] identification that the NFL couldn't stop us from using," he said.

Now for an even more unique experience, fans in California wine country can sample the wine at one of two Vermeil "wine-tasting lounges" in Calistoga or Napa. The locations are a combination of upscale sports bar and laid-back wine-tasting room. Each location has a TV for football viewing, a replica Super Bowl XXXIV trophy, and photos from Vermeil's career.

One of Vermeil's former players, Eddie Kennison, also has a wine-tasting room and club named Cellar & Loft located in the River Market area of Kansas City. Kennison's appreciation for wine came from—you guessed it—Vermeil, his former coach with the Rams and Chiefs. "Coach helped me learn that wine is one of the good things in life, like family," Kennison said.

Cellar & Loft is one of more than 40 restaurants and retailers in the Kansas City area that carries Vermeil Wines. That list and information about purchasing bottles online can be found at vermeilwines.com.

Vermeil Wines is no passing fancy; it is a respected label. The first few years of the business venture have featured great reviews

When Wine Won a Chiefs Game

In November of 2003, the 9–1 Chiefs were playing host to the hated Raiders and pushing for home-field advantage in the AFC playoffs.

The Chiefs led 21–7 at halftime and then 24–14 heading into the fourth quarter but saw that evaporate. Oakland quarterback Rick Mirer hit Jerry Rice for a 47-yard touchdown play early in the fourth. Then with two minutes, 18 seconds left in regulation, Sebastian Janikowski struck a 41-yard field goal that tied the game at 24.

On their ensuing drive, it looked as if the Chiefs were going to get stalled and send the game into overtime. On fourth and 14, however, quarterback Trent Green found Marc Boerigter for a 16-yard pass play, which set up a 35-yard field-goal attempt for the 43-year-old Morten Andersen with less than a minute left.

Before Andersen left the sideline to attempt his career 31st game-winning field goal and 500th regular-season field goal, coach Dick Vermeil offered an incentive for his kicker and fellow wine connoisseur. "You make this kick and you've got one of my Bryant Family Vineyards, and they're impossible to get," Vermeil said of the bottle of Bryant Family Vineyards Cabernet Sauvignon, which was worth about $500.

Andersen's kick inched over the crossbar with a few seconds left, giving the Chiefs the 27–24 win. Vermeil, who's one of the most honest coaches you'd ever meet—brutally honest at times—was perfectly fine to make good on the present to Andersen. The NFL, however, wasn't about to acquiesce.

After hearing of Vermeil's offer, the league ruled a few days later that he couldn't give Andersen the bottle of wine because it was seen as a performance bonus that wasn't included in Andersen's contract. "We'll have to wait until after the season to share a glass of wine at my house," Vermeil said upon hearing the NFL's ruling. "I just can hardly believe it."

Of course, the Chiefs players didn't completely cork the idea. They pitched in and purchased for Andersen a $2 screw-top bottle of Boone's Farm wine, a slight downgrade from Vermeil's very high-quality stuff.

from some of the top reviewers in the business. Vermeil Wines consistently receives scores of 90 and above on bottles that range from $18 to $225 apiece. "I'm a football guy, not a business guy, but anything we taste that doesn't fit the quality of what we want to sell, we're not going to bottle it," Vermeil said. "Not everything turns out perfect. It's just like football. You try to do it right. You try to win."

100 Watch Magical Mahomes Moments

During his MVP and Super Bowl seasons, Patrick Mahomes was must-see TV. Here are 10 must-see-to-believe plays from Mahomes' first two years as the Chiefs' starter (in chronological order) that fans can find on YouTube.

August 17, 2018 at Atlanta Falcons (preseason)
It might seem odd to have a preseason game in this list, but this was just the second preseason game with Mahomes as Kansas City's starter. So this was the game when NFL fans really glimpsed the strength of Mahomes' arm as he launched a pass 68.6 yards in the air for a touchdown to Tyreek Hill. That was longer than any completed pass during the 2017 and '18 seasons.

September 23, 2018 vs. San Francisco 49ers
With 8:54 left in the second quarter, the 49ers forced Mahomes out of the pocket. Instead of throwing it away—like most normal quarterbacks would do—Mahomes scrambled back to the 25-yard line, circled, and came back before throwing a pass that found Chris Conley in the back of the end zone. It was only a four-yard

pass, but according to Next Gen Stats, Mahomes ran 35.7 yards on the play.

October 1, 2018 at Denver Broncos
Mahomes is right-handed. And yet somehow with Broncos linebacker Von Miller starting to lunge and grab his legs, Mahomes switched the ball from his right to his left hand and completed an incredible pass to Tyreek Hill for a first down in a much-needed drive for the Chiefs.

December 9, 2018 vs. Baltimore Ravens
Toward the end of the first half against the Ravens, Mahomes scrambled out of the pocket, juked one defender, and then threw a perfect pass across his body to Demarcus Robinson…*while looking in the opposite direction.* The no-look pass to Robinson will remain on Mahomes' highlight reel for years to come.

December 13, 2018 vs. Los Angeles Chargers
On Kansas City's first drive of the game, Mahomes scrambled toward the sideline, made a quick pump fake, and looked like he was going to be taken down by a Chargers defender. While in the defender's grasp, though, Mahomes found Robinson for a touchdown.

January 20, 2019 vs. New England Patriots (AFC Championship Game)
The Chiefs trailed 17–7 late in the third quarter when Mahomes found Sammy Watkins near midfield for a 10-yard play. The impressive part of this play is that New England's Adrian Clayborn was coming so fast that all Mahomes could do was make a quick sidearm throw around Clayborn as he was being taken down. Four plays later the Chiefs scored.

October 6, 2019 vs. Indianapolis Colts

Early in the second quarter against the Colts at Arrowhead on *Sunday Night Football,* Indy's defense pushed Mahomes out of the pocket on a third and 18. He turned his back and ran toward the opposite end zone before scrambling back and throwing a 27-yard running strike to Byron Pringle for a touchdown.

November 10, 2019 at Tennessee Titans

In his first game back following a dislocated knee injury, Mahomes looked like his old self early in the fourth quarter as he jumped to avoid pressure on a third and 9 and threw a 21-yard strike to Mecole Hardman, who sprinted about 48 yards for a touchdown. He had added a jump pass to his repertoire.

January 12, 2020 vs. Houston Texans (AFC Divisional Playoffs)

After spotting the Texans 24 points, Mahomes and the Kansas City offense put together an unbelievable comeback against Houston. With less than a minute remaining in the first half and the Chiefs trailing 24–21, Mahomes scrambled back and then to his left. As he inched near the line of scrimmage, Mahomes spotted Travis Kelce at the goal line. Mahomes slowed down and dragged his left foot to stay behind the line of scrimmage and then made a cross-body shove pass to Kelce for the touchdown. That was the third of three consecutive touchdown passes from Mahomes to Kelce for five, six, and five yards, respectively.

January 19, 2020 vs. Titans (AFC Championship Game)

Out of all of Mahomes' plays, this might've been the most crucial. With 20 seconds left in the first half and the Titans leading 17–14, the Chiefs faced second and 10 from Tennessee's 27-yard line. Mahomes took the snap and ran to his left toward the sideline. It looked like he was going to go out of bounds and stop the clock. Instead, he stayed in, sprinted up the sideline, cut back in, spun between two defenders, and fell into the end zone with 11 seconds remaining. That gave the Chiefs the lead for the first time in the game. They kept the lead and advanced to Super Bowl LIV.

Acknowledgments

I'll admit it: I cried. I cried when the Chiefs beat the Titans in the 2019 AFC Championship Game. I cried during the two weeks between that game and Super Bowl LIV. And I cried toward the end of that game. Oh, and I've cried since. Watching the Chiefs end a 50-year drought—my entire lifetime—and win the Super Bowl was something that most of us longtime Chiefs fans wondered if we'd ever see. That said, this isn't about that season. Nor is it a history of the Kansas City Chiefs per se. It's a collection of stories about great (and not-so great) moments and players, along with some of the things you might enjoy doing as a Chiefs fan. All of that said, as one might imagine, putting a book like this together requires a lot of research, assistance, and support regardless of the author's knowledge—or lack thereof—of the topic. Thankfully, in my case, I grew up in the Kansas City area in the 1970s and '80s as a big Chiefs fan.

During my adult life, I've been blessed with the opportunity to write a book with former Chiefs running back Marcus Allen, a Super Bowl-related book for CBS Sports, in addition to countless Chiefs-related articles for Metro Sports' website, *The Kansas City Star*, and other outlets. That's not to mention the interviews with former Chiefs players for the radio show formerly known as *Behind the Stats*.

A special thanks to Michelle Bruton with Triumph Books, who gave me the go-ahead to write this. Thank you also to my editor, Jeff Fedotin, who's both largely responsible for me writing this book and the best editor for this project. Jeff, who's an editor at Triumph, happens to be a Kansas City native and lifelong Chiefs fan. As I've written before, I've worked with quite a few excellent editors over the years, but I don't think I've had one who's as knowledgeable and passionate about the book's subject than Jeff was with *100 Things*. We had numerous discussions, debates, and email exchanges about the contents and the order of the chapters. He had a huge (and wonderful) influence on this book. Besides Michelle and Jeff, there are multiple other people at Triumph who were responsible for this project during production or have been instrumental in publicity and marketing since its release. I thank each of them.

To Brad Gee in the Chiefs media relations department and Jodain Massad with the Chiefs' in-house production company for providing information and research assistance. To Emily McNeill, who arranged the interview with Eric Berry. To Steve Alic of USA Football, who lined up Carl Peterson. To Danni Boatwright, who helped get her husband Casey Wiegmann for the barbecue chapter. To Paige Klone and Beth Hoops, who arranged an interview with David Koechner. To Jeff Pearlman, a wonderful writer, who provided a terrific Elvis Grbac story. A special thanks to Ruth Bigus who was a tremendous help with numerous player contacts.

To Jim Chappell, Matthew Hicks, Mark Stallard, Chris Browne, and Adam Ehlert—thank you all.

To Trent Green and Deron Cherry for writing the foreword and introduction, respectively. They both have been great ambassadors for the Chiefs, but they're even better people. We're lucky to have each of them in Kansas City.

To the former Chiefs who agreed to be interviewed for this book specifically and/or provided help with the barbecue story: Kimble Anders, Shawn Barber, Eric Berry, J.J. Birden, Steve Bono, Chris Burford, Mark Collins, Brad Cottam, Len Dawson, Priest Holmes, Nick Lowery, Bill Maas, Curtis McClinton (and Margo McClinton), Ted McKnight, Mark McMillian, Rudy Niswanger, Carl Peterson, Will Shields, Mark Vlasic, Casey Wiegmann. I can't thank you enough for your time. Additionally, thank you to Rob

Riggle and David Koechner for taking time out of your schedules to talk for the book.

I owe a mountain of gratitude to the group of friends and family who serve as my core support and guidance: Jim Wissel, Tom Lawrence, Chris Garrett, Dennis and Caroline, Tim and Amy, Josh and Susan. As with past book projects, based on the amount of praying I did throughout the writing of this, without Christ this isn't possible. A final special thanks to my favorite in-laws, Todd and Pat Burwell, and my parents, Fred and Sharon. To Helen, Charlie, and Aaron, who make me thankful each day, and to my best friend, Libby, who's as eager to get home from church on an NFL Sunday as I am to watch the Chiefs.

Sources

The author would like to acknowledge the reporters and columnists who have covered the Kansas City Chiefs organization since the team's inception as the Dallas Texans. As mentioned in the acknowledgments, many of the quotations found throughout the book were taken from personal interviews between these men and the author. Some were for this book, while others were from interviews from previous books, articles, and radio shows. Most other quotes were taken from press conferences. Other quotes and information came from various sources. Those sources include:

Websites
bobgretz.com
espn.com
helmethut.com
kcchiefs.com
kchistory.org
kclibrary.org
lasportshall.com
nfl.com
nflcommunications.com
vermeilwines.com
youtube.com

Newspapers/News Services
Associated Press
The Boston Globe
Chicago Tribune
The Florida Times-Union
Houston Chronicle

The Kansas City Star
The Kansas City Times
Los Angeles Times
The New York Times
The Topeka Capital-Journal
USA TODAY

Periodicals
GQ
Sports Illustrated

Books
(Excluding books by the author)

Althaus, Bill and Rich Wolfe. *For Chiefs Fans Only!* Lenexa, Kansas: Ascend Books 2009.

Brown, Daniel. *100 Things 49ers Fans Should Know & Do Before They Die.* Chicago: Triumph Books 2013.

Eisenberg, John. *Ten-Gallon War.* New York: Houghton Mifflin Harcourt Publishing Company 2012.

Flanagan, Jeffrey and Marty Schottenheimer. *Martyball!* New York: Sports Publishing 2012.

Levy, Marv. *Where Else Would You Rather Be?* Champaign, Illinois: Sports Publishing 2004.

McGuff, Joe. *Winning It All.* New York: Doubleday & Company, Inc. 1970.

McKenzie, Michael. *Arrowhead: Home of the Chiefs.* Lenexa, Kansas: Addax Publishing 1997.

Rappoport, Ken. *The Little League That Could.* Lanham, Maryland: Taylor Trade Publishing 2010.

Stallard, Mark. *Kansas City Chiefs Encyclopedia.* Champaign, Illinois: Sports Publishing 2002.

Stallard, Mark. *Super Chiefs*. Overland Park, Kansas: Kaw Valley Books 2013.

Steidel, Dave. *Remember the AFL*. Cincinnati, Ohio: Clerisy Press 2008.

Stram, Hank with Lou Sahadi. *They're Playing My Game*. Chicago: Triumph Books 2006 (updated).

Sweet, David A.F. *Lamar Hunt: The Gentle Giant Who Revolutionized Professional Sports*. Chicago: Triumph Books 2010.

Taylor, Otis with Mark Stallard. *The Need to Win*. Champaign, Illinois: Sports Publishing 2003.

Worgul, Doug. *The Grand Barbecue*. Kansas City, Missouri: Kansas City Star Books 2001.

DVDs

Chiefs: The Complete History. NFL Films 2007.

The Story of the 2003 Kansas City Chiefs: A Team Together. NFL Films 2004.

About the Author

After growing up in the Kansas City area, Matt Fulks started his journalism career while attending Lipscomb University in Nashville, Tennessee, when his baseball career was cut short due to a lack of ability. He is the author/co-author of more than 25 books, including *The Road to Canton* with Hall of Fame running back Marcus Allen. Fulks lives in the Kansas City area with his wife, Libby, their three kids, his midlife crisis Jeep, and two Weimaraners named after Elvis. Sort of. He is the director of Royals general manager Dayton Moore's "C" You In The Major Leagues Foundation.

Other Triumph Books titles by Matt Fulks

If These Walls Could Talk: Kansas City Royals, with Jeff Montgomery, 2017

100 Things Royals Fans Should Know & Do Before They Die (Updated), 2016

More Than A Season, with Dayton Moore (Updated), 2016

Taking the Crown, 2015

More Than A Season, with Dayton Moore, 2015

Out of the Blue, 2014

100 Things Royals Fans Should Know & Do Before They Die, 2014

Coach John Wooden: 100 Years of Greatness, 2010

The Good, the Bad, & the Ugly: Pittsburgh Steelers, 2008

Echoes of Kansas Basketball, 2006

"C" You In The Major Leagues Foundation

Matt Fulks is donating a portion of his author profits from the sale of this book to Dayton Moore's "C" You In The Major Leagues Foundation. The mission of CYITML is to provide hope and support to families in crisis while reaching, teaching, and developing future character-driven leaders. Since launching in 2014, CYITML has granted more than $1 million to 62 organizations, mainly in the Kansas City area. The foundation's signature program is C-10 Mentoring & Leadership, which provides job and life skill development, educational enhancements, a sense of service in the community, and more to a select group of high school students. More information about the foundation and the C-10 program can be found at CYouInTheMajorLeagues.org.